Knitting COZY

OUTDOORSY PATTERNS FOR WARMTH AND STYLE

THERESE CHYNOWETH

Knitting COZY

Knitting Cozy

Landauer Publishing, *https://landauer.foxchapelpublishing.com*, is an imprint of Fox Chapel Publishing Company, Inc.

Project Team
Editorial Director: Brian Hurley
Acquisitions Editor: Amelia Johanson
Editor: Christa Oestreich
Designer: Leslie Hall, Wendy Reynolds
Photographer: Mike Mihalo
Proofreader: Jeremy Hauck

Shutterstock used: Netrun78 (3); Alla_vector (4–5 background, 6); New Africa (18 bottom left, 33 bottom, 74–75 bottom, 78 bottom left, 118 bottom left); Hrachova Anna (44); TojoGraphics LLC (49 bottom right); Wstockstudio (71 bottom right); Nigel Stripe (79 top right, 153 top right); Pixel-Shot (168 background).

ISBN 978-1-63981-152-6

Library of Congress Control Number: 2026940780

To learn more about the other great books from Fox Chapel Publishing, or to find a retailer near you, call toll-free at 800-457-9112 or visit us at www.FoxChapelPublishing.com.
We are always looking for talented authors.
To submit an idea, please send a brief inquiry to acquisitions@foxchapelpublishing.com.
Or write to:
Fox Chapel Publishing
903 Square Street
Mount Joy, PA 17552

Printed in China
First printing

MIX
Paper | Supporting responsible forestry
FSC® C147414

CONTENTS

INTRODUCTION

When you choose clothing that you can layer as needed, you run the risk of seriously overpacking for any extended travels. A couple of wool sweaters, along with some knit hats, cowls, and fingerless mitts are a great way to make sure you stay warm, especially in the spring and fall when temperatures and conditions can vary wildly throughout the day. With that in mind, I've brought together a collection of sweaters, hats, cowls, and fingerless mitts, along with a shawl, some practical totes, and a couple of throws that should keep you warm and comfy on any adventure.

I grew up very close to a 33,000-acre marsh that is both a state wildlife area and national wildlife refuge at a time when the preservation and protection of the natural environment was beginning to take hold in the wider public imagination. Hundreds of thousands of waterfowl, including numerous species of ducks, herons, and cranes, either pass through or nest there. The fall migration was always spectacular when large skeins of honking geese flew overhead. My sisters and I often walked up to the local Department of Natural Resources headquarters (which we referred to as "Conservation Hill") and looked out over the vast expanse of wetlands that were, at the time, still recovering from many decades of draining and farming.

Today, I live about 50 miles from there and not only get to hear the Canada geese again but also listen with awe to the sandhill cranes with their eerie, prehistoric-sounding calls. Many opportunities exist here for me to get out and explore, with county and state parks offering a wide variety of hiking and sightseeing experiences year-round. A walk through the Kettle Moraine State Forest or along the 1,200-mile-long Ice Age National Scenic Trail presents chances to trek the varied terrain left by the retreating glaciers from the last ice age. A number of Rails to Trails paths offer biking and hiking adventures, as well.

No matter where you live or visit, it's important for our souls to reconnect with the natural world around us. Quick hikes on a local nature trail or longer treks that require overnight stops are often just what you need when the world gets too crazy to handle. Whether sleeping in a tent at a no-frills campsite or glamping at a cabin in a not-too-remote area, it makes little difference where you rest after you've spent the day recharging your internal batteries. Having warm, hand-knit sweaters and accessories offers comfort to both body and soul.

The patterns in this book are worked in a variety of techniques and wide range of sizes. Four of the five sweaters (the Hedgerow Cardigan, Wanderer Pullover, Boreas Pass Pullover, and Backcountry Trails Pullover) are sized for both men and women. Additionally, six of the ten accessory patterns (North Woods Hats, Cottonwood Cowl, Pacific Crest Cabled Hat, Shadow Canyon Slouch Hat, Duality Cowls, and Starry Night Hat and Cowl) are ideal for anyone and everyone. These knits are great for wearing on the trail, while traveling, for running into town, or for just relaxing by the fire. You don't have to live the cabin life every day, but why not pretend?

TECHNIQUES, TIPS, AND TOOLS

The knitting projects in this book assume a confident beginner's level of skill, and a few include slightly more advanced techniques, but even those of us who are seasoned knitters can always use a little brushup on the standard techniques. This section highlights the techniques you'll need to know to create these warm and cozy pieces. See page 41 for the abbreviations chart.

BIND OFFS (BO)

Among the numerous methods to bind off your knitting, here are two of the most useful and easiest to work. Make sure to keep an even tension and not work too tightly to create a smooth, nonpuckering or wavy edge.

■ STANDARD BIND OFF

Knit 2 stitches *(Fig. 1)*.

*Insert the left needle from left to right into the first stitch that was worked, then lift it over the second stitch and off the right needle to bind off 1 stitch *(Fig. 2)*, k1.

Repeat from * until the required number of stitches have been bound off.

Fig. 1

Fig. 2

■ THREE-NEEDLE BIND OFF

Place the stitches to be joined onto two separate needles. Hold the needles together in your left hand, with either the knit sides out or the purl sides out as called for in the pattern.

Using a third needle, knit the first stitch on both needles together as 1 stitch.

*Knit the next stitch on both needles together in the same way *(Fig. 3)*.

Insert the left needle closest to you from left to right into the first stitch that was worked *(Fig. 4)* and lift it over the second stitch and off the right needle to bind off 1 stitch from both needles *(Fig. 5)*.

Repeat from * until all the stitches on the left needles have been worked and 1 stitch remains on the right needle. Cut the yarn and pull the tail through the remaining stitch.

Fig. 3

Fig. 4

Fig. 5

BUTTONHOLES

One-row buttonholes are easy to make and can be worked over any stitch pattern. It may seem a bit fiddly at first, but it is really quite useful.

■ ONE-ROW BUTTONHOLE

Work to the spot where the buttonhole will be made, bring the yarn to the front of the work, and slip 1 stitch purlwise *(Fig. 6)*, then bring the yarn to the back of the work and drop it *(Fig. 7)*.

*Slip 1 stitch purlwise, insert the left needle into the first slipped stitch from left to right, and lift it over the second slipped stitch and off the right needle to bind off 1 stitch.

Repeat from * until the required number of stitches have been bound off.

Return the last slipped stitch to the left needle and turn.

Pick up the yarn and hold it in back. *Insert the right needle between the first two stitches on the left needle *(Fig. 8)*, yarn over and draw through a loop, then place the new stitch on the left needle and tighten it slightly, being careful not to pull it too tight.

Repeat from * until the same number of stitches have been cast on that were bound off, then cast on 1 more stitch, and before placing that stitch on the left needle, bring the yarn to the front. Turn.

Slip the first stitch on the left needle purlwise, lift the last cast-on stitch over the slipped stitch and off the right needle *(Fig. 9)*.

Fig. 6

Fig. 7

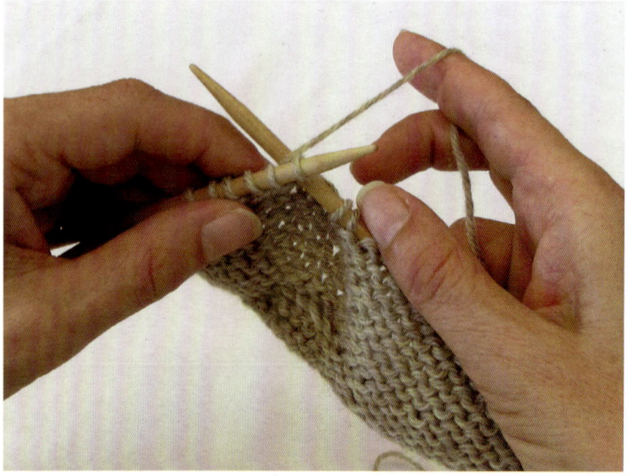

Fig. 8

Fig. 9

CABLES

Cables can be worked in a variety of ways, with all stitches being knit, purled, in ribbing, or worked in some other pattern.

BASIC CABLES

Slip the stated number of stitches to a cable needle and hold them in front for a left-cross cable *(Fig. 10)* or in back for a right-cross cable.

Work the stated number of stitches in the pattern from the left needle *(Fig. 11)*, then work the stitches on the cable needle *(Fig. 12)*.

Fig. 10

Fig. 11

Fig. 12

MULTIPLE CROSS CABLES

Slip the first given number of stitches to a cable needle and hold them in front for a left-cross cable or in back for a right-cross cable.

Slip the second given number of stitches to a second cable needle and hold that cable needle either in front or back as stated in the pattern *(Fig. 13)*.

Work the third given number of stitches from the left needle *(Fig. 14)*.

Work the stitches from the second cable needle *(Fig. 15)*.

Finally, work the stitches from the first cable needle *(Fig. 16)*.

Fig. 13

Fig. 14

Fig. 15

Fig. 16

CAST ONS (CO)

As with ending your knitted item, there are many ways to begin. Each cast on has its ideal uses, but the three described here are basic versions every knitter should get to know.

■ BACKWARD LOOP CAST ON

*Form a loop with the working strand (the strand coming from the ball of yarn).

With the strand in front of your thumb *(Fig. 17)*, slip the loop onto the needle *(Fig. 18)* and tighten it.

Repeat from * until the desired number of stitches are cast on.

> ***Note***
>
> The cast-on edge can be loose after the first row has been worked over these stitches, so make sure to cast them on fairly tightly.

Fig. 17

Fig. 18

■ LONG TAIL CAST ON

Leaving a long yarn tail (about ½" to 1" [1.3 to 2.5cm] for each stitch you need to cast on), make a slip knot in the yarn and place it on the needle *(Fig. 19)*. Pull the tail to snug the stitch up to the needle.

Holding the needle in your right hand, pick up both the long tail and the strand coming from the ball of yarn in your left hand. Insert your thumb and index finger between the strands, with the long tail over your thumb and the strand coming from the ball of yarn over your index finger, and grasp both strands with the other three fingers. Turn your left palm up slightly so that the yarn strands from the needle form a V between your fingers *(Fig. 20)*.

*Bring the needle up through the loop on your thumb *(Fig. 21)*, then reach the needle over the strand on your index finger and scoop it through the loop on your thumb *(Fig. 22)*. Remove your thumb from the loop, then insert your thumb back under the tail strand and use it to tighten the stitch on the needle *(Fig. 23)*.

Repeat from * until the desired number of stitches are cast on.

Fig. 19

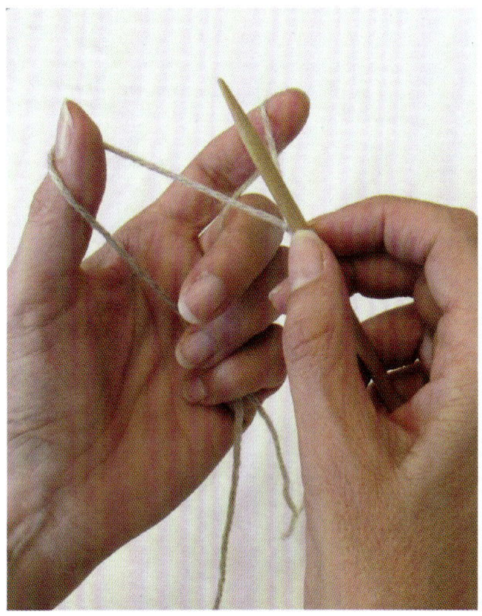

Fig. 20

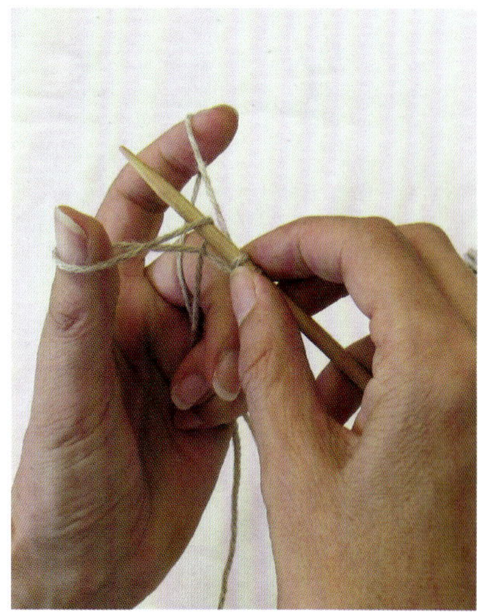

Fig. 21

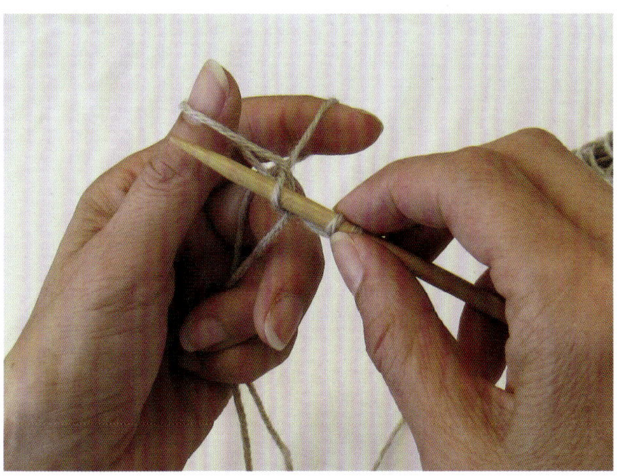

Fig. 22

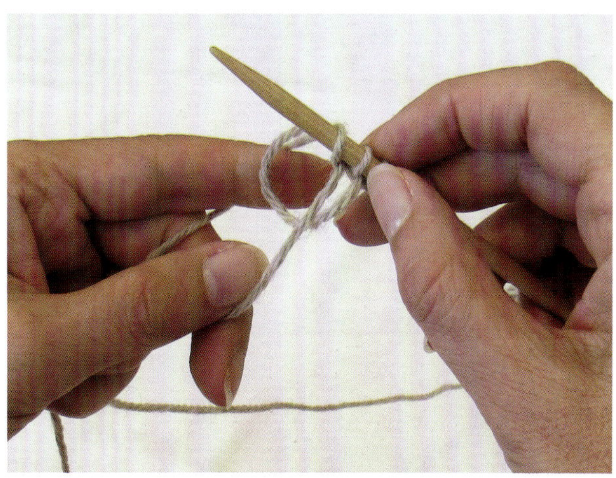

Fig. 23

■ PROVISIONAL CAST ON

With a crochet hook that is larger than the needles you'll be using, loosely make a chain that is 4 to 8 links longer than the number of stitches you need *(Fig. 24)*.

Cut the yarn and pull it through the last chain. Pull on the tail to close the last stitch but do not tighten it.

Using your needle and the working yarn, begin a few chains from one end and *insert the needle into the bump at the back of the chain *(Fig. 25)*.

Wrap the yarn around the needle and draw through a loop *(Fig. 26)*.

Repeat from * until the desired number of stitches are on the needle, making sure to end a few links from the end of the chain.

When you need to remove the chain, remove the tail from the last stitch at the end of the chain, then slowly pull on the tail to release each stitch, placing each one on the needle as you go.

Fig. 24

Fig. 25

Fig. 26

DECREASES (DEC)

Decreases are used to shape your knitting, whether it's along an edge or farther in from an edge. When multiple decreases are worked in the same row or round, the shaping is more dramatic, and when repeated over multiple rows or rounds, it can be used to create a directional line.

■ KNIT TWO TOGETHER (K2TOG)

Knit two stitches together as if they were one stitch *(Fig. 27)*—1 stitch decreased.

Fig. 27

■ PURL TWO TOGETHER (P2TOG)

Purl two stitches together as if they were one stitch *(Fig. 28)*—1 stitch decreased.

Variations on Decreases

k3tog = Knit the next three stitches together as if they were one stitch—2 stitches decreased.

p3tog = Purl the next three stitches together as if they were one stitch—2 stitches decreased.

Fig. 28

■ SLIP ONE, KNIT TWO TOGETHER, PASS SLIPPED STITCH OVER (SK2P)

Slip one stitch knitwise *(Fig. 29)*.

Knit two stitches together *(Fig. 30)*.

Finally, lift the slipped stitch over the decrease stitch and off the right needle *(Fig. 31)*—2 stitches decreased.

Fig. 29

Fig. 30

Fig. 31

■ SLIP, SLIP, KNIT (SSK)

Slip two stitches knitwise, one at a time *(Fig. 32)*.

Insert the left needle into the fronts of both slipped stitches and knit them together through the back of the loops *(Fig. 33)*—1 stitch decreased.

Fig. 32

Fig. 33

■ SLIP, SLIP, PURL (SSP)

Slip two stitches knitwise, one at a time *(Fig. 34)*, then return them to the left needle in their turned positions *(Fig. 35)*.

Insert the right needle through the back of the loops and purl them together *(Fig. 36)*—1 stitch decreased.

Fig. 34

Fig. 35

Fig. 36

Variations on Decreases

sssk = Slip three stitches knitwise, one at a time, then knit all three together through the back of the loops—2 stitches decreased.

sssp = Slip three stitches knitwise, one at a time, then purl all three together through the back of the loops—2 stitches decreased.

TWO OVER TWO RIGHT CROSS DECREASE (2/2 RC DEC)

Slip two stitches onto a cable needle and hold in back of the work as for a right cross cable *(Fig. 37)*.

*Insert the right needle into the first stitch on both the left needle and the cable needle, then knit them together *(Fig. 38)*.

Repeat from * once more—2 stitches decreased.

Fig. 37

Fig. 38

INCREASES

Like decreases, increases are used to shape your knitting. Some are meant to be nearly invisible, while others can be used to create their own design elements within the pattern.

KNIT ONE FRONT AND BACK (K1FB)

Knit into the front of the stitch but do not slip the stitch from the left needle *(Fig. 39)*.

Reach around the back of the stitch with the right needle and knit into the back of the stitch on the left needle *(Fig. 40)*, then slip the stitch from the left needle—1 stitch increased.

Fig. 39

Fig. 40

■ MAKE ONE (M1)

Insert the left needle from front to back under the strand between the last stitch worked and the next stitch *(Fig. 41)*.

Knit this strand through the back of the loop *(Fig. 42)*—1 stitch increased.

Variations on Increases

An **M1L** (make one left leaning) is the same as an M1; the instructions to make it left leaning are typically used only when right-leaning increases are also used in the same pattern.

■ MAKE ONE PURLWISE (M1P)

Insert the left needle from front to back under the strand between the last stitch worked and the next stitch *(Fig. 43)*.

Purl this strand through the back of the loop *(Fig. 44)*—1 stitch increased.

Variations on Increases

An **M1Lp** (make one left-leaning purlwise) is the same as an M1p; the instructions to make it left leaning are typically used only when right-leaning increases are also used in the same pattern.

Fig. 41

Fig. 42

Fig. 43

Fig. 44

■ MAKE ONE RIGHT LEANING (M1R)

Insert the left needle from back to front under the strand between the last stitch worked and the next stitch *(Fig. 45)*.

Knit this strand through the front of the loop *(Fig. 46)*—1 stitch increased.

Fig. 45

Fig. 46

■ MAKE ONE RIGHT-LEANING PURLWISE (M1RP)

Insert the left needle from back to front under the strand between the last stitch worked and the next stitch *(Fig. 47)*.

Purl this strand through the front of the loop *(Fig. 48)*—1 stitch increased.

Fig. 47

Fig. 48

PURL ONE FRONT AND BACK (P1FB)

Purl into the front of the stitch but do not slip the stitch from the left needle *(Fig. 49)*.

Reach around the back of the stitch with the right needle and purl into the back of the stitch on the left needle *(Fig. 50)*, then slip the stitch from the left needle—1 stitch increased.

Fig. 49

Fig. 50

PICKING UP STITCHES

Knowing how to efficiently pick up stitches is essential to creating smooth, clean edges along a neckline or armhole, or when working modularly for the Cabin Fever Tote and Dark Skies Bag.

PICK UP AND KNIT

With the right side of the work facing you and using the correct size needle, insert the needle from front to back between the first and second stitches of the first row.

Wrap the yarn around the needle and pull through a loop to make a stitch.

*Insert the needle between the first and second stitches of the next row *(Fig. 51)*.

Wrap the yarn around the needle and pull through a loop to make a stitch *(Fig. 52)*.

Repeat from * until the required number of stitches is picked up.

Fig. 51

Fig. 52

Tip

You don't always want to pick up stitches for every row worked, and sometimes you'll need to skip a row to keep the edge from stretching out. If a specific number of stitches to pick up isn't stated in the pattern, an easy way to estimate how many stitches you'll need is to base it on the gauge of the stitch pattern you'll be working and place markers every 2" (5.1cm) along the edge where the stitches will be picked up.

For example, if the gauge for your ribbing is 20 stitches per 4" (10.2cm), you will need to pick up 5 stitches for every 1" (2.5cm). So, with markers placed every 2" (5.1cm) along the edge, you'll know to pick up 10 stitches between each pair of markers.

■ PICK UP AND PURL

With the wrong side of the work facing you and using the correct size needle, insert the needle from back to front between the first and second stitches of the first row.

Wrap the yarn around the needle and pull through a loop to make a stitch.

*Insert the needle between the first and second stitches of the next row *(Fig. 53)*.

Wrap the yarn around the needle and pull through a loop to make a stitch *(Fig. 54)*.

Repeat from * until the required number of stitches is picked up. See the tip above about determining how many stitches you need to pick up and how often to skip a row.

Fig. 53

Fig. 54

SHORT ROWS

Another very useful shaping method, short rows are just that, worked over only a portion of the row or round. There are several methods for working short rows, and I've shared my favorites here.

■ GERMAN SHORT ROWS

Work to the spot where your knitting will be turned, then turn your work. Making sure the yarn is in front, slip one stitch purlwise *(Figs. 55 and 56)*.

Lift the yarn up over the top of the needle to the back and pull tightly so both legs of the slipped stitch lay over the top of the needle to form a double stitch, abbreviated as "DS" *(Figs. 57 and 58)*.

If the next stitch is a knit stitch, leave the yarn in back; if the next stitch is a purl stitch, bring the yarn to the front between the needles.

On subsequent rows/rounds, work both legs of each double stitch together as one *(Figs. 59 and 60)*.

Fig. 55

Fig. 56

Fig. 57

Fig. 58

Fig. 59

Fig. 60

■ SIMPLE SHORT ROWS

Work to the spot where your knitting will be turned, then turn your work.

Making sure the yarn is in the correct position to work the next row, slip 1 stitch purlwise *(Fig. 61)* and tighten the stitch to prevent leaving a big loop *(Fig. 62)*.

Fig. 61

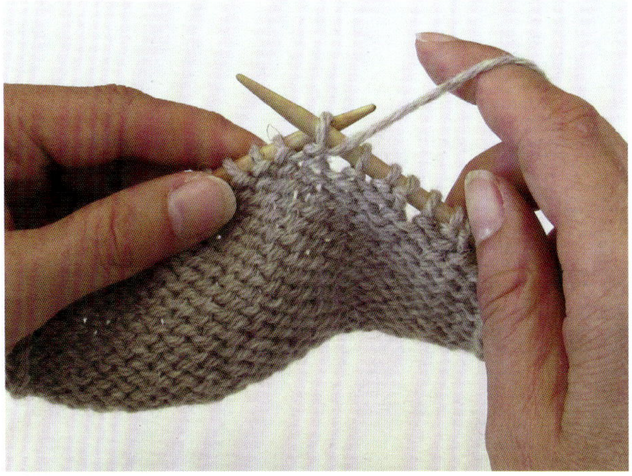

Fig. 62

■ WRAP-AND-TURN SHORT ROWS (W&T)

On right-side rows, work to the spot where your knitting will be turned. With the yarn in back, slip one stitch purlwise *(Fig. 63)*.

Move the yarn to the front between the needles *(Fig. 64)*, return the slipped stitch to the left needle and return the yarn to the back *(Fig. 65)*, then turn your work.

To hide the wrap on a right-side row, insert the right needle below the wrap and into the stitch it wraps *(Fig. 66)*. Knit the stitch and the wrap together as one stitch and so that the wrap falls to the wrong side.

Fig. 63

Fig. 64

Fig. 65

Fig. 66

On wrong-side rows, work to the spot where your knitting will be turned. With the yarn in front, slip one stitch purlwise *(Fig. 67)*.

Move the yarn to the back between the needles *(Fig. 68)*, return the slipped stitch to the left needle, return the yarn to the front *(Fig. 69)*, then turn your work.

To hide the wrap on a wrong-side row, lift the back loop of the wrap to the left needle *(Fig. 70)*, then purl the stitch and the wrap together so that the wrap falls to the wrong side.

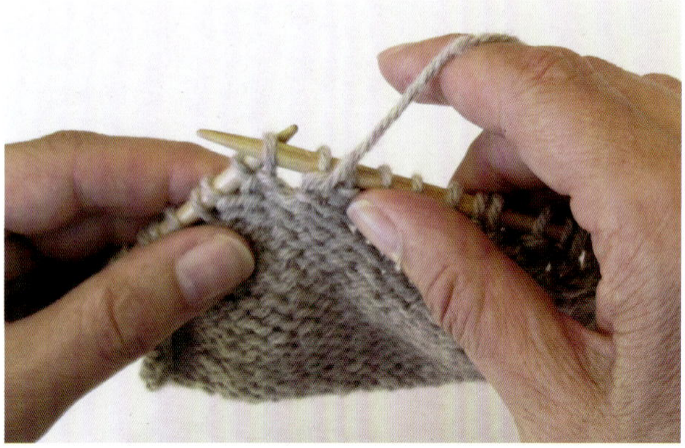

Fig. 67

Fig. 68

Fig. 69

Fig. 70

TWIST STITCHES

Twist stitches are actually two-stitch-wide mini cables. They're easiest to work without a cable needle; just twist the upper stitch to either the right or left.

■ LEFT TWIST (LT)

With the right needle to the back of your work, skip the first stitch on the left needle and knit the second stitch through the back of the loop *(Fig. 71)*. Do not slip the stitch from the needle.

Knit the first stitch on the left needle as usual *(Fig. 72)*, then slip both stitches from the left needle.

Fig. 71

Fig. 72

■ RIGHT TWIST (RT)

Knit two stiches together *(Fig. 73)* but do not slip the stitches from the left needle.

Knit the first stitch again *(Fig. 74)*, then slip both stitches from the left needle.

Fig. 73

Fig. 74

STRANDED COLORWORK

Knitting with two colors at the same time is frequently referred to as "Fair Isle" knitting, named for a style of knitting originating in the Shetland Islands northeast of Scotland. Best used when working in the round with only two colors in each round, you can hold both colors in one hand or hold one color in each hand. I really like using the latter method because the yarns never tangle, and it's easy to hold one strand of yarn in each hand as you work, knitting some stitches English/American-style with the yarn in the right hand, and knitting the other stitches Continental-style with the yarn held in the left hand. It does take some practice to become comfortable knitting with the hand you're not accustomed to using but with time and patience, you'll become a pro.

■ BASIC TECHNIQUE

Hold the needles with your stitches as you normally would, and with one color in each hand.

To work a stitch with the color in your right hand, insert the right needle into the next stitch and wrap the yarn around the needle, then pull through a stitch *(Fig. 75)*.

To work a stitch with the color in your left hand, insert the right needle into the next stitch, then use the right needle to catch the yarn in your left hand and draw through a loop *(Fig. 76)*.

■ SWITCHING COLORS

Whenever you switch colors, spread the stitches near the right needle tip apart slightly so that they're not too close together (this will help to make sure the unused yarn doesn't pull those stitches close together and cause your work to pucker), then knit the next stitch with the new color.

Fig. 75

Fig. 76

Fig. 77

Fig. 78

■ WEAVING IN

Whenever you have a large number of stitches where the yarn floated across the back must cross before it will be worked with again, it's a good idea to "weave in" or "trap" that unused strand so it doesn't become too long (and create the ideal place to snag fingers, jewelry, or buttons while putting on or taking off the item). A general rule of thumb is about 1" (2.5cm) or more worth of stitches.

To weave in the strand from your left hand, insert the right needle into the next stitch and under the strand in your left hand *(Fig. 77)*, then knit the stitch as you normally would and continue as usual. The strand that's been woven in will lie over the top of the stitch you just knit.

To weave in the strand from your right hand, bring the yarn in your right hand up over the left needle and hold it in place with your right index finger *(Fig. 78)*.

Insert the right needle into the next stitch and above the strand from your right hand, catch the yarn in your left hand and draw through a loop, letting the strand from your right hand return to its normal position. The strand that's been woven in will lie below the stitch that's just been knit.

SUPPLIES AND TIPS

Mastering the techniques is certainly key to falling in love with this craft, but the following advice will help you turn those stitches into finished projects you'll want to cuddle up in proudly.

■ CHOOSING A SIZE

Many knitting patterns are written for specific sizes. Always look at the given measurements to make sure you knit a garment that will fit in the same way it's shown in the photos. In the past, patterns were often written for a very limited size range, but I've tried to include women's sizing from XS (extra small) through 4XL and men's sizing from S (small) through 3XL for each of the garments as needed.

The amount of "ease" or extra width is also sometimes noted. This will also affect how the garment fits. "Ease" is the amount of extra width calculated into a design to achieve a certain look. Cardigans will need to be a little larger than pullovers to accommodate the layers worn under them. Pullovers can range from very close fitting (with no extra ease) to oversized (with a lot of extra ease).

The ease in various fits will generally follow some set dimensions:

A **very close-fitting** sweater is the *actual* bust/chest measurement or less

A **close-fitting** sweater has 1" to 2" (2.5 to 5.1cm) of extra width

A **standard-fitting** sweater has 2" to 4" (5.1 to 10.2cm) of extra width

A **loose-fitting** sweater has 4" to 6" (10.2 to 15.2cm) of extra width

An **oversized-fitting** sweater has 6" (15.2cm) or more of extra width

If the size that you want to make leaves less than the suggested amount of ease needed for your own bust/chest measurement and you don't want the sweater to fit too snuggly, consider making the next size up. When measuring your bust or chest to determine which size to knit, measure around the fullest part of the bust or chest since this is the circumference that the sweater needs to fit around.

Hats should fit relatively snugly to make sure they stay on. One-size hats will fit most adults. The fingerless mitts in the Visions Cowl and Fingerless Mitts pattern should fit with little or no extra ease.

CHOOSING YARNS AND COLORS

One of the most important choices you can make when knitting something is choosing the yarn for your project. The fiber content of the yarn you use is also very important. Although a rugged wool yarn is ideal for cool weather outerwear, it would not be a good choice for an elegant evening top (where an extra-fine Merino wool or smooth silk is better suited). However, you don't need a PhD in textile science to choose the right yarn for your next project, and with a little experience you can become confident when it comes to picking out the right yarn for your next creation.

Commercially produced yarns carry a symbol on their labels indicating the "weight" or thickness of the yarn. The Craft Yarn Council (CYC) introduced a numbering system in the early 2000s to help

Some of the yarns used for the projects in the book. From left to right: #2 fine weight (Leading Men Fiber Arts Callback and Wonderland Yarns Mad Hatter), #3 light weight (Knit One Crochet Too Hand Painted Batiste, Berroco Spree, and Plymouth Yarns Merino Del Sol), and #4 medium weight (Gazzal Unicorn, Green Mountain Spinnery Weekend Wool, and Cascade Yarns Cantata).

knitters when it comes to choosing the correct weight yarn. These numbers range from #0 for lace to #7 for jumbo and, just as these numbers suggest, it helps you determine not only what needle size should work for your yarn, but it also gives you a rough idea of the number of stitches per 1" (2.5cm) you can expect to achieve with stockinette stitch.

An older system uses terms like fingering, sport, DK, worsted, Aran, and bulky to describe the yarns, and is often still included in patterns, but unless you're familiar with the yarns classified under this system it can sometimes be a bit confusing; "worsted" is not only a yarn weight but also a spinning process, so make sure to check if your yarn is "worsted weight" or "worsted spun." And "4-ply" (a British term) often leaves me puzzled as to how thin or thick the yarn is. Even when you have several yarns with the same CYC weight, the thickness and density of a strand of each yarn can vary quite a bit and is influenced not only by the fiber content but also by how it was processed and spun. This means that recommended needle sizes and gauges can differ from one yarn to another within the same weight category. Make sure to read the label, compare yarns side by side, and swatch them whenever possible (more on that in the gauge section on page 31).

Ideal for any outdoor adventure, I used mostly wool or wool blend yarns to achieve the cozy, cabin-living vibe for this book, ranging from a coarse wool from Green Mountain Spinnery for the Cabin Fever

A side-by-side comparison of nine of the eleven #4 medium weight yarns I used in this book. From left to right: Green Mountain Spinnery Cotton Comfort, Green Mountain Spinnery Weekend Wool, Studio Donegal Soft Donegal, Berroco Ultra Alpaca, Malabrigo Rios, Gazzal Unicorn, Acorn and Oak Fibers Scholar, Valley Yarns Becket, and Cascade Yarns Cantata.

Yarn Weight	Numerical Weight	Type of Yarns in Category	Ply Count	Gauge in Stockinette Stitch	Recommended Needle Size
Lace	0	Fingering 10-count crochet thread	1-2	33-40 sts	US 000-1 (1.5-2.25mm)
Super Fine	1	Sock, Fingering, Baby	3-4	27-32 sts	US 1-3 (2.25-3.25mm)
Fine	2	Sport, Baby	5	23-26 sts	US 3-5 (3.25-3.75mm)
Light	3	DK, Light Worsted	8	21-24 sts	US 5-7 (3.75-4.5mm)
Medium	4	Worsted, Afghan, Aran	10-12	16-20 sts	US 7-9 (4.5-5.5mm)
Bulky	5	Chunky, Craft, Rug	14	12-15 sts	US 9-11 (5.5-8mm)
Super Bulky	6	Super Bulky, Roving	16	7-11 sts	US 11-17 (8-12.75mm)
Jumbo	7	Jumbo, Roving	16 & up	6 sts & fewer	US 17 (12.75mm) and larger

Tote, to a classic wool from Acorn and Oak Fibers for the Pacific Crest Cabled Hat, to a light and cozy cotton/wool blend from Cascade Yarns for the South Fork Throw. Colors from nature and time-honored color combinations were my main source of inspiration when it came to choosing colors for the designs. (Though I did have fun exploring some other possibilities as well, especially when working on the Maywood Shawl and Dark Skies Bag.) When picking your own colors, don't be afraid to venture outside your comfort zone (at least a little bit) and find inspiration all around you.

■ GAUGE

Tip

Do you have to knit a gauge swatch? The short answer is: YES!

For projects that need to fit in a specific way, it's important to get as close to the gauge stated in the pattern as possible; even a small variation can affect the fit and drape of a sweater. I once put together a chart showing how even a small amount of difference in gauge can affect the finished measurements. On smaller projects, the discrepancy might not be too evident, but once you get into sweater territory, the differences are very obvious.

The number of stitches per 1" (2.5cm) is often much more important than the number of rows per 1" (2.5cm), but you should also make sure to check your row gauge as well. It will affect the shaping for sleeves and V-neck lines and may affect the frequency at which your work increases or decreases.

If the pattern you want to make uses two or more different types of stitch patterns (such as the Hedgerow Cardigan, which uses the stockinette stitch and mosaic knitting, or the Wanderer Pullover, which mixes a knit/purl texture with stranded knitting), make sure to work a gauge swatch for *both* stitch patterns. You may need to change needle sizes when transitioning from one to the other to maintain the correct measurements. Most knitters will work stranded colorwork patterns more tightly than stockinette stitch or textured patterns, so it's important to know if you will need to adjust your needle sizes between each technique.

Measuring the number of stitches per 1" (2.5cm).

Measuring the number of rows per 1" (2.5cm).

When knitting up a gauge swatch, use the needle size listed in the pattern as your starting point. You may need to change to larger or smaller needles to achieve the correct number of stitches per 1" (2.5cm). If you get more stitches across 1" (2.5cm), try a larger size needle. If you get fewer stitches across 1" (2.5cm), try a smaller needle size.

Also make sure to occasionally check the gauge of the garment as you work. The true test of how accurate your gauge swatch was is how closely your project matches the swatch. If it's off, rip out the stitches you need to and switch to larger or smaller needles as needed.

■ USING CIRCULAR AND DOUBLE-POINTED NEEDLES

For the most part, the designs in this book were knit using circular needles. Available in every size and in a number of different materials, they come in a variety of lengths that can easily accommodate a large number of stitches when working back and forth, as well as smaller numbers of stitches when working in the round.

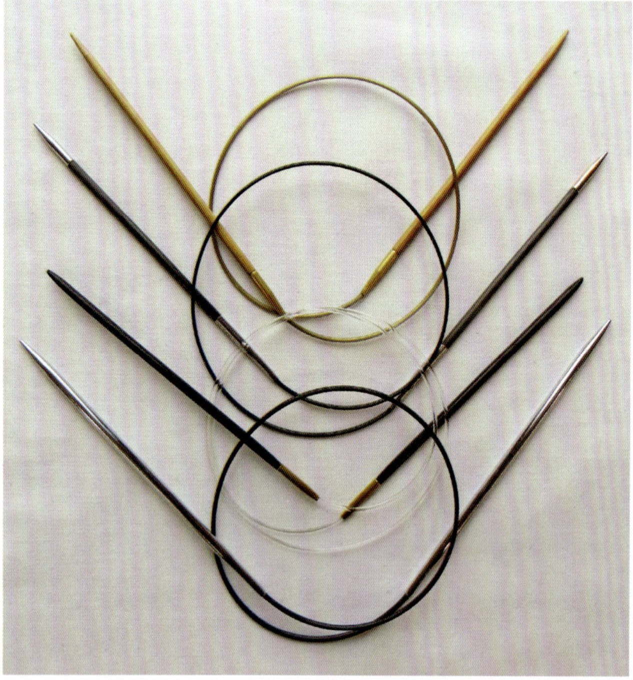

Circular needles are made in many materials. From top to bottom: bamboo, carbon fiber with nickel-plated tips, wood, and aluminum.

Double-pointed needles are useful for working with a smaller number of stitches. From left to right: aluminum, bamboo, wood, and plastic.

Hats often start out on a short circular needle that is 16" (40.6cm) long then are changed to double-pointed needles as you shape the top. At that point, the number of stitches decreases so much that it's no longer possible to work on the circular needle. Cowls are nice because you use the same circular needle for the entire project. Designs like the Maywood Shawl and the Lehigh Cowl start on a longer circular needle, then change to a short circular needle as the number of stitches decreases. Sweater sleeves usually begin on double-pointed needles, then change to short circular needles as you increase the number of stitches.

Frequently, when you first take circular needles out of their package, the cable will be fairly tightly coiled and unwilling to straighten out. To remedy this, bring water to a boil either on the stove or in a microwave, then carefully place the pan or bowl on a heat-resistant pad. Holding the circular needle by both tips near where they're attached to the cable, lower the cable into the heated water, and you should see the cable relax immediately. Hold the cable in the water for 10 to 15 seconds, then lift it out of the water and straighten it. If there's still a little more curl to the cable than you prefer, place it back into the hot water for another 10 to 15 seconds. Wipe off the cable when you're satisfied with how much it has relaxed.

■ USING STITCH MARKERS

When working in the round, stitch markers are essential for marking where your rounds begin and end. Frequently on sweater patterns, they're also used to mark the right side of the body (since the left side of the body is where rounds most often begin and end). Markers can also be used to indicate where a particular patterned panel is placed within a larger ground of stockinette or another basic stitch pattern. For example, the diamond centered on the front, back, and sleeves of the Boreas Pass Pullover on page 160.

They also come in handy for marking the length of each pattern repeat across a row or round, making it easier to see where you might have made any mistakes in reading your chart.

Stitch markers are available in a wide range of colors, shapes, and materials. Clockwise from upper left: metal rings with beads, removable clips, soft plastic rings, and thick plastic rings.

■ WORKING FROM CHARTS

Most of the stitch patterns used in this book are charted out rather than written out line by line. Charts are a great visual reference that can easily tell you where you are in a pattern. When worked in the round, all chart rows are read from right to left (the direction of the knitting if you knit right-handed). When worked back and forth, all right-side rows are read from right to left, and all wrong-side rows are read from left to right (again, the direction of the knitting as seen from the right side if you're working right-handed). Whether right-side rows are even-numbered or odd-numbered depends on how the chart begins.

The charts represent what you see on the right side of your knitting (even when you're working wrong-side rows back and forth). The chart key will indicate how to work each symbol; for instance, a blank chart square (a box with no symbol in it) will be knit on the right side and purled on the wrong side, often abbreviated as "k on RS; p on WS." Reading charts where you work back and forth may seem counterintuitive at first, but with practice, you'll become more comfortable with it.

The charts for the side panels in the Winter Trails Throw on page 69 include gray squares labeled "no stitch." This indicates that one or more stitches have been decreased out of the work or that stitches will be added on another row, and they're included in the chart so that the sections of the chart will line up. This makes it much easier to read the chart and to follow your knitting as well.

Chart A2 is from the Wanderer Pullover.

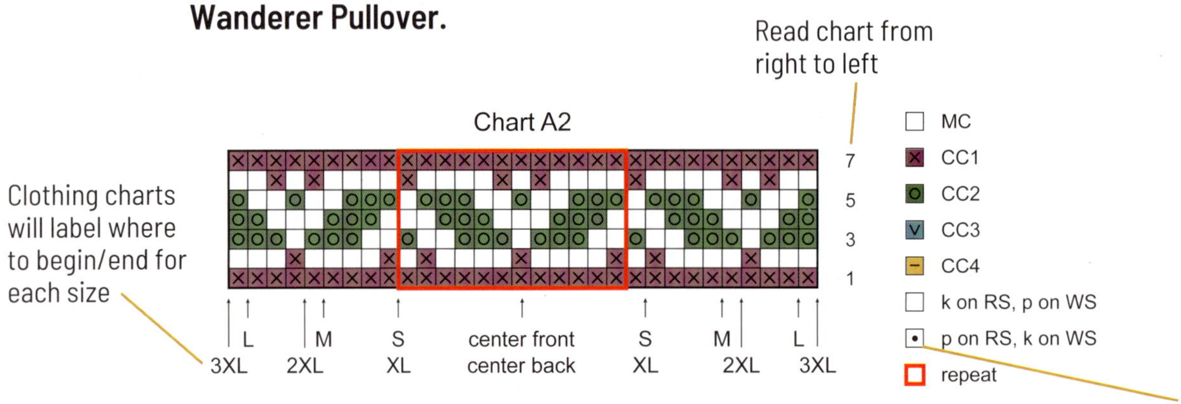

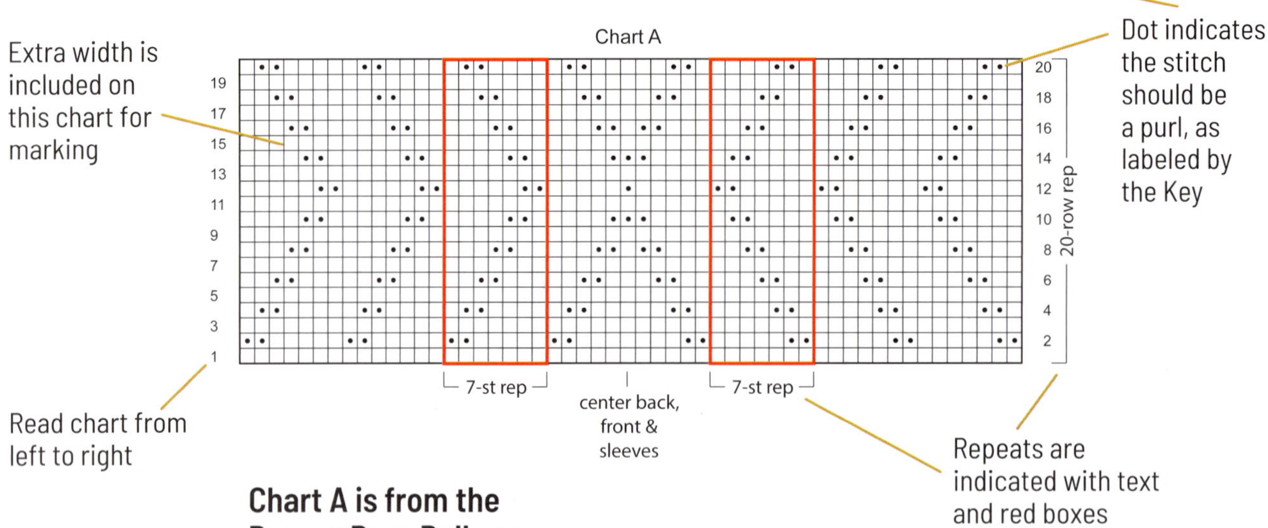

Chart A is from the Boreas Pass Pullover.

Pay attention to the Key for each pattern. The colors may change between projects.

Some charts have a repeat indicated, with additional stitches outside of the repeat on both the left and right sides of the repeat. These sections on each side of the repeat are used to indicate the beginning and ending points of the pattern when a full repeat is not worked all the way across the row/round. For some designs, such as the Wanderer Pullover and the Boreas Pass Pullover, extra width is included in the chart so that you can use that area to mark where you will be working your raglan increases or sleeve increases/decreases.

One of the most versatile tools to have, stitch holders come in a range of lengths to accommodate almost any number of stitches.

■ WHETHER TO USE STITCH HOLDERS OR SCRAP YARN

Sometimes when working in the round, you will need to place a few stitches on hold while you work just a section of the garment. Whether you should use a stitch holder or scrap yarn depends on how many stitches you need to place on hold and the circumference of the knitting.

Using scrap yarn is ideal if you're dividing a body at the armholes when working from the bottom up, or if you're dividing the body and sleeves when working from the top down. The large number of stitches makes it difficult to place that many stitches onto holders. Scrap yarn is also ideal for placing stitches for a thumb gusset, such as for the Visions Fingerless Mitts on page 54, on hold because of the very small circumference involved.

Using stitch holders is ideal for holding shoulder stitches that will later be joined using Three-Needle Bind Off (see page 9).

■ USING SHORT ROWS

One of the best knitting techniques I've ever learned is short rows. They can be used to shape the neck for a garment worked in the round from the top down, to add more length when the row gauges of two or more stitch patterns being worked at the same time are not identical, to add bust darts, and to shape shoulders before binding off. They can also be worked in different colors to add contrast-colored wedges to a design.

I particularly like short rows for shoulder shaping, as they prevent "stair steps" as you bind off stitches to shape shoulders.

Short rows are ideal when adding a shawl collar to a garment, such as the one on the Hedgerow Cardigan. They allow you to pick up all the stitches you need for button bands and a collar at the same time. Once the collar is shaped, you can just work over all the stitches to complete the button bands and collar without the need to sew any seams.

Another great use is for working in sections. The Dark Skies Bag is worked in sections so that you're not sewing together a lot of pieces to complete the bag. Two of the squares on both the front and back of the bag are worked by picking up stitches along an edge (the vertical needle) to your working stitches (the horizontal needle) *(Fig. 79)*. Then, as you work back and forth over the working (green) stitches, the last stitch nearest the vertical needle is joined using either ssk, k2tog, or p2tog to the next stitch on the vertical needle *(Fig. 80)*.

Fig. 79

Fig. 80

■ PICKING UP STITCHES ALONG A VERTICAL EDGE

Some of the designs in this book (such as the Crosshatch Tunic, the South Fork Throw, and the Winter Trails Throw) require you to pick up stitches along a vertical edge. There's no hard-and-fast rule for how many stitches to pick up for every 1" (2.5cm), but the stitch gauge is a good guide, and the pattern will often specify how many stitches are needed over a specific number of rows. For example, the South Fork Throw instructs you to pick up two stitches for every three rows. Some patterns list a specific number of stitches, especially if the number of stitches picked up needs to accommodate a stitch pattern.

A good way to make sure the number of stitches you pick up is correct is to find the gauge for the edging you'll be adding to the vertical edge, and then measure the length of the edge where the stitches will be added. Multiply the length of the edge by the number of stitches to the 1" (2.5cm) you need, and you'll get the number of stitches to pick up. However, you may have to fudge that number slightly to get the exact number required.

■ BUTTONS

Occasionally you will need to sew buttons onto a project. The number and size of the buttons you need will be listed with the materials for the project. Button diameter is often specified in millimeters (mm) and the nearest fraction of an inch (sometimes down to the 16th or 32nd of an inch). Buttons for knit pieces tend to be larger than regular shirt buttons. If the buttons you intend to use are not exactly the same size that's called for in the pattern, just make sure they are at least slightly larger than the buttonholes but slightly smaller than the width of the button band. Buttons that are too small will easily slip out of the buttonholes.

When sewing a button to a piece of knitting, use sewing thread that is the same color as the button (or as close as you can find). This will ensure that the thread is less noticeable once the button is attached, and it will be sturdier than if you use the project yarn. However, if you're using shank buttons (buttons that have a metal or plastic loop under the button face), sewing thread that is the same color as the yarn is fine.

Buttons come in a wide variety of sizes and materials, from vintage to contemporary.

Fig. 81

Fig. 82

Shank buttons are great for use with knitting because the length of the shank allows the button to sit neatly above the buttonhole without distorting the button band. Flat buttons (those without a shank) will need a little extra help. To sew these buttons to a button band with minimal distortion, you can add a thread "shank." Hold a heavy tapestry needle, toothpick, or similar object under the button as you sew it on. Once you've passed the sewing needle and thread through the holes in the button three or four times, and before you knot off the thread, insert the sewing needle into one of the holes in the button but not through the band *(Fig. 81)*. Instead, with the sewing needle and thread between the button and the button band, remove the object you're holding under the button, then tightly wrap the thread around the strands of thread under the button three or four times *(Fig. 82)*. Insert the needle through the button band to the wrong side, making sure your wrapping is tight, then knot off the thread on the wrong side.

Looking for buttons can be a challenge (I often refer to them as the bane of my existence because I always seem to have trouble finding options in the color, size, and quantity that will work). If you don't have a fabric or craft store in your area or a local yarn shop that stocks buttons, try looking at resale shops or antique stores for some amazing vintage buttons. There are also a number of good online sources that sell a wide variety of both new and vintage buttons.

■ HANDLES

Two of the designs featured in this collection (the Cabin Fever Tote and Dark Skies Bag) need handles. The style and length of the handles should be compatible with the size and function of the individual design. While it might be attractive to knit or braid straps from the same yarn that you used to knit the bag, they will stretch and may not be well suited to the needs of your bag.

For a tote, you want sturdy handles that can help support the weight of anything you intend to carry with you. Natural materials like leather are more traditional and ideal for this purpose, coming in a several colors and styles. If you're vegan or just don't like the idea of using leather, choosing sturdy straps woven of cotton, linen, or hemp are a great alternative, but you do want to make sure the material you use is at least 1" (2.5cm) wide.

When you have a smaller piece, such as a shoulder bag, the handles don't need to be as substantial. There are lots of options available in all sorts of materials, colors, and styles. You can find either a ready-to-attach assemblage or get individual components, depending on your style preferences. Using a metal chain may or may not be a good choice and depends on the thickness or weight of the chain, so keep that in mind when you see that attractive chain strap. The same goes for leather: some of the leather straps that you'll find may be too heavy and thick for a lighter weight knitted shoulder bag, so you may want to consider a braided leather cord instead.

Shopping for bag handles online, while convenient, can be overwhelming. If you're having trouble visualizing what the handle would look like when attached to your bag, look at what you already have in your closet, or go on a quick shopping trip to see what has been used by ready-to-wear manufacturers. Make sure to take some quick measurements and notes on what you like. That will simplify the process so that you can eliminate those things that won't work.

Some handles come with post and screw attachments, ideal for small bags, making them easy to add to the body of the bag. Other handles, especially those intended for totes, need to be sewn onto the bag. Many have pre-punched holes, making the sewing simpler and ensuring even stitches. To sew the handles to the bag, be sure to use a double strand of button thread, which is sturdier than regular sewing thread.

Place one handle on each side of the bag, with the inner edges about one-third of the way from each end. Sew one handle to each side of the tote through all layers as follows: Insert the needle from the wrong side up through the first hole and pull the thread to the right side. Insert the needle from the right side down through the second hole and pull the thread to the wrong side. Make another stitch through the first two holes again to reinforce the stitching. Continue stitching through the remaining holes in the tab, pulling the thread up to the right side in the next hole, then down to the wrong side in the next hole (the stitches will alternate right side and wrong side, and only half of them will be visible). Make two stitches at the other end of the tab to reinforce the stitching. Then work back along the edge of the tab to the beginning, making sure to make the stitch on the right side where the previous stitch was on the wrong side, and vice versa; you'll have what looks like a continuous line of stitching *(Fig. 83)*. Knot the thread securely on the wrong side.

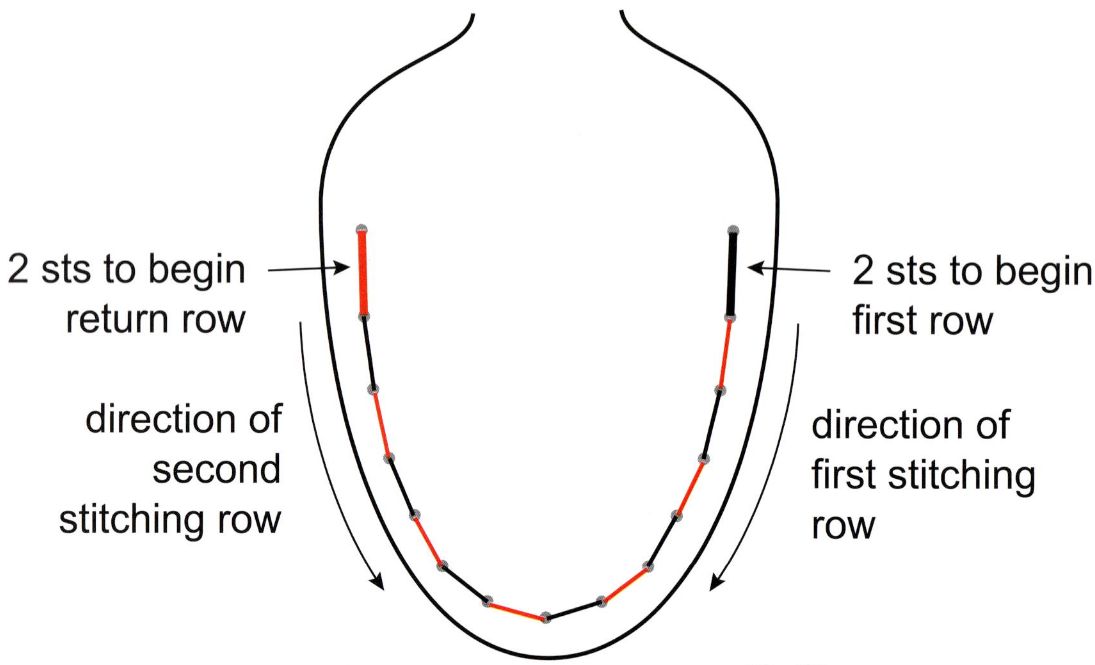

Fig. 83

ABBREVIATIONS

*	repeat instructions following the single asterisk as directed
†	repeat instructions following the single dagger as indicated
2/2 RC dec	two over two right cross decrease
approx	approximately
beg	begin(ning)
BO	bind off
CC	contrast color
CO	cast on
cont	continu(e/ed/es/ing)
dec	decreas(e/ed/es/ing)
DS	double stitch
inc	increas(e/ed/es/ing)
k	knit
k1fb	knit into front and back of same stitch—1 stitch increased
k2tog	knit 2 stitches together—1 stitch decreased
k3tog	knit 3 stitches together—2 stitches decreased
LH	left-hand
LT	left twist
M1 (M1L)	make 1 (make 1 left): insert left needle from front to back, knit in back of loop—1 stitch increased
M1p (M1Lp)	make 1 left purl: insert left needle from front to back, purl in back of loop—1 stitch increased
M1R	make 1 right: insert left needle from back to front, knit in front of loop—1 stitch increased
M1Rp	make 1 right purl: insert left needle from back to front, purl in front of loop—1 stitch increased
MC	main color
p	purl
p1fb	purl into front and back of same stitch—1 stitch increased
p2tog	purl 2 stitches together—1 stitch decreased
p3tog	purl 3 stitches together—2 stitches decreased
patt(s)	pattern(s)
pm	place marker
psso	pass slipped stitch(es) over
rem	remain(ing)
rep	repeat(s)
RH	right-hand
rnd(s)	round(s)
RS	right side
RT	right twist
sk2p	slip 1 stitch knitwise, knit 2 stitches together, pass slipped stitch over—2 stitches decreased
sl	slip(ped)
sm	slip marker
ssk	slip 2 stitches knitwise and knit 2 together through the back loops—1 stitch decreased
ssp	slip 2 stitches knitwise and purl 2 together through the back loops—1 stitch decreased
sssk	slip 3 stitches knitwise and knit 3 together through the back loops—2 stitches decreased
sssp	slip 3 stitches knitwise and purl 3 together through the back loops—2 stitches decreased
st(s)	stitch(es)
tbl	through back loop(s)
w&t	wrap and turn
WS	wrong side
wyib	with yarn in the back
wyif	with yarn in the front
yo	yarn over

SOUTH FORK *Throw*

Inspired by classic Western blankets, the combination of cotton and wool in this yarn can be used year-round. The smallest size is perfect for one person curling up with a good book; the larger sizes are great for couples snuggling in front of a cozy fire or while binge-watching your favorite new series.

SKILL LEVEL: EASY

FINISHED MEASUREMENTS:

35 ½ [43 ½, 51 ½]" (90.2 [110.5, 130.8]cm) wide x 39 ¾ [52, 63 ¾]" (101 [132.1, 161.9]cm) long

SIZES

S [M, L]

YARN

715 [1261, 1938] yds (654 [1153, 1772]m) #4 medium weight yarn in Main Color (MC)

82 [101, 120] yds (75 [92, 110]m) #4 medium weight yarn in Contrast Color 1 (CC1)

72 [89, 106] yds (66 [81, 97]m) #4 medium weight yarn in Contrast Color 2 (CC2)

86 [107, 127] yds (79 [98, 116]m) #4 medium weight yarn in Contrast Color 3 (CC3)

82 [101, 120] yds (75 [92, 110]m) #4 medium weight yarn in Contrast Color 4 (CC4)

MATERIALS

US Size 9 (5.5mm) circular needles, or size needed for gauge, in length of 32" (81.3cm)

Stitch holders or scrap yarn

US Size I/9 (5.5mm) crochet hook, or larger for provisional cast on

Scissors

Tapestry needle

YARN INFORMATION

Sample uses Cantata from Cascade Yarns (70% cotton, 30% superwash Merino wool; 3.5oz [100g]; 218yds [200m]) in colors #16 Sand (MC—4 [6, 9] skeins), #10 Navy (CC1—1 skein), #42 Ginger (CC2—1 skein), #28 Antique Moss (CC3—1 skein) and #35 Pine (CC4—1 skein)

GAUGE

15 sts and 23 rows = 4" (10.2cm) in stockinette stitch, blocked

33-row stripe bands measure approx 5" (12.7cm) wide

PATTERN NOTES

This throw is worked in one piece, beginning with a provisional cast on.

When working the stripes, do not cut the main color. Instead, carry it loosely up along the side edge and twist it with the contrast color at the beginning of each RS row.

SPECIAL STITCHES

St st (stockinette stitch) = Knit RS rows and purl WS rows.

Rev St st (reverse stockinette stitch) = Purl RS rows and knit WS rows.

Shown in size Small.

THROW

Using crochet hook and scrap yarn, loosely make a chain 132 [162, 192] chains long. Cut yarn and pull end through last chain, but do not tighten.

Using circular needle and MC, beg a couple chains from one end, pick up and knit 127 [157, 187] sts in back loops of the chain. Do not join.

Beg with a RS row, work 42 [68, 92] rows of St st, ending with a WS row.

*Join CC1 to beg with a RS row. Work 6 rows of Rev St st, ending with a WS row.

Cut CC1.

Using MC, work 3 rows of St st, ending with a RS row.

Join CC2 to beg with a WS row. Work 6 rows of Rev St st, ending with a RS row.

Cut CC2.

Using MC, work 3 rows of St st, ending with a WS row.

Join CC3 to beg with a RS row. Work 6 rows of Rev St st, ending with a WS row.

Cut CC3.

Using MC, work 3 rows of St st, ending with a RS row.

Join CC4 to beg with a WS row. Work 6 rows of Rev St st, ending with a RS row.

Cut CC4.

Using MC, beg with a WS row and work 33 [49, 65] rows of St st, ending with a WS row.

Rep from * once more, then work the stripes again.

Using MC, beg with a WS row and work 21 [33, 45] rows of St st, ending with a WS row.

Place sts on scrap yarn.

■ SIDE BORDERS

Using CC2 and with RS facing, pick up and knit 2 sts for every 3 rows along one side edge of the throw—152 [199, 244] sts.

Next Row (WS): Knit.

Cut CC2.

Join MC and knit 6 rows.

BO knitwise.

■ TOP BORDER

Return held sts to circular needle.

Using CC1 and with RS facing, pick up and knit 5 sts in end of one side border (1 st in each "valley" in the garter ridges; last st should be in same st where side border was picked up), k2tog, knit to last 2 sts, ssk, then pick up and knit 5 sts in end of side border (first stitch is picked up in same stitch where side border was picked up)—135 [165, 195] sts.

Knit 1 row.

Cut CC1.

Join MC and knit 6 rows.

BO knitwise.

■ BOTTOM BORDER

Remove provisional CO and place resulting 127 [157, 187] sts on circular needle.

Using CC4 and with RS facing, pick up and knit 5 sts in end of side border same as top border, k2tog, knit to last 2 sts, ssk, then pick up and knit 5 sts in end of side border—135 [165, 195] sts.

Knit 1 row.

Cut CC4.

Join MC and knit 6 rows.

BO knitwise.

■ FINISHING

Weave in ends.

Block to 36 [44, 52]" (91.4 [111.8, 132.1]cm) wide x 41 [53, 65]" (104.1 [134.6, 165.1]cm) long. *Note: The throw will relax slightly after blocking.*

DUALITY *Cowls*

I like playing with opposites and contrasts when designing. Sometimes, even subtle differences in texture and appearance are very intriguing as well as fun to knit. The dual nature of these cowls (both are short, but they can be combined to form one long infinity scarf) was the highlight of this design. Knit and purl texture along with oversized garter rib stitch patterns make for a quick-to-knit study of the dual nature of everyday things.

SKILL LEVEL: EASY

FINISHED MEASUREMENTS:

Garter Rib Cable Cowl: 23 ½" (59.7cm) long x 10 ½" (26.7cm) wide / **Mosaic Rib Cowl:** 23 ½" (59.7cm) long x 11" (27.9cm) wide

When both cowls are buttoned together, they measure 44" (111.8cm) long.

YARN

Garter Rib Cable Cowl: 269 yds (246m) #4 medium weight yarn

Mosaic Rib Cowl: 245 yds (224m) #4 medium weight yarn

MATERIALS

US Size 8 (5mm) needles, or size required for gauge

Stitch markers

Two cable needles

Scissors

Tapestry needle

1" (2.54cm) diameter buttons, five for each shorter cowl or ten for the long cowl

Sewing needle and thread

YARN INFORMATION

Sample uses Ultra Alpaca from Berroco (50% superfine alpaca/50% Peruvian wool; 3.5oz [100g]; 219yds [200m]) in color #6299 Lichen Mix—2 skeins for each shorter cowl, or 3 skeins for both cowls

GAUGES

20 ½ sts and 25 rows = 4" (10.2cm) in the Garter Rib Cable patt, blocked

17 sts and 23 rows = 4" (10.2cm) in the Mosaic Rib patt, blocked

PATTERN NOTES

The two shorter cowls can be worn separately or joined to be worn as a long infinity scarf.

Yarn overs are added when crossing the cables of the Garter Rib Cable pattern, then dropped on the following row to allow the extra-wide cable crossings to open up slightly.

A different number of stitches are cast on for each cowl because of the nature of each stitch pattern, though both should be very close to the same width after blocking.

SPECIAL STITCHES

6/2/6 LC (6 over 2 over 6 left cross) = Sl 6 sts to first cable needle and hold in front, sl next 2 sts to second cable needle and hold in back, k6, yo, k2 from second cable needle, yo, then k6 from first cable needle. On the next row, drop the yarn overs.

6/2/6 RC (6 over 2 over 6 right cross) = Sl 6 sts to first cable needle and hold in back, sl next 2 sts to second cable needle and hold in back, k6, yo, k2 from second cable needle, yo, then k6 from first cable needle. On the next row, drop the yarn overs.

Shown is Mosaic Rib Cowl.

GARTER RIB CABLE COWL

CO 54 sts.

Row 1 (RS): Knit.

Row 2 (WS): Sl 1 wyif, knit to end of row.

Rep last row 2 more times, ending with a WS row.

Work Rows 1–28 of Garter Cable Chart 5 times.

Buttonhole Row 1 (RS): Sl 1 wyif, k3, *BO 2 sts, work 8 more sts in established patt (there should be 9 sts after buttonhole gap); rep from * 3 more times, BO 2 sts, then knit to end of row.

Buttonhole Row 2 (WS): Sl 1 wyif, k3, *CO 2 sts over buttonhole gap using Backward Loop method (see page 12), work in established patt over next 9 sts; rep from * 3 more times, CO 2 sts over gap, then knit to end of row.

Next Row: Sl 1 wyif, knit to end of row.

Rep last row 4 more times.

BO knitwise.

■ FINISHING

Weave in ends. Block piece to 11" (28cm) wide and 24" (61cm) long.

Sew buttons about ¾" (1.9cm) above the CO edge to match placement of buttonholes.

MOSAIC RIB COWL

CO 48 sts.

Row 1 (RS): Knit.

Row 2 (WS): Sl 1 wyif, knit to end of row.

Rep last row 3 more times, ending with a RS row.

Work Rows 1–20 of Mosaic Rib Chart 5 times, then work Rows 1–18 again.

Garter Cable Chart

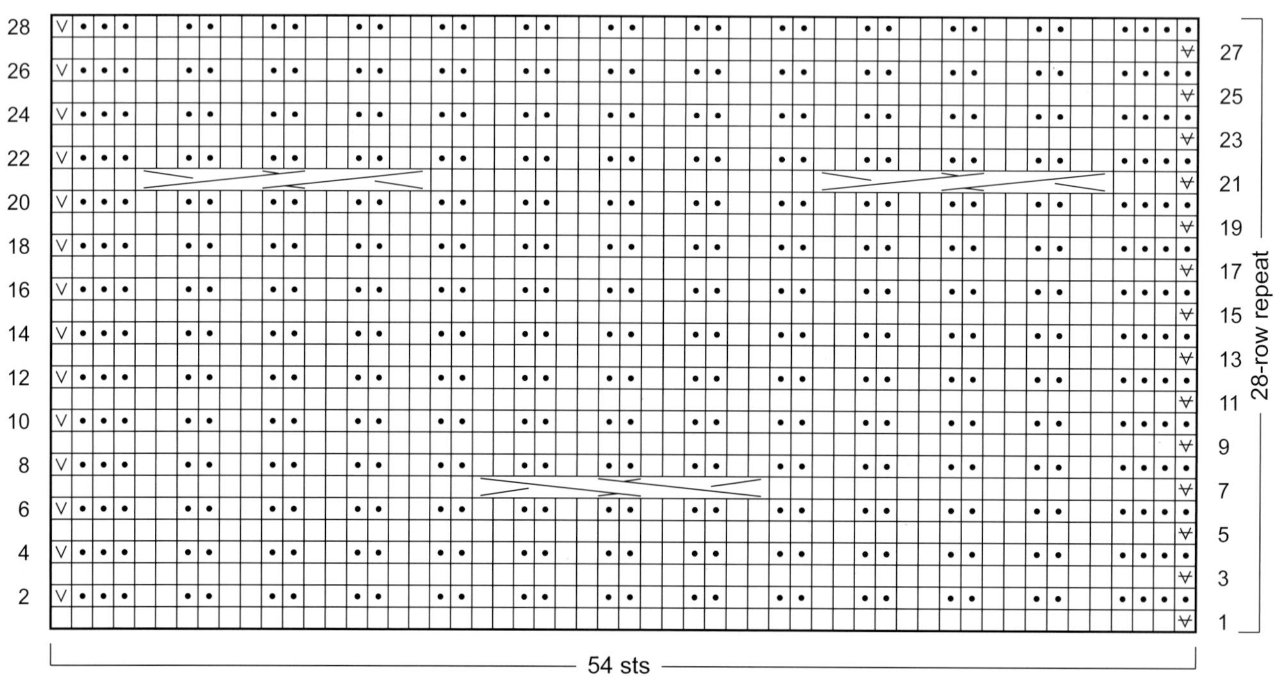

Buttonhole Row 1 (WS): Sl 1 wyif, k2, sm, *BO 2 sts, work 7 more sts in established patt (there should be 8 sts after buttonhole gap); rep from * 3 more times, BO 2 sts, then knit to end of row.

Buttonhole Row 2 (RS): Sl 1 wyif, k2, *CO 2 sts over buttonhole gap using Backward Loop method (see page 12), work in established patt over next 8 sts; rep from * 3 more times, CO 2 sts over gap, then knit to end of row.

Next Row: Sl 1 wyif, knit to end of row.

Rep last row 3 more times.

BO knitwise.

FINISHING

Weave in the ends. Block piece to 11" (28cm) wide and 24" (61cm) long.

Sew buttons about ¾" (1.9cm) above the CO edge to match placement of buttonholes.

Mosaic Rib Chart

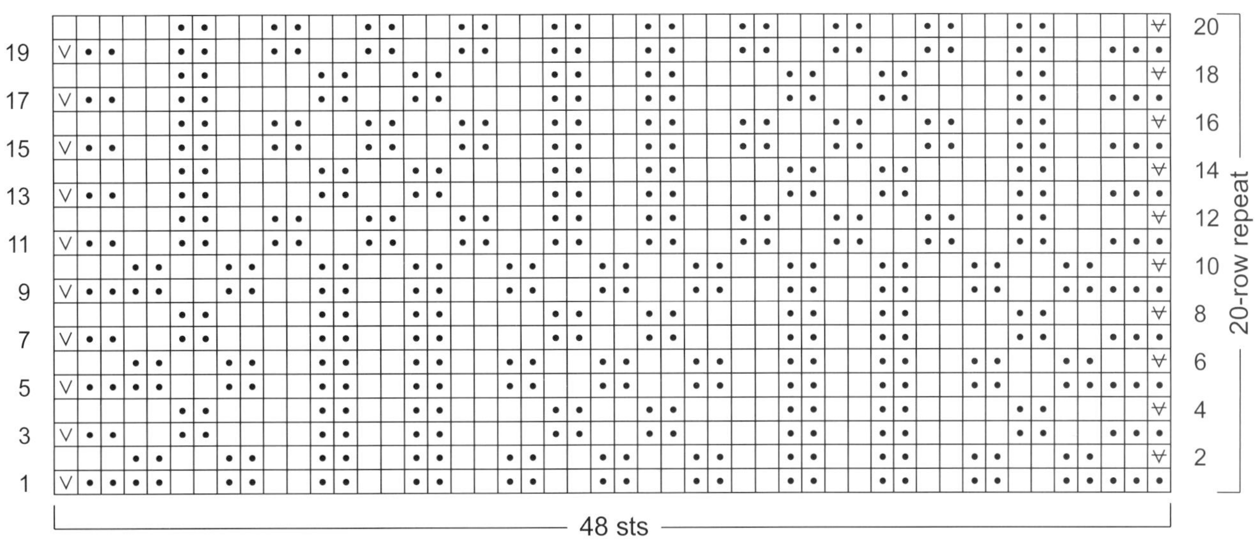

Key

- k on RS, p on WS
- p on RS, k on WS
- sl 1 wyif on WS
- sl 1 wyif on RS
- 6/2/6 LC
- 6/2/6 RC

SHADOW CANYON *Slouch Hat*

Rich with texture, the solid and painted colors play nicely together in this slouch hat. No matter what colors you use, this piece will be easy to customize for anyone on your gift list—or plan on making several to suit your different moods.

SKILL LEVEL: EASY

FINISHED MEASUREMENTS

17 ¾ [19 ¼, 20 ¾]" (45.1 [48.9, 52.7]cm) circumference above the brim and 10 ¾ [11, 11]" (27.3 [28, 28]cm) high

SIZES

S [M, L]

YARN

123 [133, 143] yds (112 [122, 131]m) #4 medium weight yarn in Main Color (MC)

60 [66, 71] yds (55 [60, 65]m) #4 medium weight yarn in Contrast Color (CC)

MATERIALS

US Size 6 (4mm) circular needle, or size required for gauge, in length of 16" (40.6cm)

Four or five US 6 (4mm) double-pointed needles, or size required for gauge

Stitch marker

Scissors

Tapestry needle

YARN INFORMATION

Sample uses Rios from Malabrigo Yarn (100% superwash Merino wool; 3.5oz [100g]; 210yds [192m]), in colors #215 Cowboy (MC—1 skein) and #288 Aquarius (CC—1 skein)

GAUGE

21 ½ sts and 36 rnds = 4" (10.2cm) in patt

PATTERN NOTE

Make sure to drop the extra yarn overs every time you work Rnds 3, 11, and 19.

Shown in size Medium.

HAT

Using circular needle and MC, CO 96 [104, 112] sts. Pm and join to work in the rnd, being careful not to twist sts.

Rnd 1: *K1, p1; rep from * around.

Rep last rnd until ribbing measures 2" (5.1cm).

Join CC.

Work Rnds 1–6 of Shadow Box patt 3 times.

Using MC, work Rnds 7 and 8 of patt.

Using MC only, knit 4 rnds.

Work Rnds 9–14 of Shadow Box patt 3 times.

Using MC, work Rnds 15 and 16 of patt.

Using MC only, knit 3 rnds.

Dec Rnd 1: Using MC, *k4 [4, 5], k2tog, k4 [5, 5], k2tog; rep from * around—80 [88, 96] sts rem.

Work Rnds 17–22 of Shadow Box patt 3 times.

Using MC, work Rnds 23 and 24 of patt.

Cut CC. Piece should measure approx 9 ½" (24.1cm) from beg.

■ SHAPE TOP

Using MC only, knit 1 rnd.

Dec Rnd 2: *K3 [3, 4], k2tog, k3 [4, 4], k2tog; rep from * around—64 [72, 80] sts rem.

Knit 1 rnd.

Dec Rnd 3: *K2 [2, 3], k2tog, k2 [3, 3], k2tog; rep from * around—48 [56, 64] sts rem.

Knit 1 rnd.

Dec Rnd 4: *K1 [1, 2], k2tog, k1 [2, 2], k2tog; rep from * around—32 [40, 48] sts rem.

Knit 1 rnd.

Sizes M and L Only

Dec Rnd 5: *K3 [1], k2tog; rep from * around—32 sts rem.

Knit 1 rnd.

Shadow Box Chart

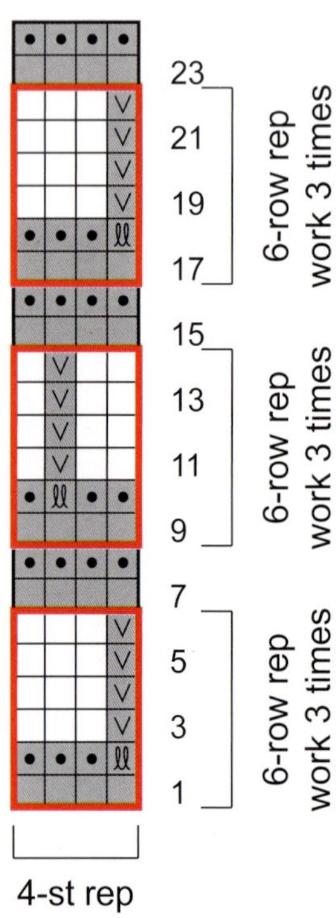

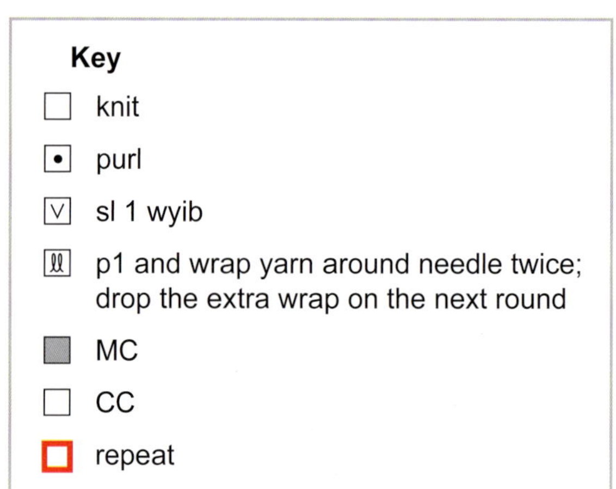

All Sizes

Dec Rnd 6: *K2, k2tog; rep from * around—24 sts rem.

Dec Rnd 7: *K1, k2tog; rep from * around—16 sts rem.

Dec Rnd 8: *K2tog; rep from * around—8 sts rem.

Cut yarn and pull tail through rem sts twice. Pull tight to close hole and fasten off on WS.

■ FINISHING

Weave in ends. Block lightly if desired.

VISIONS COWL AND *Fingerless Mitts*

Elegant enough to wear out on the town, these fingerless mitts and cowl are relaxed enough to wear wherever your adventures take you. Use vintage buttons for a one-of-a-kind look.

SKILL LEVEL: EASY

FINISHED MEASUREMENTS:

Mitts: 6 ¾ [7 ¼, 7 ¾]" (17.1 [18.4, 19.7]cm) circumference x 6 [6 ½, 7]" (15.2 [16.5, 17.8]cm) long

Cowl: 19 ½" (49.5cm) circumference x 5 ¾" (14.6cm) high

SIZES

Mitts: S [M, L]

Cowl: One size

YARN

Mitts: 115 [135, 158] yds (105 [123, 144]m) #3 light weight yarn

Cowl: 140yds [128m] #3 light weight yarn

MATERIALS

US Size 5 (3.75mm) circular needle, or size required for gauge, in length of 16" (40.6cm)

US Size 5 (3.75mm) double-pointed needles, or size required for gauge

Cable needle

Stitch marker

Stitch holders or scrap yarn

US Size F/5 (3.75mm) crochet hook

Scissors

Tapestry needle

9⁄16" (1.4cm) diameter buttons, two for cowl and two for mitts

Sewing needle and thread

YARN INFORMATION

Samples use Sueño from HiKoo (80% superwash Merino wool/20% viscose from bamboo; 3.5oz [100g]; 255yds [233m]) in color #1135 Indigo (1 skein for each)

GAUGES

21 sts and 33 rnds = 4" (10.2cm) in rib patt for cowl, blocked

25 sts and 33 rnds = 4" (10.2cm) in rib patt for mitts

10-st cable measures approx 1" (2.5cm) wide

PATTERN NOTES

The fingerless mitts begin flat, then join at the top of the cuff to work in the round to the finished hand length.

The cowl begins flat, joins to work in the round to the top border, then the stitches are divided to work back and forth again before binding off.

SPECIAL STITCHES

3/3 LC (3 over 3 left cross) = Sl 3 sts to cable needle and hold in front, k3, then k3 from cable needle.

3/3 RC (3 over 3 right cross) = Sl 3 sts to cable needle and hold in back, k3, then k3 from cable needle.

Interrupted Rib (multiple of 3 sts + 2)

Rnd 1: Knit.

Rnd 2: *K2, p1; rep from * to the last 2 sts, k2.

Rep Rnds 1 and 2 for patt.

Mitts shown in size Medium.

COWL

Using circular needle, CO 134 sts. Do not join.

Row 1 (WS): *K2, p2; rep from * to last 2 sts, k2.

Row 2 (RS): *P2, k2; rep from * to last 2 sts, p2.

Rep last 2 rows until ribbing measures approx 1 ¼" (3.2cm), ending with a WS row.

Dec Row (RS): P2tog, k2, p2, (k2, p2tog) 30 times, k2, p2, k2, p2tog—102 sts rem. Do not turn.

Joining Rnd: K3, p2, pm for beg of rnd, k92, p2, k6, p2.

Next Rnd: *K2, p1; rep from * to last 12 sts, k2, pm, work Rnd 1 of Right Cable over next 10 sts.

Cont in Interrupted Rib, with Right Cable over last 10 sts of every rnd until piece measures approx 4 ¼" (10.8cm) from beg, ending with at least 1 rnd above a cable crossing.

Inc Row (RS): (K2, p1fb) 30 times, k2, p2, k2, p1fb, then turn and leave last 5 sts unworked—133 sts.

Set-Up Row (WS): *K2, p2; rep from * to last st, k1fb—134 sts.

Next Row (RS): *P2, k2; rep from * to last 2 sts, p2.

Cont in K2, P2 Rib for approx 1 ¼" (3.2cm).

BO loosely in ribbing.

■ FINISHING

Weave in ends. Block to measurements.

Sew a button to side opening near both CO and BO edges.

Button Loops

Using a crochet hook, join yarn to edge of side opening near CO or BO edge opposite button, make a chain about 6 chains long, or long enough for button to slip through. Join with a slip st to side of opening approx ½" (1.3cm) from join and fasten off. Weave in ends.

Make a button loop on rem opening side edge to match.

RIGHT FINGERLESS MITT

Using circular needle, CO 50 [54, 58] sts. Do not join.

Row 1 (WS): *K2, p2; rep from * to last 2 sts, k2.

Row 2 (RS): *P2, k2; rep from * to last 2 sts, p2.

Rep last 2 rows until cuff measures 1 ¼" (3.2cm), ending with a WS row.

Dec Row (RS): P2tog, k2, p2, (k2, p2tog) 9 [10, 11] times, k2, p2, k2, p2tog, do not turn—39 [42, 45] sts rem.

With RS facing, distribute sts evenly over 3 or 4 double-pointed needles. Join to work in the rnd and work k3, p2, then pm for beg of rnd.

Next Rnd: Knit to last 10 sts, p2, k6, p2.

Next Rnd: (K2, p1) 9 [10, 11] times, k2, work Row 1 of Right Cable over last 10 sts.

■ THUMB GUSSET

Inc Rnd 1: K11, pm, k1fb, pm, then work to end of rnd—40 [43, 46] sts.

Next Rnd: Work in established patt to marker, sm, p2, sm, then work to end of rnd.

Inc Rnd 2: Work to marker, sm, k1, M1L, k1, sm, then work to end of rnd—41 [44, 47] sts.

Right Cable

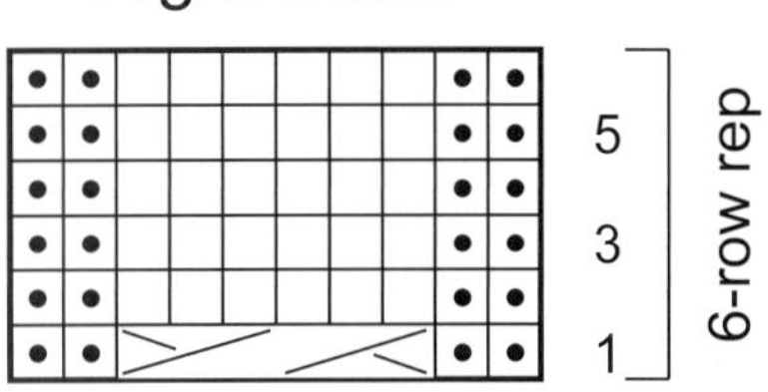

Left Cable

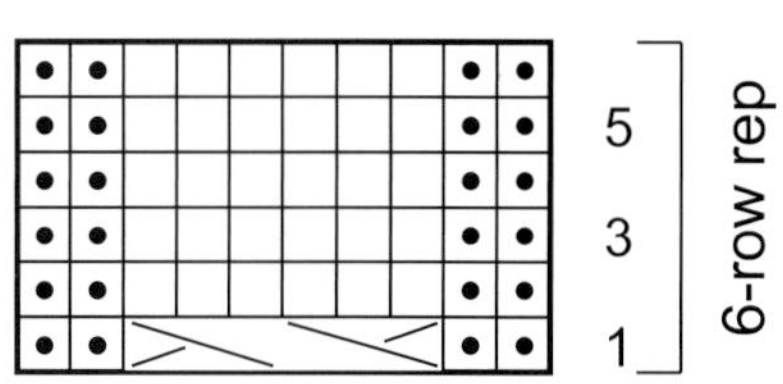

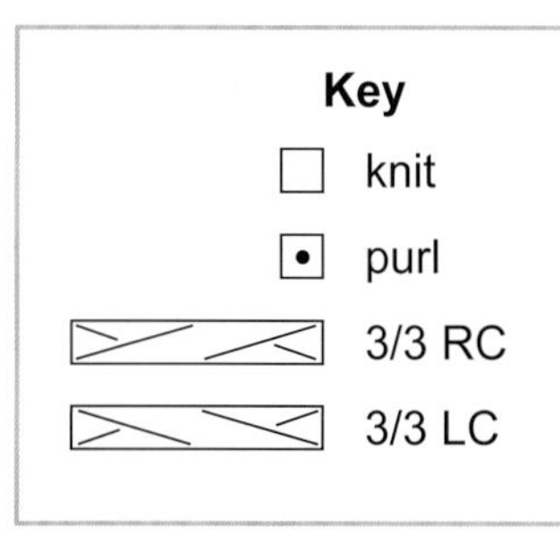

Next Rnd: Work to marker, sm, p1, knit to 1 st before marker, p1, sm, then work to end of rnd.

Inc Rnd 3: Work to marker, sm, k1, M1L, knit to 1 st before marker, M1R, k1, sm, then work to end of rnd—2 sts inc.

Rep last 2 rnds 6 [7, 7] more times—55 [60, 63] sts, with 17 [19, 19] sts between markers for gusset.

Work 2 [2, 4] rnds even.

Hand

Next Rnd: Work to marker, remove marker, place 17 [19, 19] gusset sts on holder or scrap yarn, remove marker, CO 4 sts using the Backward Loop method (see page 12), join, then work to end of rnd—42 [45, 48] sts rem.

Working new sts into Interrupted Rib, cont even until piece measures approx 5 ¼ [5 ¾, 6 ¼]" (13.3 [14.6, 15.9]cm), ending with a knit rnd.

Dec Rnd: (K2, p1) 10 [11, 12] times, (k2, p2tog) 3 times—39 [42, 45] sts rem.

Next 2 Rnds: *K2, p1; rep from * around.

BO all sts in patt.

■ THUMB

Return held 17 [19, 19] gusset sts to 2 double-pointed needles.

Using a third double-pointed needle, beg at center of CO sts at top of thumb opening, pick up and knit 2 sts, pick up side leg of mitt st in gap next to thumb gusset and place it twisted on LH needle, k2tog, k15 [17, 17] gusset sts, sl 1, pick up side leg of mitt st in gap next to thumb gusset and place it twisted on LH needle, return slipped st to LH needle, k2tog tbl, pick up and knit 2 sts in rem CO sts at top of opening—21 [23, 23] sts.

Dec Rnd: Sl 1, k2tog, (p1, k1) twice, p2tog, (k1, p1) 1 [2, 2] time(s), k1, p2tog, (k1, p1) twice, k1, sl 1, knit together last st of rnd with first st of rnd, psso—16 [18, 18] sts rem.

Next Rnd: *K1, p1; rep from * around.

BO in patt.

■ FINISHING

Weave in ends, using yarn tails to close any holes at sides of the thumb opening. Block mitts if desired.

Sew a button to right edge of cuff opening of Right Mitt. *Note: Sew to left edge of cuff opening of Left Mitt.*

Button Loops

Using a crochet hook, join yarn to edge of side opening near CO edge opposite button, make a chain about 6 chains long, or long enough for button to slip through. Join with a slip st to side of opening about ½" (1.3cm) from join and fasten off. Weave in rem ends.

LEFT FINGERLESS MITT

Using circular needle, CO 50 [54, 58] sts. Do not join.

Row 1 (WS): *K2, p2; rep from * to last 2 sts, k2.

Row 2 (RS): *P2, k2; rep from * to last 2 sts, p2.

Rep last 2 rows until cuff measures 1 ¼" (3.2cm), ending with a WS row.

Dec Row (RS): P2tog, k2, p2, (k2, p2tog) 9 [10, 11] times, k2, p2, k2, p2tog, do not turn—39 [42, 45] sts rem.

With RS facing, distribute sts evenly over 3 or 4 double-pointed needles. Join to work in the rnd and work k3, p2, then pm for beg of rnd.

Next Rnd: Knit to last 10 sts, p2, k6, p2.

Next Rnd: (K2, p1) 9 [10, 11] times, k2, work Row 1 of Left Cable over last 10 sts.

■ THUMB GUSSET

Inc Rnd 1: K21, pm, k1fb, pm, then work to end of rnd—40 [43, 46] sts.

Complete Left Mitt same as Right Mitt.

DARK SKIES *Bag*

A little boho, this cute shoulder bag is still sophisticated enough to take you out on the town. Although it's perfect for using up leftover yarn from other projects, it's also a great opportunity to play with a curated collection of colors from your favorite indie dyer.

SKILL LEVEL: EASY

FINISHED MEASUREMENTS: 8" (20.3cm) wide x 9" (22.9cm) tall

YARN

61 yds (56m) #2 fine weight yarn in Color 1

61 yds (56m) #2 fine weight yarn in Color 2

55 yds (50m) #2 fine weight yarn in Color 3

55 yds (50m) #2 fine weight yarn in Color 4

49 yds (45m) #2 fine weight yarn in Color 5

MATERIALS

US Size 2 (2.75mm) needles, or size required for gauge

Scissors

Tapestry needle

Sewing needle and thread

⅝" (16mm) diameter sew-in magnetic clasp

36" (91.4cm) long piece of 8mm braided leather cord or ready-to-attach shoulder strap with connectors

2 strap connectors, if using braided leather cord

2 end caps with clasps to fit cord

⅜ yd (34cm) fabric

Button thread, if using strap connectors

Leather epoxy, if using braided leather cord

YARN INFORMATION

Sample uses Mad Hatter Minis from Wonderland Yarns (100% superwash Merino wool; 5oz [142g]; 430yds [393m]), in color Magical Menagerie (1 set of mini skeins)

Each mini skein is 1oz (28.35g) and contains 86yds (78.6m), the colors included are: Folkloric (Color 1, green), Merfolk (Color 2, turquoise multi), Incantation (Color 3, purple multi), Serendipitous (Color 4, red), and Kitsune (Color 5, gold)

GAUGES

26 ½ sts and 52 rows = 4" (10.2cm) in Stripe patt, blocked

25 ½ sts and 61 rows = 4" (10.2cm) in Border patt, blocked

Square 1 measures 3" (7.6cm) wide x 3" (7.6cm) long

PATTERN NOTES

This bag is worked in two sections, then sewn together along the side and bottom edges. The striped blocks on the lower part of the bag are worked modularly, with each successive square beginning off a previous square. Stitches for the top band are picked up along one long edge.

If desired, a ready-made shoulder strap can be used in place of the individual components listed above. Make sure that you have a means of connecting the strap to the sides of the bag.

TOTE

■ SIDE 1

Square 1

Using Color 1, CO 21 sts.

Purl 1 row.

Join Color 2.

*Using Color 2, knit 2 rows. Using Color 1, knit 1 row, then purl 1 row.

Rep from * 8 more times—18 stripes, with 9 of each color.

Cut Color 2.

BO purlwise until 1 st rem on the RH needle. Pull rem st into a loop large enough to pass ball of yarn through, pull yarn through and tighten the st but do not cut yarn.

Fig. 1

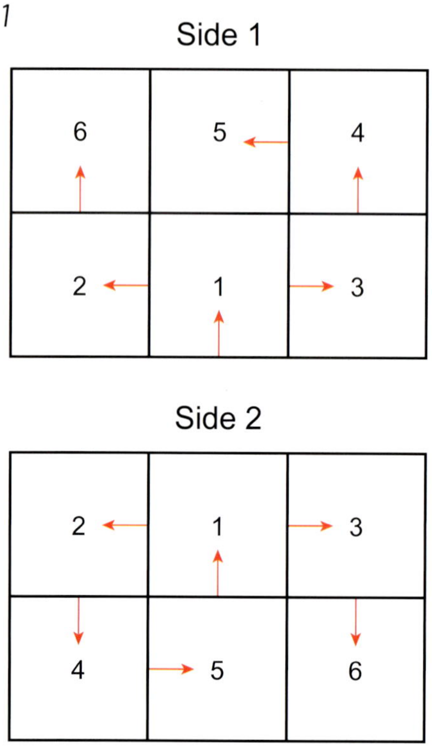

Red arrows indicate the direction of work for each square. The numbers indicate the order in which the squares are worked.

Square 2

Using Color 1 and with RS facing, pick up and knit 21 sts along left side edge of Square 1.

Purl 1 row.

Join Color 2.

*Using Color 2, knit 2 rows. Using Color 1, knit 1 row, then purl 1 row.

Rep from * 8 more times—18 stripes, with 9 of each color.

Cut Color 2.

BO purlwise. Cut yarn and fasten off rem st.

Square 3

Using Color 1 and with RS facing, pick up and knit 21 sts along right side edge of Square 1.

Purl 1 row.

Join Color 2.

*Using Color 2, knit 2 rows. Using Color 1, knit 1 row, then purl 1 row.

Rep from * 8 more times—18 stripes, with 9 of each color.

Cut Color 2.

BO purlwise. Cut yarn and fasten off rem st.

Square 4

Using Color 3 and with RS facing, pick up and knit 21 sts along left side edge of Square 3.

Purl 1 row.

Join Color 4.

*Using Color 4, knit 2 rows. Using Color 3, knit 1 row, then purl 1 row.

Rep from * 8 more times—18 stripes, with 9 of each color.

Cut Color 4.

BO purlwise until 1 st rem on RH needle. Pull rem st into a loop large enough to pass ball of yarn through, pull yarn through and tighten the st but do not cut yarn.

Square 5

Using Color 3 and with RS facing, pick up and knit 20 sts along left side edge of Square 4.

Using a second needle, pick up 18 sts along top edge of Square 1 by lifting lower loops of purl bumps onto needle, turn.

Working across stitches picked up in Color 3, purl 1 row.

Join Color 4.

Next Row (RS): Using Color 4, k19, ssk (last picked up st with first loop on LH needle), turn.

Next Row (WS): Using Color 4, k20.

Next Row: Using Color 3, k19, ssk, turn.

Next Row: Using Color 3, p20.

Rep last 4 rows 8 more times. Cut Color 4.

BO purlwise until 1 st rem on RH needle. Pull rem st into a loop large enough to pass ball of yarn through, pull yarn through and tighten the st, but do not cut yarn.

Square 6

Using Color 3 and with RS facing, pick up and knit 20 sts along right side edge of Square 2.

Using a second needle, pick up 18 sts along top edge of Square 5 by lifting lower loops of purl bumps onto needle, turn.

Working across stitches picked up in Color 3, purl 1 row.

Join Color 4.

Next Row (RS): Using Color 4, k19, ssk (last picked up st with first loop on LH needle), turn.

Next Row (WS): Using Color 4, k20.

Next Row: Using Color 3, k19, ssk, turn.

Next Row: Using Color 3, p20.

Rep last 4 rows 8 more times. Cut Color 4.

BO purlwise. Cut yarn and fasten off rem st.

Border

Using Color 5 and with RS facing, pick up and knit 57 sts along edges of Squares 4, 5, and 6.

Knit 1 row.

Join Color 1 and knit 2 rows. Cut Color 1.

Join Color 3 and knit 1 row.

Work Rows 1–40 of the Border Chart patt, carrying unused color along right edge of work. Cut Color 2 after Row 9, Color 3 after Row 17, and Color 4 after Row 29.

Next Row (WS): Using Color 2, knit. Cut Color 2.

Join Color 1 and knit 2 rows. Cut Color 1.

Using Color 5, knit 2 rows.

BO knitwise.

■ SIDE 2

Square 1

Using Color 3, CO 21 sts.

Purl 1 row.

Join Color 4.

*Using Color 4, knit 2 rows. Using Color 3, knit 1 row, then purl 1 row.

Rep from * 8 more times—18 stripes, with 9 of each color.

Cut Color 4.

BO purlwise until 1 st rem on RH needle. Pull rem st into a loop large enough to pass ball of yarn through, pull yarn through, and tighten the st but do not cut yarn.

Border Chart

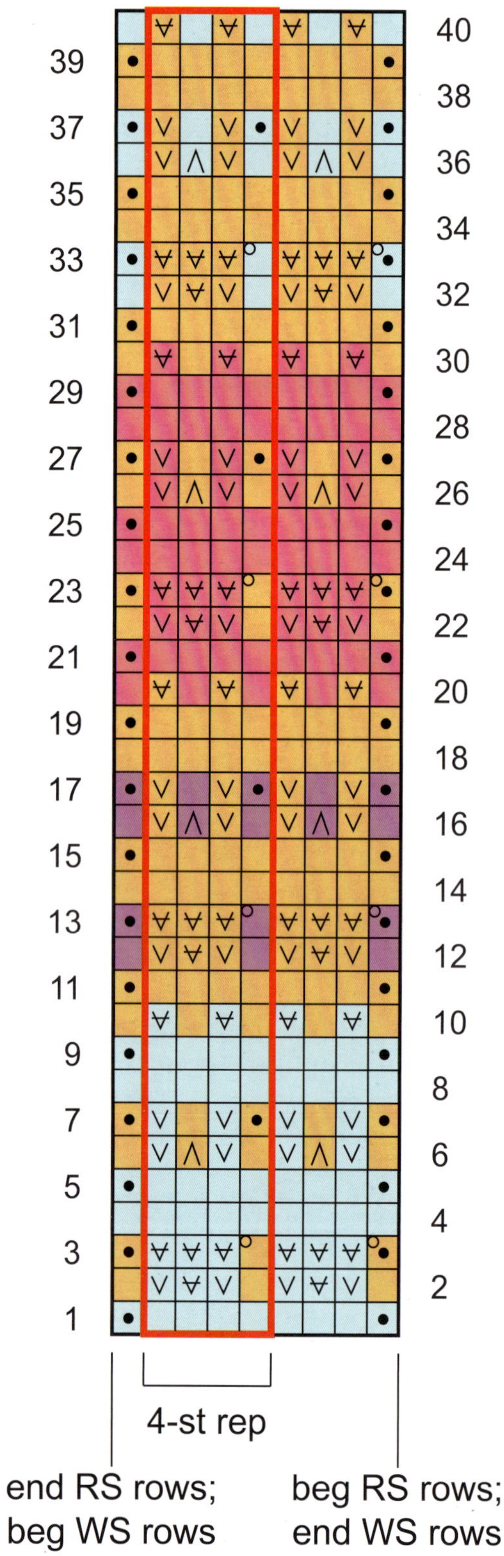

Key

- k on RS; p on WS
- p on RS; k on WS
- sl wyib on RS; sl wyif on WS
- sl wyif on RS; sl wyib on WS
- yo and p1 on WS; drop yo on next row
- yo and k1 on WS; drop yo on next row
- insert RH needle under float from 3 rows below and knit with next st on LH needle
- Color 5
- Color 2
- Color 4
- Color 3
- repeat

Square 2

Using Color 3 and with RS facing, pick up and knit 21 sts along left side edge of Square 1.

Purl 1 row.

Join Color 4.

*With Color 4, knit 2 rows. With Color 3, knit 1 row, then purl 1 row.

Rep from * 8 more times—18 stripes, with 9 of each color.

Cut Color 4.

BO purlwise. Cut yarn and fasten off the rem st.

Square 3

Using Color 3 and with RS facing, pick up and knit 21 sts along right side edge of Square 1.

Purl 1 row.

Join Color 4.

*Using Color 4, knit 2 rows. Using Color 3, knit 1 row, then purl 1 row.

Rep from * 8 more times—18 stripes, with 9 of each color.

Cut Color 4.

BO purlwise. Cut yarn and fasten off rem st.

Square 4

Using Color 1 and with RS facing, pick up and knit 21 sts along left side edge of Square 2.

Purl 1 row.

Join Color 2.

*Using Color 2, knit 2 rows. Using Color 1, knit 1 row, then purl 1 row.

Rep from * 8 more times—18 stripes, with 9 of each color.

Cut Color 2.

BO purlwise until 1 st rem on RH needle. Pull rem st into a loop large enough to pass ball of yarn through, pull yarn through and tighten the st but do not cut yarn.

Square 5

Using Color 1 and with RS facing, pick up and knit 20 sts along left side edge of Square 4.

Using second needle, pick up 18 sts along cast-on edge of Square 1 by lifting loops of cast-on edge onto needle, turn.

Working across stitches picked up in Color 1, purl 1 row.

Join Color 2.

Next Row (RS): Using Color 2, k19, ssk (last picked up st with first loop on LH needle), turn.

Next Row (WS): Using Color 2, k20.

Next Row: Using Color 1, k19, ssk, turn.

Next Row: Using Color 1, p20.

Rep last 4 rows 8 more times. Cut Color 2.

BO purlwise until 1 st rem on RH needle. Pull rem st into a loop large enough to pass ball of yarn through, pull yarn through and tighten the st, then fasten off but do not cut yarn.

Square 6

Using Color 1 and with RS facing, pick up and knit 20 sts along right side edge of Square 3.

Using second needle, pick up 19 sts along top edge of Square 5 by lifting lower loops of purl bumps onto needle, turn.

Next Row (WS): Working across stitches picked up in Color 1, p19, p2tog (last picked up st with first loop on LH needle), turn.

Join Color 2.

Next Row (RS): Using Color 2, k20.

Next Row: Using Color 2, k19, k2tog, turn.

Next Row: Using Color 1, k20.

Next Row: Using Color 1, p19, p2tog, turn.

Rep last 4 rows 8 more times. Cut Color 2.

BO purlwise. Cut yarn and fasten off rem st.

Border

Work same as for Side 1.

■ FINISHING

Weave in ends. Block both pieces to 8 ½" (21.6cm) wide x 9 ½" (24.1cm) long.

Sew both pieces together along the side and lower edges.

Lining

Trim fabric to 9" (22.9cm) wide x 19 ½" (49.5cm) long *(Fig. 2)*.

Fold fabric in half across the width, with RS held together. Sew a ⅜" (1cm) wide seam along each side edge, leaving the top open. Press each seam open as far as possible.

Fold 1" (2.5cm) at top edge to WS and press.

With WS of lining still facing, open out bag and insert lining into bag. Place several pins to hold the pieces together, making sure folded edge of lining is about ¾" (1.9cm) below top edge of bag. Sew lining in place.

Sew one half of magnetic snap at center of both top edges and just below the edge of the lining.

Following the epoxy manufacturer's instructions, glue the end caps to the ends of the braided cord and allow to cure.

Attach a strap connector to each side of the bag. Attach an end of the strap to the loops on the connectors.

Alternatively, if you purchased a ready-made shoulder strap, attach one end of the strap to each side of the bag.

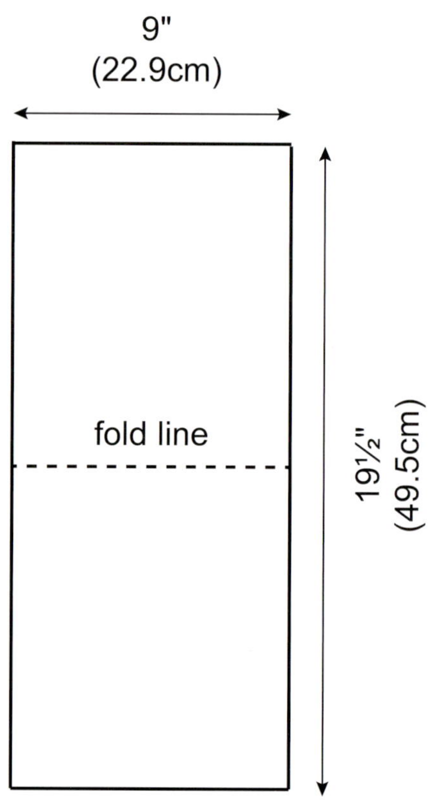

Fig. 2

WINTER TRAILS *Throw*

This throw is perfect for curling up with a good book or after a daylong hike. The smallest size is ideal for one person, while the two larger sizes make good couple snuggling or as an extra layer of warmth on particularly cold nights. While the colors shown in the photo are sure to pair well with any decor color scheme, customize your throw using any two colors that look great together.

SKILL LEVEL: INTERMEDIATE

FINISHED MEASUREMENTS

35 ¼ [42 ¼, 48 ¾]" (89.5 [107.3, 123.8]cm) wide x 36 ½ [47 ½, 59 ½]" (92.7 [120.7, 151.1]cm) long

SIZES

S [M, L]

YARN

717 [1130, 1815] yds (656 [1033, 1660]m) #4 medium weight yarn in Color A

563 [896, 1122] yds (515 [819, 1026]m) #4 medium weight yarn in Color B

MATERIALS

US Size 7 (4.5mm) circular needles, or size needed for gauge, in lengths of 24" (61cm) and 32" (81.3cm)

Cable needle

Scissors

Tapestry needle

YARN INFORMATION

Sample uses Northampton from Valley Yarns (100% wool; 3.5oz [100g]; 247yds [226m]) in colors #05 Light Grey (Color A–3 [5, 8] balls) and #50 Medium Grey (Color B–3 [4, 5] balls)

GAUGE

21 ½ sts and 26 rows = 4" (10.2cm) in chart patterns, blocked

PATTERN NOTES

This throw is worked in three pieces, then all the pieces are sewn together.

The number of stitches will vary from row to row on the Right and Left Side Panels.

Circular needles are used to accommodate the number of stitches cast on, especially for the larger sizes.

SPECIAL STITCHES

LPT (left purl twist) = Sl 1 st to cable needle and hold in front, p1, then k1 from cable needle.

RPT (right purl twist) = Sl 1 st to cable needle and hold in back, k1, then p1 from cable needle.

2/1 LPC (2 over 1 left purl cross) = Sl 2 sts to cable needle and hold in front, p1, then k2 from cable needle.

2/1 RPC (2 over 1 right purl cross) = Sl 1 st to cable needle and hold in back, k2, then p1 from cable needle.

2/2 LC (2 over 2 left cross) = Sl 2 sts to cable needle and hold in front, k2, then k2 from cable needle.

2/2 LPC (2 over 2 left purl cross) = Sl 2 sts to cable needle and hold in front, p2, then k2 from cable needle.

2/2 RC (2 over 2 right cross) = Sl 2 sts to cable needle and hold in back, k2, then k2 from cable needle.

2/2 RPC (2 over 2 right purl cross) = Sl 2 sts to cable needle and hold in back, k2, then p2 from cable needle.

THROW

■ RIGHT PANEL

Using shorter circular needle and Color A, CO 43 [51, 67] sts. Do not join.

Work 15 [15, 19] rows in Border Rib patt, ending with a RS row.

Sizes S [M] Only

Inc Row (WS): K1, p2, M1p, p1, k2, (p1, M1L, k6, M1L, p1) 1 [2] time(s), k2, p3, M1L, k2, p1, k4, p2, M1L, k3, p5, k2, M1L, p3, k2—49 [59] sts.

Size L Only

Inc Row (WS): K1, p2, M1p, p1, k2, (p1, M1L, k6, M1L, p1) 2 times, k2, p3, k3, p1, k4, p2, M1L, k3, p5, k3, p3, k2, p1, M1L, k6, M1L, p1, k2, p1, M1p, p2, k1—76 sts.

All Sizes

Work Rows 1–24 of Right Panel chart 8 [11, 14] times, then work Rows 1–17 once more—49 [59, 76] sts. Piece should measure approx 34 ½ [45 ¾, 57 ½]" (87.6 [116.2, 146]cm) from beg.

Sizes S [M] Only

Dec Row (WS): K1, k2tog, p2, k3, (k2tog, p4, k2tog, k2) 1 [2] time(s), k1, p2, k2tog, k4, p1, k1, p2, k2tog, k2, p7, k1, k2tog, p2, k2—43 [51] sts rem.

Size L Only

Dec Row (WS): K1, k2tog, p2, k3, (k2tog, p4, k2tog, k2) 2 times, k1, p2, k6, p1, k1, p2, k2tog, k2, p7, k3, p2, k3, k2tog, p4, k2tog, k3, p2, k2tog, k1—67 sts rem.

All Sizes

Work 15 [15, 19] rows in Border Rib. BO all sts knitwise.

Right Edging

Using longer circular needle and Color A, beg at lower right edge and pick up and k183 [235, 295] sts evenly along right edge of panel.

Beg with Row 2, work 6 [6, 10] rows of Border Rib.

BO all sts knitwise.

■ LEFT PANEL

Using shorter circular needle and Color A, CO 43 [51, 67] sts. Do not join.

Work 15 [15, 19] rows in Border Rib.

Sizes S [M] Only

Inc Row (WS): K2, p3, M1L, k2, p5, k3, M1L, p2, k4, p1, k2, M1L, p3, k2, (p1, M1L, k6, M1L, p1) 1 [2] time(s), k2, p1, M1p, p2, k1—49 [59] sts.

Size L Only

Inc Row (WS): K1, p2, M1p, p1, k2, p1, M1L, k6, M1L, p1, k2, p3, k3, p5, k3, M1L, p2, k4, p1, k3, p3, k2, (p1, M1L, k6, M1L, p1) 2 times, k2, p1, M1p, p2, k1—76 sts.

Border Rib

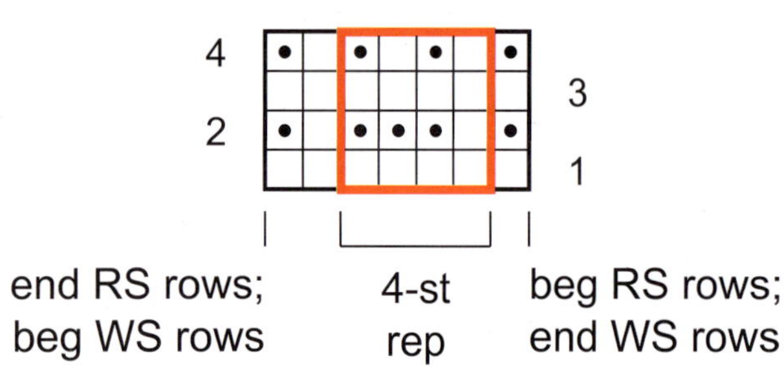

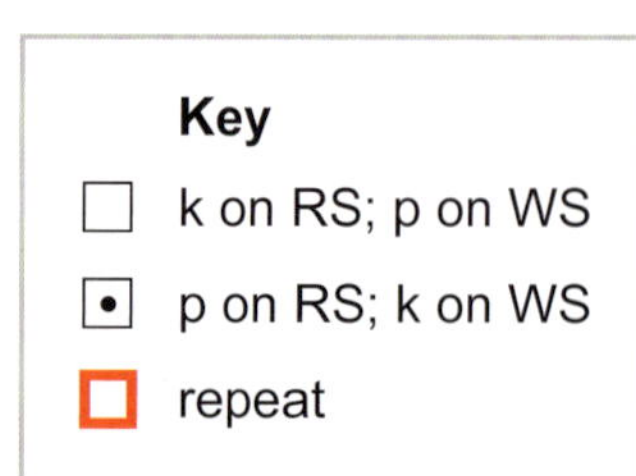

Shown in size Small.

All Sizes

Work Rows 1–24 of Left Panel chart 8 [11, 14] times, then work Rows 1–17 once more—49 [59, 76] sts. Piece should measure approx 34 ½ [45 ¾, 57 ½]" (87.6 [116.2, 146]cm) from beg.

Sizes S [M] Only

Dec Row (WS): K2, p2, k2tog, k1, p7, k2, k2tog, p2, k1, p1, k4, k2tog, p2, k3, (k2tog, p4, k2tog, k2) 1 [2] time(s), k1, p2, k2tog, k1—43 [51] sts rem.

Size L Only

Dec Row (WS): K1, k2tog, p2, k3, k2tog, p4, k2tog, k3, p2, k3, p7, k2, k2tog, p2, k1, p1, k6, p2, k3, (k2tog, p4, k2tog, k2) 2 times, k1, p2, k2tog, k1—67 sts rem.

All Sizes

Work 15 [15, 19] rows in Border Rib. BO all sts knitwise.

Left Edging

Using longer circular needle and Color A, beg at upper left edge and pick up and k183 [235, 295] sts evenly along left edge of panel.

Beg with Row 2, work 6 [6, 10] rows of Border Rib.

BO all sts knitwise.

■ CENTER PANEL

Using shorter circular needle and Color B, CO 79 [91, 91] sts. Do not join.

Work 15 [15, 19] rows in Border Rib.

Size S Only

Inc Row (WS): K1, p2, M1p, p1, k2, (p2, k6, M1p, p1) 2 times, k2, p3, k2, p2, k3, p2, k2, M1L, k1, p2, k3, p2, k2, p3, k2, (p1, M1L, k6, p2) 2 times, k2, p1, M1p, p2, k1—86 sts.

Sizes M [L] Only

Inc Row (WS): K1, p2, M1p, p1, k2, (p1, M1p, k6, M1p, p1) 3 times, k2, p3, k2, p2, k3, p2, k2, M1L, k1, p2, k3, p2, k2, p3, k2, (p1, M1p, k6, M1p, p1) 3 times, k2, p1, M1p, p2, k1—106 [106] sts.

All Sizes

Work Rows 1–24 of Center Panel chart 8 [11, 14] times, then work Rows 1–17 once more—84 [104, 104] sts. Piece should measure approx 34 ½ [45 ¾, 57 ½]" (87.6 [116.2, 146]cm) from beg.

Size S Only

Dec Row (WS): K1, k2tog, p2, k5, p4, k6, p4, k5, p2, k2, p2, k1, k2tog, p2, k1, k2tog, k1, p2, k2tog, k1, p2, k2, p2, k5, p4, k6, p4, k5, p2, k2tog, k1—79 sts rem.

Sizes M [L] Only

Dec Row (WS): K3, p2, k3, (k2tog, p4, k2tog, k2) 3 times, k1, p2, k2, p2, k3, p2, k1, k2tog, k1, p2, k3, p2, k2, p2, k3, (k2tog, p4, k2tog, k2) 3 times, k1, p2, k3—91 [91] sts rem.

All Sizes

Work 15 [15, 19] rows in Border Rib. BO all sts knitwise.

■ FINISHING

Weave in ends.

Block both side panels to 10 ½ [12 ¼, 15 ½]" (26.7 [31.1, 39.4]cm) wide x 38 [49, 61]" (96.5 [124.5, 154.9]cm) long, and center panel to 16 ½ [20, 20]" (41.9 [50.8, 50.8]cm) wide x 38 [49, 61]" (96.5 [124.5, 154.9]cm) long. *Note: The pieces will relax slightly after blocking.*

Sew side panels to center panel, making sure edgings on each side panel are at outside edges of throw, and lining up cables where pieces meet.

Right Panel

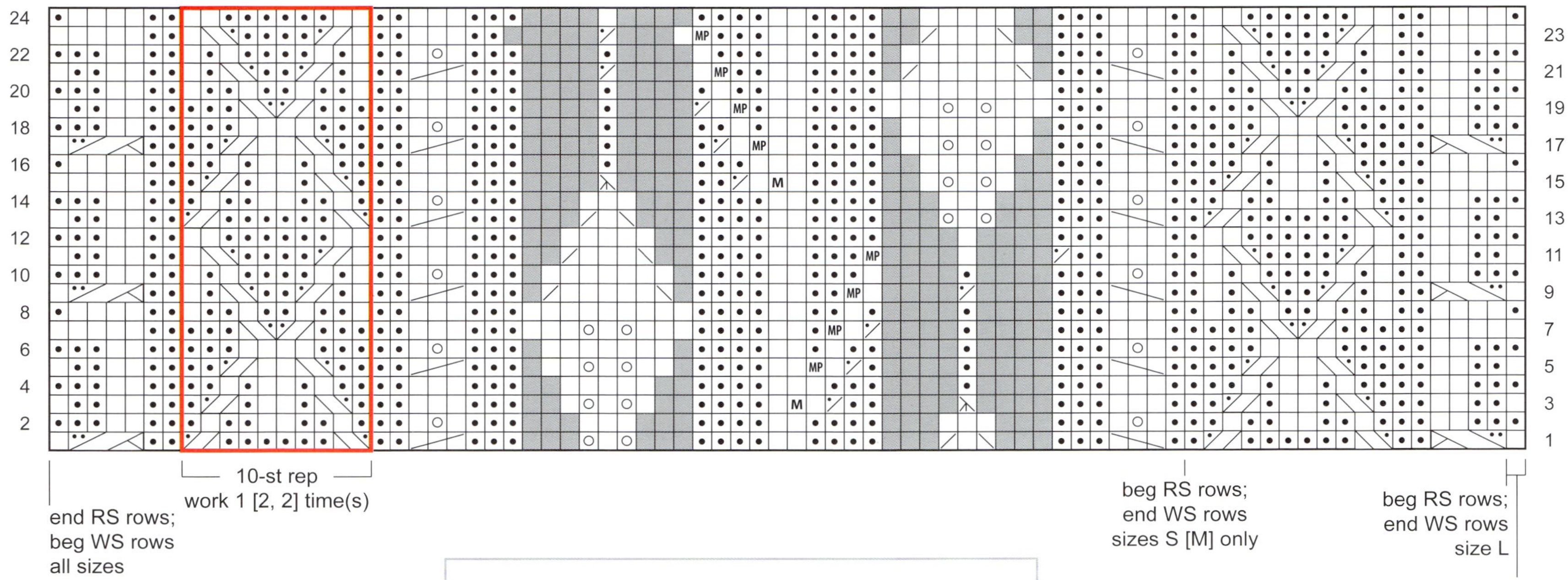

Key

(blank square)	k on RS; p on WS
(dot)	p on RS; k on WS
(circle)	yo
(right-slanting line)	k2tog
(right-slanting line with dot)	p2tog
(left-slanting line)	ssk
(sk2p symbol)	sk2p
M	make 1 knitwise
MP	make 1 purlwise
(3-st left-slanting line)	sl 1, k2, psso
(3-st right-slanting line)	lift 3rd st on LH needle over first 2 sts, k2
(2-st cable symbol)	LPT
(2-st cable symbol)	RPT
(3-st cable symbol)	2/1 LPC
(3-st cable symbol)	2/1 RPC
(4-st cable symbol)	2/2 LC
(4-st cable symbol)	2/2 RC
(4-st cable symbol)	2/2 LPC
(4-st cable symbol)	2/2 RPC
(grey square)	no stitch
(red box)	repeat

Left Panel

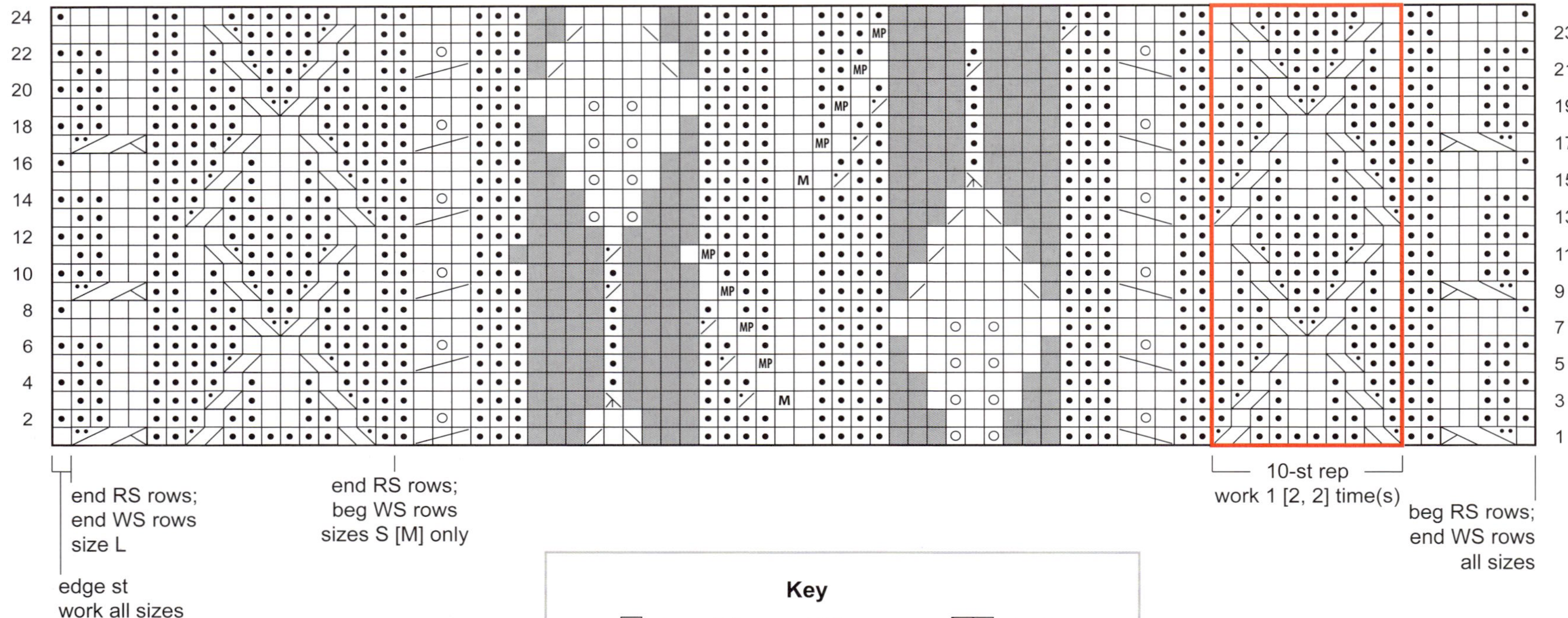

Key

- k on RS; p on WS
- p on RS; k on WS
- yo
- k2tog
- p2tog
- ssk
- sk2p
- make 1 knitwise
- make 1 purlwise
- sl 1, k2, psso
- lift 3rd st on LH needle over first 2 sts, k2
- LPT
- RPT
- 2/1 LPC
- 2/1 RPC
- 2/2 LC
- 2/2 RC
- 2/2 LPC
- 2/2 RPC
- no stitch
- repeat

Center Panel

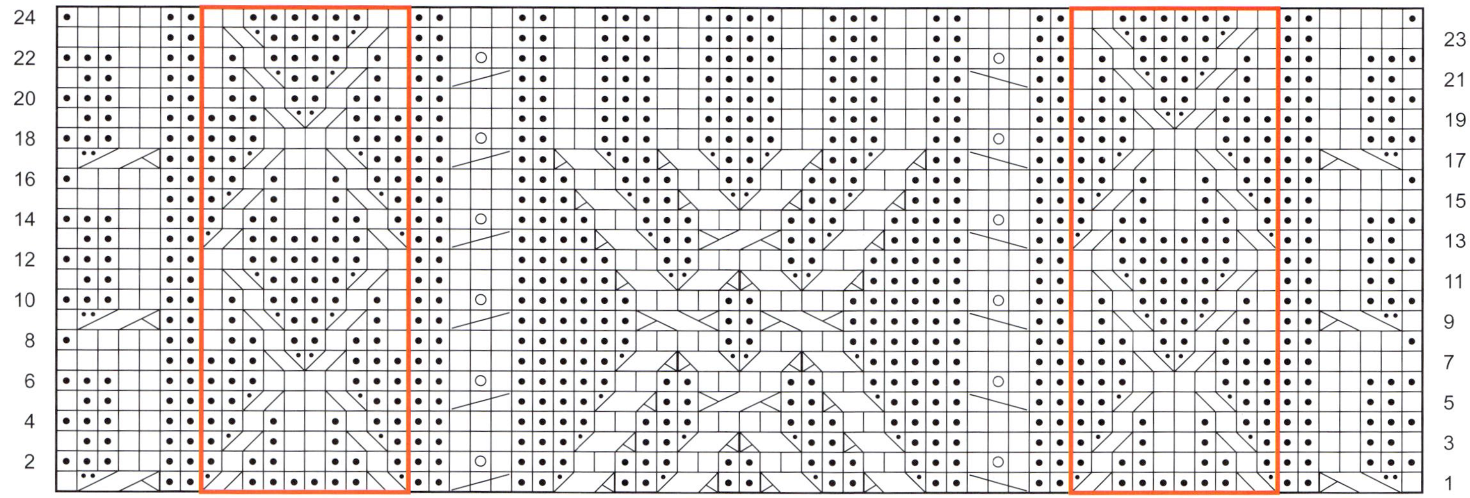

Key

- k on RS; p on WS
- p on RS; k on WS
- yo
- k2tog
- p2tog
- ssk
- sk2p
- make 1 knitwise
- make 1 purlwise
- sl 1, k2, psso
- lift 3rd st on LH needle over first 2 sts, k2
- LPT
- RPT
- 2/1 LPC
- 2/1 RPC
- 2/2 LC
- 2/2 RC
- 2/2 LPC
- 2/2 RPC
- no stitch
- repeat

PACIFIC CREST *Cabled Hat*

Cables reminiscent of the steep peaks of the Sierra Nevada mountain range add loads of visual interest to this hat. Worked in the round from the bottom up, the lower half of the ribbing is folded up to add an extra layer of warmth around your ears. Although it's the perfect hat for any man, don't be afraid to steal it from him!

SKILL LEVEL: INTERMEDIATE

FINISHED MEASUREMENTS: 19 ½" (49.5cm) circumference above rib and 8" (20.3cm) high with brim folded

YARN

190yds (174m) #4 medium weight yarn

MATERIALS

US Size 6 (4mm) circular needle in length of 16" (40.6cm)

US Size 7 (4.5mm) circular needle, or sized required for gauge, in length of 16" (40.6cm)

Four or five US 7 (4.5mm) double-pointed needles, or sized required for gauge

Stitch marker

Cable needle

Scissors

Tapestry needle

YARN INFORMATION

Sample uses Scholar from Acorn and Oak Fibers (85% US Targhee wool, 15% gray mixed wool; 3.5oz [100g]; 244yds [223m]), in color Shoreline—1 skein

GAUGE

24 ½ sts and 31 rnds = 4" (10.2cm) in Chevron Cable patt, blocked

PATTERN NOTES

Rounds 1, 11, and 21 of the Chevron Cable pattern begin with the last two stitches of the previous round to cross a cable. Make sure to remove the beginning-of-round marker when you begin the cable and replace it in the correct spot at the center of the cable.

The shaping for the top of the hat continues the right cross cable up to the top, decreasing two stitches in each repeat around.

SPECIAL STITCHES

2/1 LC (2 over 1 left cross) = Sl 2 sts to cable needle and hold in front, k1, then k2 from cable needle.

2/1 LPC (2 over 1 left purl cross) = Sl 2 sts to cable needle and hold in front, p1, then k2 from cable needle.

2/1 RC (2 over 1 right cross) = Sl 1 st to cable needle and hold in back, k2, then k1 from cable needle.

2/1 RPC (2 over 1 right purl cross) = Sl 1 st to cable needle and hold in back, k2, then p1 from cable needle.

2/2 LC (2 over 2 left cross) = Sl 2 sts to cable needle and hold in front, k2, then k2 from cable needle.

2/2 RC (2 over 2 right cross) = Sl 2 sts to cable needle and hold in back, k2, then k2 from cable needle.

2/2 RC dec (2 over 2 right cross decrease) = Sl 2 st to cable needle and hold in back, (knit together 1 st from LH needle with 1 st from cable needle) twice—2 sts dec.

HAT

Using smaller circular needle, CO 120 sts. Pm and join to work in the rnd, being careful not to twist sts.

Rnd 1: *K1, p1; rep from * around.

Rep last rnd until ribbing measures approx 4 ½" (11.4cm).

Change to larger circular needle.

Next Rnd: Knit to last 2 sts—2 sts rem unworked.

Work Rnds 1–31 of Chevron Cable Chart once—100 sts rem.

Knit 1 rnd.

■ SHAPE TOP

Dec Rnd 1: K2, 2/2 RC dec, *k6, 2/2 RC dec; rep from * to last 4 sts, k4—80 sts rem.

Knit 1 rnd.

Dec Rnd 2: *2/2 RC dec, k4; rep from * to last 8 sts, 2/2 RC dec, sl 4, remove marker, return sl sts to LH needle, pm for new beg of rnd—60 sts rem.

Knit 1 rnd.

Change to double-pointed needles.

Dec Rnd 3: *K2, 2/2 RC dec; rep from * around—40 sts rem.

Knit 1 rnd.

Dec Rnd 4: *2/2 RC dec; rep from * around—20 sts rem.

Knit 1 rnd.

Next Rnd (dec): Rep Dec Rnd 4—10 sts rem.

Cut yarn and pull tail through rem sts twice. Pull tight to close hole and fasten off on WS.

■ FINISHING

Weave in ends. Block lightly if desired.

Fold half of ribbing to RS to form a brim.

Chevron Cable Chart

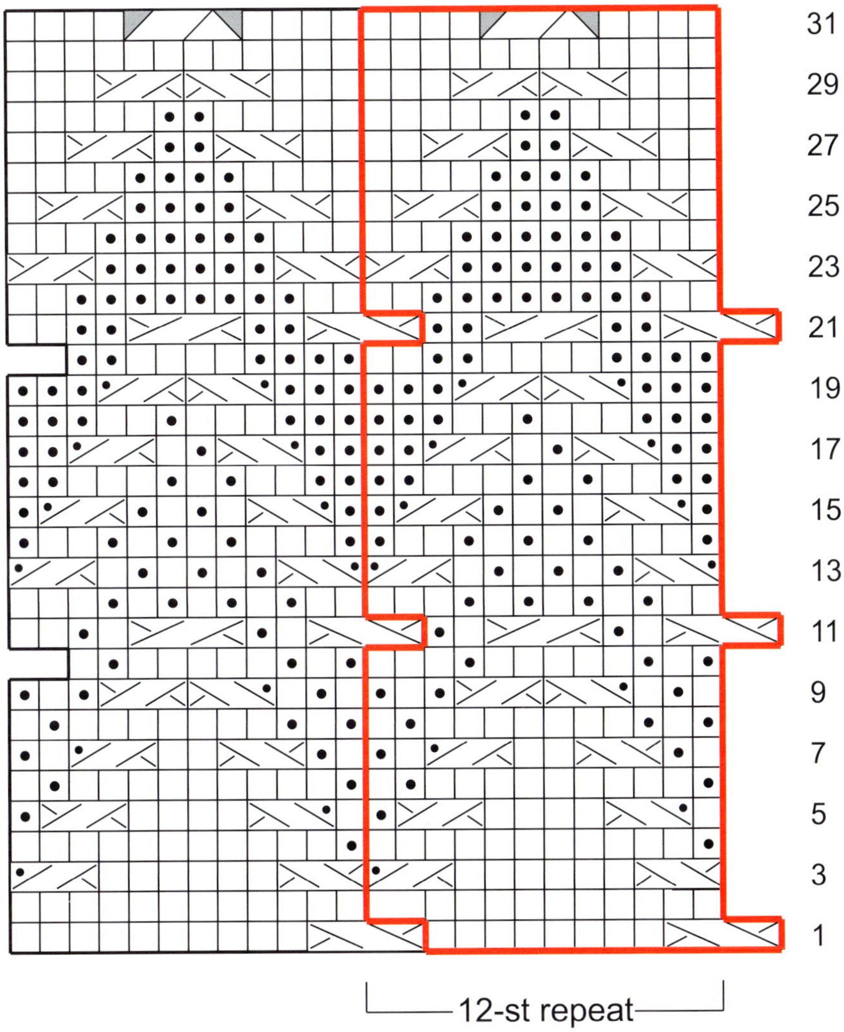

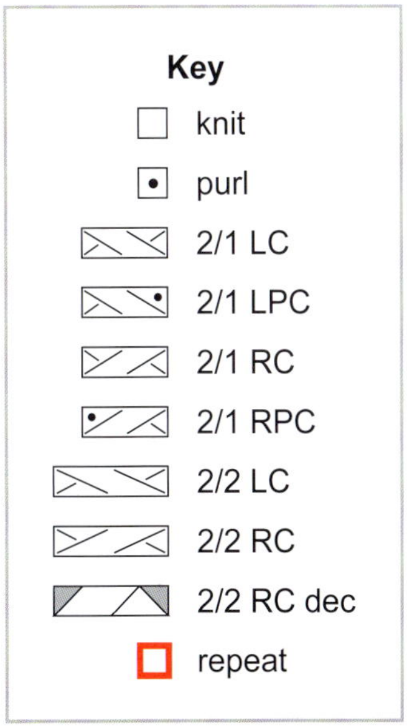

Note: The beginning and end of the round shifts on Rounds 1, 11, and 21 to accommodate the cable that crosses at that point.

NORTH WOODS *Hats*

These hats are the perfect accompaniment to the Hedgerow Cardigan, but they're also a great accessory to go with any outer gear whenever you need to keep your head warm. They're an ideal way to use up leftover yarn or to make a quick gift. They'll knit up so fast, it'll feel like near-instant gratification.

SKILL LEVEL: INTERMEDIATE

FINISHED MEASUREMENTS: 17 ¾" (45.1cm) circumference x 8 [10]" (20.3 [25.4]cm) long

YARN

101 [115] yds (92 [105]m) #4 medium weight yarn in Main Color (MC)

43 [71] yds (39 [65]m) #4 medium weight yarn in Contrast Color (CC)

YARN INFORMATION

Samples use Cozy Cotton from Green Mountain Spinnery (20% organic cotton/80% fine wool; 2oz [56.7g]; 140yds [128m]), in colors Cocoa Bean #10197 [Echo #10199] (MC—1 skein) and Maple #10196 [Pomelo #10200] (CC—1 skein)

MATERIALS

US Size 7 (4.5mm) circular needle in length of 16" (40.6cm)

US Size 8 (5mm) circular needle, or size required for gauge, in length of 16" (40.6cm)

US Size 8 (5mm) double-pointed needles

Stitch markers

Tapestry needle

GAUGE

18 sts and 36 rnds = 4" (10.2cm) in Hat Chart 1 or 2 patt using larger needles, blocked

Shown is Hat 2.

HAT 1

Using the smaller circular needle and MC, CO 80 sts. Pm and join to work in the rnd, being careful not to twist sts.

Rnd 1: *K2, p2; rep from * to end of rnd.

Rep last rnd until ribbing measures 1 ½" (3.8cm).

Change to the larger circular needle and knit 1 rnd.

Join CC.

Work Rnds 1–43 of Hat 1 Chart.

■ SHAPE TOP

Changing to double-pointed needles when there are too few sts to work on the circular needle, work Rnds 44–62 of Hat 1 Chart—10 sts rem.

Cut yarn and pull tail through rem sts twice. Pull tight to close hole and fasten off on WS.

■ FINISHING

Weave in ends. Block lightly if desired.

HAT 2

Using the smaller circular needle and MC, CO 84 sts. Pm and join to work in the rnd, being careful not to twist sts.

Rnd 1: *K2, p2; rep from * to end of rnd.

Rep last rnd until ribbing measures 3 ½" (8.9cm).

Change to the larger circular needle.

Dec Rnd: *K19, k2tog; rep from * 3 more times—80 sts rem.

Join CC.

Work Rnds 1–42 of Hat 2 Chart.

■ SHAPE TOP

Changing to double-pointed needles when there are too few sts to work on the circular needle, work Rnds 43–61 of Hat 2 Chart—10 sts rem.

Cut yarn and pull tail through rem sts twice. Pull tight to close hole and fasten off on WS.

■ FINISHING

Weave in ends. Block lightly if desired.

Fold brim up to the RS at middle of ribbing.

Shown is Hat 1.

Hat 1 Chart

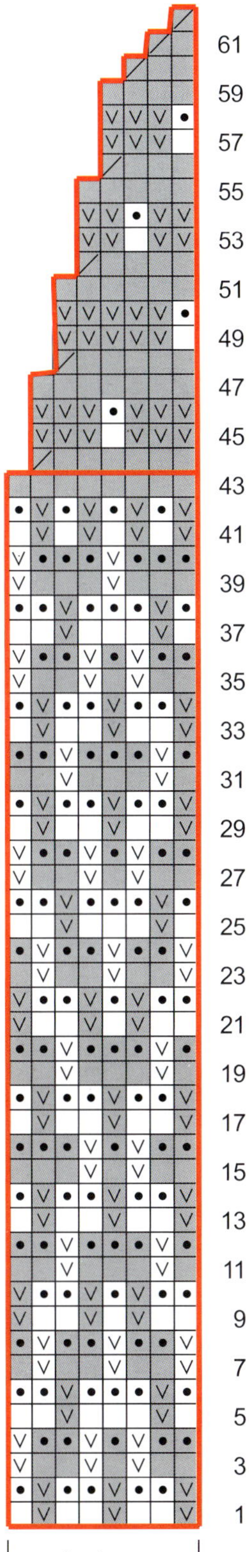

Hat 2 Chart

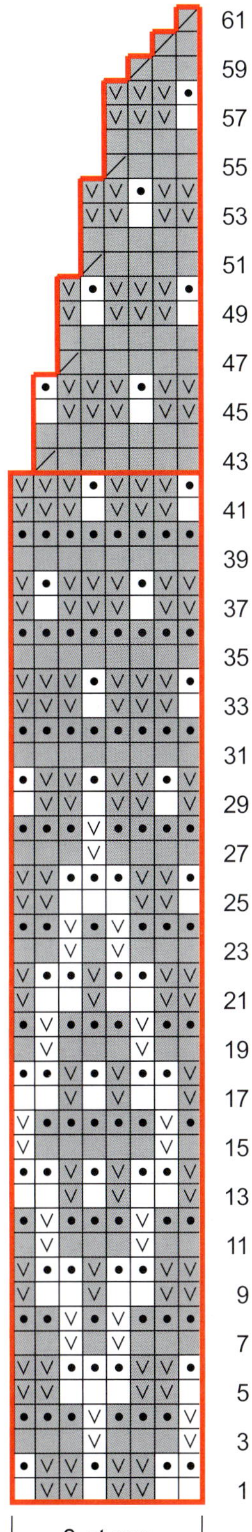

Key

- MC
- CC
- knit
- purl
- sl 1 wyib
- k2tog
- repeat

LEHIGH HAT AND *Cowl*

A close-fitting hat and cowl are ideal for chilly days or evenings when the weather is turning from summer to autumn. Easier to knit than they might appear, this hat and cowl will wow your friends with your knitting prowess.

SKILL LEVEL: INTERMEDIATE

FINISHED MEASUREMENTS:

Hat: 15 [17, 19 ¼]" (38.1 [43.2, 48.9]cm) circumference x 7 ½ [8, 8 ½]" (19 [20.3, 21.6]cm) tall

Cowl: 32 ½" (82.6cm) wide x 14" (35.6cm) tall

SIZES

Hat: S [M, L]

Cowl: One Size

YARN

Hat: 131 [161, 196] yds (120 [147, 179]m) #3 light weight yarn

Cowl: 262 yds (240m) #3 light weight yarn

MATERIALS

US Size 5 (3.75mm) circular needles, or size required for gauge, in lengths of 16" (40.6cm) and 24" (61cm)

US Size 5 (3.75mm) double-pointed needles, or size required for gauge

Stitch markers

Scissors

Tapestry needle

YARN INFORMATION

Samples use Spree from Berroco (56% wool/44% cotton; 1.75oz [50g]; 142yds [130m]), in color #9406 Juniper (Hat—1 [2, 2] skein[s]; Cowl—2 skeins)

GAUGES

30 sts and 31 rnds = 4" (10.2cm) in Hat Chart patt, blocked

28 ½ sts and 28 rows = 4" (10.2cm) in Cowl Chart patt, blocked

Hat shown in size Small.

HAT

Using shorter circular needle, CO 112 [128, 144] sts. Pm and join to work in the rnd, being careful not to twist the sts.

Rnd 1: *K1, p1; rep from * around.

Rep last rnd until ribbing measures approx ¾" (1.9cm).

Work Rows 1–4 of the Hat Chart 10 [11, 12] times. Piece should measure approx 6 [6 ½, 7]" (15.2 [16.5, 17.8]cm) from beg.

SHAPE TOP

Change to double-pointed needles when there are too few sts to work on the circular needle.

Dec Rnd 1: *K1-tbl, p3tog, (k1, p1) twice, M1R, k1, M1L, (p1, k1) twice, sssp; rep from * around—98 [112, 126] sts rem.

Next Rnd: *K1-tbl, (p1, k1) twice, p1, k3, (p1, k1) twice, p1; rep from * around.

Dec Rnd 2: *K1-tbl, p3tog, k1, p1, k1, M1Rp, k1, M1Lp, k1, p1, k1, sssp; rep from * around—84 [96, 108] sts rem.

Next Rnd: *K1-tbl, (p1, k1) 5 times, p1; rep from * around.

Dec Rnd 3: *K1-tbl, p3tog, k1, p1, M1R, k1, M1L, p1, k1, sssp; rep from * around—70 [80, 90] sts rem.

Next Rnd: *K1-tbl, p1, k1, p1, k3, p1, k1, p1; rep from * around.

Dec Rnd 4: *K1-tbl, p3tog, k1, M1Rp, k1, M1Lp, k1, sssp; rep from * around—56 [64, 72] sts rem.

Next Rnd: *K1-tbl, (p1, k1) 3 times, p1; rep from * around.

Dec Rnd 5: *K1-tbl, p3tog, k1, sssp; rep from * around—28 [32, 36] sts rem.

Next Rnd: *K1-tbl, p1, k1, p1; rep from * around.

Dec Rnd 6: *K1-tbl, p3tog; rep from* around—14 [16, 18] sts rem.

Dec Rnd 7: *K2tog-tbl; rep from* around—7 [8, 9] sts rem.

Cut yarn and pull tail through rem sts twice. Pull tight to close hole and fasten off on WS.

FINISHING

Weave in ends. Block lightly if desired.

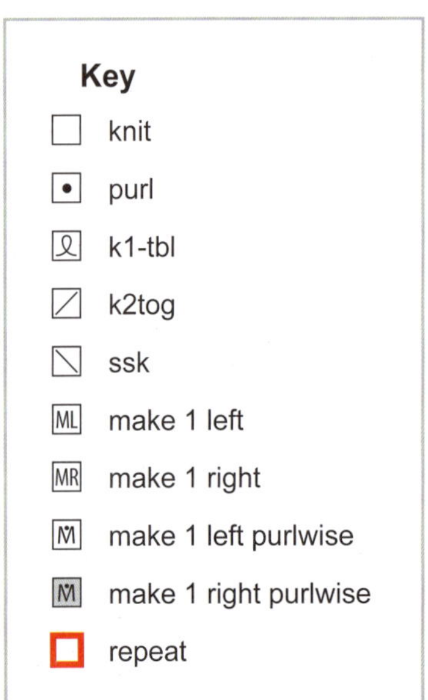

Hat Chart

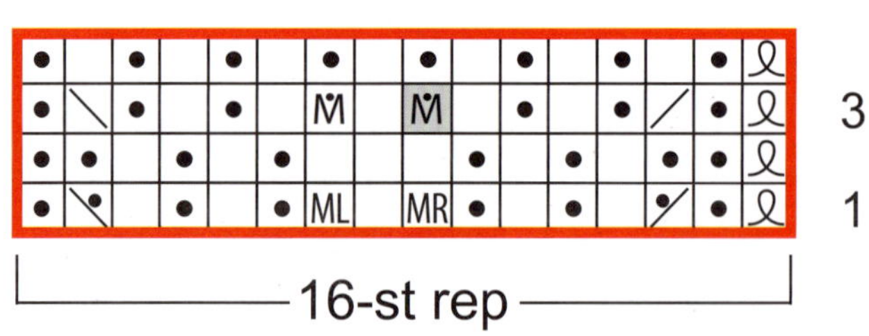

Key

- k on RS, p on WS
- p on RS, k on WS
- k1-tbl on RS, p1-tbl on WS
- sl 1 wyib
- k2tog
- p2tog
- ssk
- ssp
- k3tog
- sk2p
- make 1 left
- make 1 right
- make 1 left purlwise
- make 1 right purlwise
- repeat

Cowl Chart

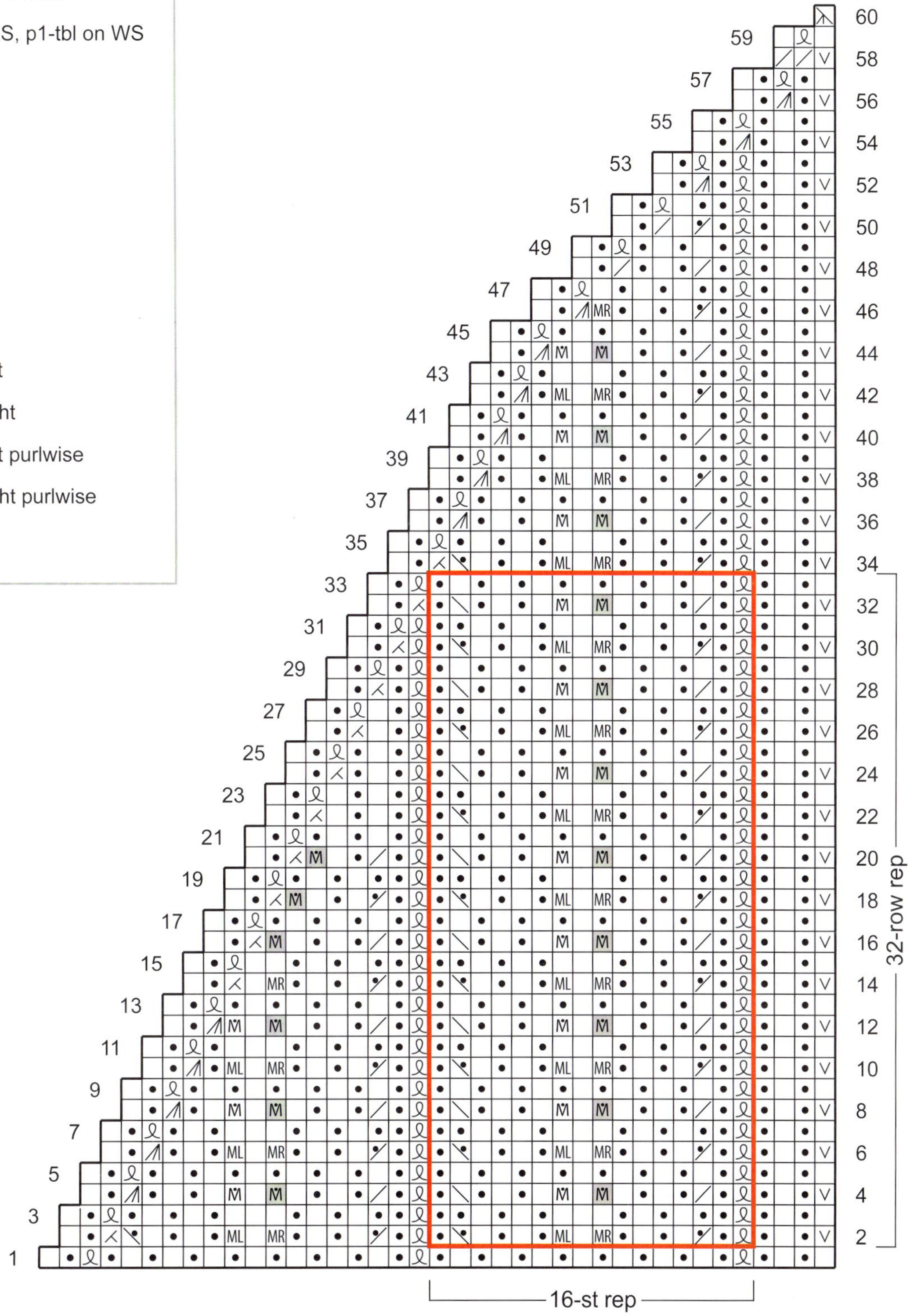

COWL

Using longer circular needle, CO 85 sts. Do not join.

Knit 2 rows.

Dec Row (RS): Sl 1 wyib, p1, k1, p1, knit to the last 4 sts, k2tog, k2—84 sts rem.

Next Row (WS): Knit to last 3 sts, p1, k1, p1.

Buttonhole Row (dec): Sl 1 wyib, p1, k1, p1, knit to last 14 sts, work One-Row Buttonhole (see page 9) over next 8 sts, then knit to last 4 sts, k2tog, k2—83 sts rem.

Next Row: Knit to last 3 sts, p1, k1, p1.

Set-Up Row (RS): Sl 1 wyib, p1, k1, p1, (M1L, k4) 19 times, M1L, k3—103 sts.

Work Rows 1–33 of Cowl Chart, then rep Rows 2–33 four more times—23 sts rem.

Work Rows 34–60 of Cowl Chart—1 st rem.

Cut yarn and fasten off rem st.

■ FINISHING

Weave in ends. Block to measurements *(Fig. 1)*. *Note: The cowl will relax slightly after blocking.*

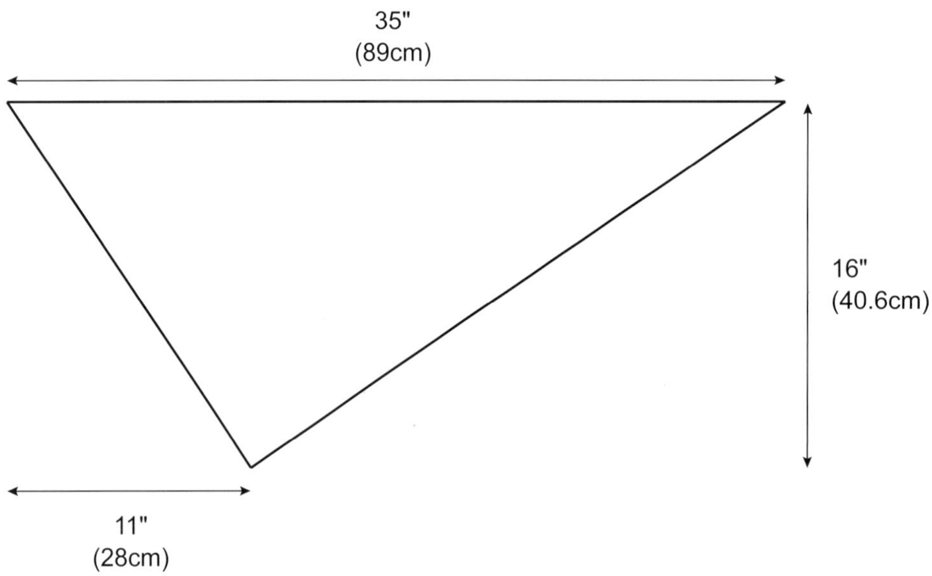

Fig. 1

VALLEY TRAIL *Hat and Cowl*

An ideal chance to play with color, this duo would look amazing in just about any color combination you can come up with, from jewel tones to graphic black-and-white to pastels. Another quick knit; you'll be out exploring the great outdoors in no time.

SKILL LEVEL: INTERMEDIATE

FINISHED MEASUREMENTS:

Hat: 16 ¾ [18, 19 ¼]" (42.5 [45.7, 48.9]cm) circumference above the brim and 7 ¾ [8, 8 ½]" (19.7 [20.3, 21.6]cm) long with the brim folded

Cowl: 20 ½" (52cm) circumference x 6 ¾" (17.1cm) high

SIZES

Hat: S [M, L]

Cowl: One size

FINISHED MEASUREMENTS

Hat: 16 ¾ [18, 19 ¼]" (42.5 [45.7, 48.9]cm) circumference above the brim and 7 ¾ [8, 8 ½]" (19.7 [20.3, 21.6]cm) long with the brim folded

Cowl: 20 ½" (52cm) circumference x 6 ¾" (17.1cm) high

YARN

Hat

110 [116, 125] yds (101 [106, 114]m) #4 medium weight yarn in Main Color (MC)

24 [26, 28] yds (22 [24, 26]m) #4 medium weight yarn in Contrast Color (CC)

Cowl

104 yds (95m) #4 medium weight yarn in Main Color (MC)

47 yds (43m) #4 medium weight yarn in Contrast Color (CC)

MATERIALS

US Size 9 (5.5mm) circular needle, or size required for gauge, in length of 16" (40.6cm)

Four or five US 9 (5.5mm) double-pointed needles

Stitch markers

Two cable needles

Scissors

Tapestry needle

YARN INFORMATION

Samples use Unicorn from Gazzal Yarns (100% wool; 3.5oz [100g]; 215yds [197m]) in colors #1356 Tiger's Eye (MC—1 [2, 2] skein[s]) and #1358 Picasso Lily (CC—1 skein)

GAUGES

20 sts and 32 rnds = 4" (10.2cm) in Crossed Stitches patt, blocked

17 ½ sts and 24 rnds = 4" (10.2cm) in stockinette stitch, blocked

PATTERN NOTES

Both pieces are worked in the round from the bottom up, beginning with a circular needle.

Because only one stitch is being placed on each cable needle while crossing the cables, a J-shaped cable needle will come in very handy here.

SPECIAL STITCHES

1/1/1 LC (1 over 1 over 1 left cross) = Sl 1 st to first cable needle and hold in front, sl 1 st to second cable needle and hold in back, k1 from left needle, k1 from second cable needle, then k1 from first cable needle.

Hat shown in size Medium.

HAT

Using circular needle and MC, CO 84 [92, 96] sts. Pm and join to work in the rnd, being careful not to twist sts.

Rnd 1: *K2, p2; rep from * to end of rnd.

Rep last rnd until ribbing measures 4" (10.2cm).

Knit 1 rnd.

Join CC, knit 1 rnd and dec 0 [2, 0] sts evenly spaced—84 [90, 96] sts rem.

Work Rnds 1–12 of Crossed Sts Chart patt twice.

With CC, purl 1 rnd. Cut CC.

With MC only, knit 1 rnd and dec 4 [2, 0] sts evenly spaced—80 [88, 96] sts rem.

■ SHAPE TOP

Dec Rnd 1: *K8 [9, 10] sts, k2tog, pm; rep from * around—72 [80, 88] sts rem.

Next Rnd: Knit.

Dec Rnd 2: *Knit to 2 sts before marker, k2tog; rep from * around—8 sts dec.

Rep last 2 rnds 3 [4, 5] more times, changing to double-pointed needles when there are too few sts to work on circular needle—40 sts rem.

Rep Dec Rnd 2 every rnd 4 times—8 sts rem.

Cut yarn and pull through rem sts twice. Pull tight to close hole and fasten off on the WS.

■ FINISHING

Weave in the ends. Block lightly if desired.

COWL

Using circular needle and MC, CO 104 sts. Pm and join to work in the rnd, being careful not to twist sts.

Rnd 1: *K2, p2; rep from * to end of rnd.

Rep last rnd 4 more times.

Knit 1 rnd.

Join CC. Knit 1 rnd and dec 2 sts evenly spaced—102 sts rem.

Work Rnds 1–12 of Crossed Sts Chart patt 3 times.

With CC, purl 1 rnd. Cut CC.

With MC only, knit 1 rnd and inc 2 sts evenly spaced—104 sts.

Next Rnd: *K2, p2; rep from * to end of rnd.

Rep last rnd 3 more times.

BO in patt.

■ FINISHING

Weave in the ends. Block lightly if desired.

Crossed Sts Chart

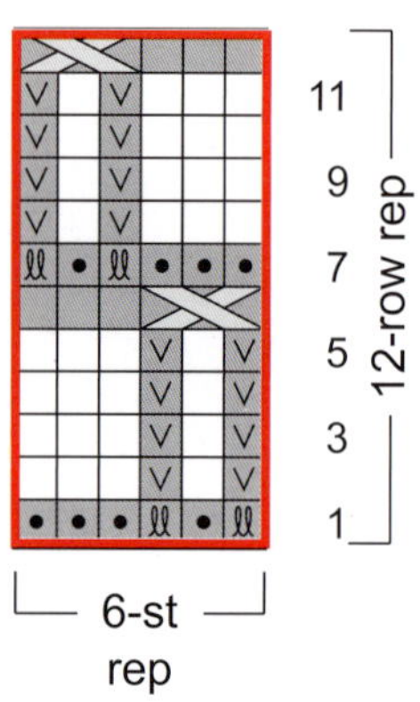

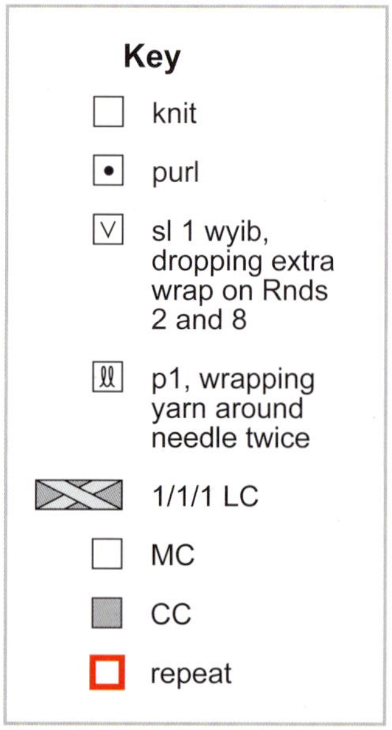

STARRY NIGHT *Hat and Cowl*

Great in just about any color combination, this set is the perfect chance to show off your favorite hand-painted yarns. Though they look complicated, with one color used for every two rounds, this hat-and-cowl set is a quick knit that's perfect for gift giving or just to satisfy your craving for new accessories.

SKILL LEVEL: INTERMEDIATE

FINISHED MEASUREMENTS:

Hat: 17 ½ [19 ¾, 21 ¾]" (44.5 [50.2, 55.2]cm) circumference x 7 ¾ [8 ½, 8 ¾]" (19.7 [21.6, 22.2]cm) high

Cowl: 20 ¾" (52.7cm) circumference x 8" (20.3cm) high

SIZES

Hat: S [M, L]

Cowl: One size

YARN

Hat

110 [135, 149] yds (101 [123, 136]m) #2 fine weight yarn in Main Color (MC)

54 [67, 73] yds (49 [61, 67]m) #2 fine weight yarn in Contrast Color (CC)

Cowl

155yds (142m) #2 fine weight yarn in Main Color (MC)

76yds (69m) #2 fine weight yarn in Contrast Color (CC)

MATERIALS

US Size 4 (3.5mm) circular needle, or size required for gauge, in length of 16" (41cm) long

Four or five US 4 (3.5mm) double-pointed needles, or size required for gauge

Stitch markers

Scissors

Tapestry needle

YARN INFORMATION

Note: One skein of each color will make both pieces.

Sample uses Callback from Leading Men Fiber Arts (100% superwash Merino wool; 3.5oz [100g]; 328yds [300m]) in colors Total Eclipse (MC—1 skein) and Street Art (CC—1 skein)

GAUGE

22 sts and 52 rnds = 4" (10.2cm) in Two-Color Sand St patt, blocked

PATTERN NOTES

Both pieces are worked in the round from the bottom up, beginning with a circular needle. When beginning the shaping at the top of the hat, change to the double-pointed needles when there are too few stitches to work comfortably on the circular needle.

Hat shown in size Medium.

HAT

Using circular needle and MC, CO 96 [108, 120] sts. Pm and join to work in the rnd, being careful not to twist sts.

Rnd 1: *P1, k1; rep from * around.

Rep last rnd until ribbing measures 1 ½" (3.8cm).

Beg Two-Color Sand St Chart and work Rnds 1–4 three times, then rep Rnds 5–8 until piece measures approx 5 ¾ [6 ¼, 6 ¼]" (14.6 [15.9, 15.9]cm) from beg, ending with 1 rnd of CC.

Set-Up Rnd: With CC, *work 16 [18, 20] sts in established patt, pm; rep from * 4 more times, then work to end of rnd.

■ SHAPE TOP

Dec Rnd 1: With MC, *k1, sk2p, knit to marker, sm; rep from * around—12 sts dec.

Work 3 rnds even.

Rep last 4 rnds 5 [6, 7] more times, then rep Dec Rnd 1 once more and remove markers on the last rnd, leaving only the beg-of-rnd marker—12 sts rem.

Cut CC.

Dec Rnd 2: With MC, *k1, sk2p; rep from * 2 more times—6 sts rem.

Cut yarn and pull through rem sts twice. Pull tight to close hole and fasten off on WS.

■ FINISHING

Weave in ends. Block lightly if desired.

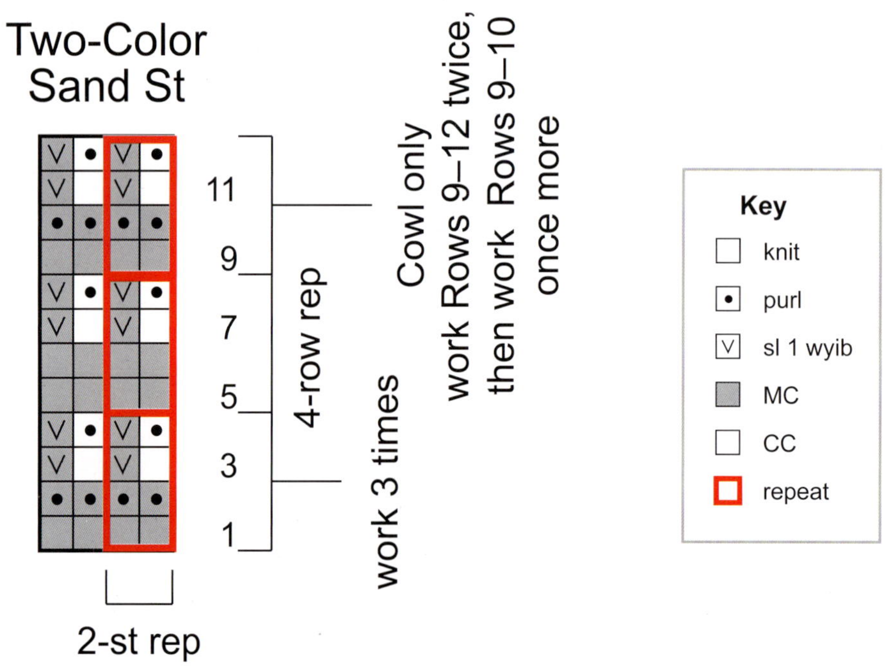

COWL

Using circular needle and MC, CO 114 sts. Pm and join to work in the rnd, being careful not to twist sts.

Rnd 1: *P1, k1; rep from * around.

Rep last rnd until ribbing measures ¾" (1.9cm).

Beg Two-Color Sand St Chart and work Rnds 1–4 three times. Rep Rnds 5–8 until piece measures approx 6 ¼" (15.9cm) from beg, ending with Rnd 8 of patt.

Work Rnds 9–12 of patt twice, then rep Rnds 9 and 10 once more.

Cut CC.

With MC only, knit 1 rnd.

Next Rnd: *P1, k1; rep from * around.

Rep last rnd until ribbing measures approx ¾" (1.9cm).

BO in ribbing.

FINISHING

Weave in ends. Block lightly if desired.

TANGLED ROPES *Hat and Cowl*

Every so often, I like to make something that's just a little different from what you see everywhere else. A short row cuff at the bottom of the hat and top edge of the cowl add that little zip that takes this set out of the ordinary. The stitch pattern I chose looks good in any color, making it easy to customize.

SKILL LEVEL: INTERMEDIATE

FINISHED MEASUREMENTS:

Hat: 17 [18 ½, 20]" (43.2 [47, 50.8]cm) circumference x 7 ½ [8 ¼, 8 ¼]" (19 [21, 21]cm) high

Cowl: 20" (50.8cm) circumference x 7 ¼" (18.4cm) high

SIZES

Hat: S [M, L]

Cowl: One size

YARN

Hat: 143 [166, 181] yds (131 [152, 166]m) #4 medium weight yarn

Cowl: 180yds (165m) #4 medium weight yarn

MATERIALS

US Size 7 (4.5mm) circular needle, or size required for gauge, in length of 16" (40.6cm)

Four or five US 7 (4.5mm) double-pointed needles, or size required for gauge

Stitch markers

Scissors

Tapestry needle

¾" (19mm) diameter buttons, two each for hat and cowl

Sewing needle and thread

YARN INFORMATION

Samples use Lucky Tweed from Kelbourne Woolens (100% Merino wool; 3.5oz [100g]; 210yds [190m]) in color #345 Sea Glass (1 skein for Hat, and 1 skein for Cowl)

GAUGE

22 ½ sts and 24 rows/rnds = 4" (10.2cm) in Twist Rib, blocked

PATTERN NOTES

The hat begins with wrap-and-turn short rows to shape the folded edge, then continues in the round to the top.

The cowl is worked in the round from the bottom up, ending with wrap-and-turn short rows to shape the folded edge at the top of the cowl.

Hat shown in size Medium.

HAT

Using circular needle, CO 96 [104, 112] sts. Do not join.

Row 1 (WS): *K2, p2; rep from * to end of row.

Short Row 1 (RS): Work 8 [9, 10] sts in established rib, w&t.

Note: On each following odd-numbered (WS) Short Row, make sure to pick up the wrap and work it together with the stitch it wraps.

Short Rows 2, 4, 6, 8, 10, 12, 14, and 16 (WS): Work to end of row.

Short Row 3: Work 16 [18, 20] sts, w&t.

Short Row 5: Work 24 [27, 30] sts, w&t.

Short Row 7: Work 32 [36, 40] sts, w&t.

Short Row 9: Work 40 [45, 50] sts, w&t.

Short Row 11: Work 48 [54, 60] sts, w&t.

Short Row 13: Work 56 [63, 70] sts, w&t.

Short Row 15: Work 64 [72, 80] sts, w&t.

Short Row 17: Work 72 [81, 90] sts, w&t.

Short Row 18: Work to end of row.

Next Row (RS): Work to end of row, working last wrap together with st it wraps, but do not turn. Pm and join to work in the rnd.

Work 1 rnd of established ribbing over all sts.

Work Rnds 1–20 of Twist Rib patt, then work Rnds 1–13 [17, 17] again. Piece should measure approx 5 ¾ [6 ½, 6 ½]" (14.6 [16.5, 16.5]cm) from CO edge at shorter side where work was joined.

■ SHAPE TOP

Dec Rnd 1: *K2, p2tog; rep from * around—72 [78, 84] sts rem.

Note: Change to the double-pointed needles when there are too few stitches to work on the circular needle.

Size S Only

Next Rnd: *RT, p1, k2, p1; rep from * around.

Next Rnd: *K2, p1; rep from * around.

Next Rnd: *RT, p1, k2, p1; rep from * to last 6 sts, RT, p1, k2, sl 1, remove marker, return sl st to LH needle, replace marker for new beg of rnd.

Dec Rnd 2: *Ssp, p2tog, k2; rep from * around—48 sts rem.

Next 2 Rnds: *P2, k2; rep from * around.

Dec Rnd 3: *P2tog, LT; rep from * around—36 sts rem.

Twist Rib

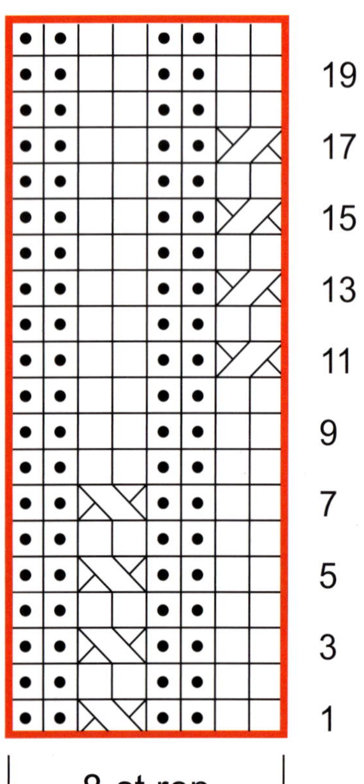

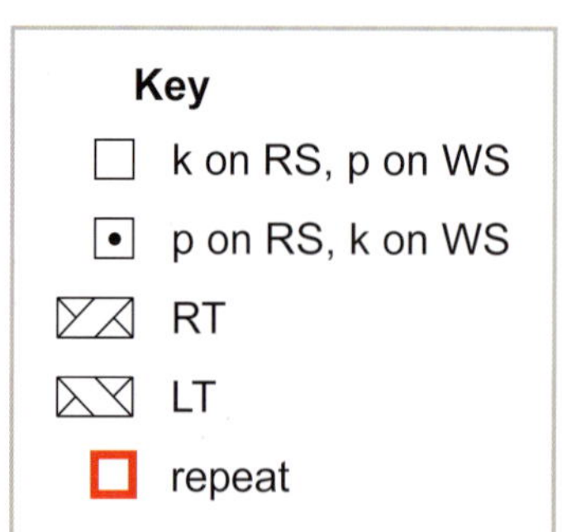

Next Rnd: *P1, k2; rep from * to last 3 sts, p1, k1, sl 1, remove marker, return sl st to LH needle, replace marker for new beg of rnd.

Dec Rnd 4: *Sk2p; rep from * around—12 sts rem.

Dec Rnd 5: *K1, k2tog; rep from * around—8 sts rem.

Size M Only

Next 2 Rnds: *K2, p1; rep from * around.

Next Rnd: *K2, p1, LT, p1; rep from * to last st, sl 1, remove marker, return sl st to LH needle, replace marker for new beg of rnd.

Dec Rnd 2: *Ssp, p2tog, k2; rep from * around—52 sts rem.

Next Rnd: *P2, LT; rep from * around.

Next Rnd: *P2, k2; rep from * around.

Dec Rnd 3: *P2tog, LT; rep from * around—39 sts rem.

Next Rnd: *P1, k2; rep from * to last 3 sts, p1, k1, sl 1, remove marker, return sl st to LH needle, replace marker for new beg of rnd.

Dec Rnd 4: *Sk2p; rep from * around—13 sts rem.

Dec Rnd 5: *K1, k2tog; rep from * to the last st, k1—9 sts rem.

Size L Only

Next 2 Rnds: *K2, p1; rep from * around.

Next Rnd: *K2, p1, LT, p1; rep from * to last st, sl 1, remove marker, return sl st to LH needle, replace marker for new beg of rnd.

Dec Rnd 2: *Ssp, p2tog, k2; rep from * around—56 sts rem.

Next Rnd: *P2, LT; rep from * around.

Next Rnd: *P2, k2; rep from * around.

Dec Rnd 3: *P2tog, LT; rep from * around—42 sts rem.

Next Rnd: *P1, k2; rep from * to last 3 sts, p1, k1, sl 1, remove marker, return sl st to LH needle, replace marker for new beg of rnd.

Dec Rnd 4: *Sk2p; rep from * around—14 sts rem.

Dec Rnd 5: *K2tog, k1; rep from * to the last 2 sts, k2tog—9 sts rem.

All Sizes

Cut yarn. Thread tail through rem sts twice and pull tight to close hole. Fasten off on WS.

■ FINISHING

Weave in ends. Lightly block to measurements if desired.

Fold shaped edge to RS to form a cuff. Sew 2 buttons to side edge of cuff through both layers to secure in place.

Lightly steam the fold, then finger-press the folded edge to set fold.

COWL

Using circular needle, CO 112 sts. Pm and join to work in the rnd, being careful not to twist sts.

Next Rnd: *K2, p2; rep from * around.

Work 2 more rnds in established ribbing.

Work Rnds 1–20 of Twist Rib twice. Piece should measure approx 7 ¼" (18.4cm) from beg.

■ SHAPE TOP EDGE

Short Row 1 (RS): Work 85 sts, w&t.

Short Row 2 and all other WS rows: Work to beg of row.

Short Row 3: Work 77 sts, w&t.

Short Row 5: Work 69 sts, w&t.

Short Row 7: Work 61 sts, w&t.

Short Row 9: Work 53 sts, w&t.

Short Row 11: Work 45 sts, w&t.

Short Row 13: Work 37 sts, w&t.

Short Row 15: Work 29 sts, w&t.

Short Row 17: Work 21 sts, w&t.

Short Row 19: Work 13 sts, w&t.

Short Row 21: Work 5 sts, w&t.

Short Row 22: Work to end of row and work each wrap together with st it wraps.

Next Row (RS): BO all sts in K2, P2 Ribbing.

■ FINISHING

Weave in ends. Lightly block to measurements.

Fold shaped edge of top to RS to form a cuff and sew 2 buttons near side edge of cuff through both layers to secure.

Lightly steam fold, then finger-press folded edge to set fold.

MAYWOOD *Shawl*

One way to enjoy a gradient yarn colorway is to knit a design that has a naturally varying pattern, especially if it's a shawl. I like working a triangular shawl from the wide end to the narrow end because I love the idea that you start out with a lot of stitches, then decrease so that the rows work faster and faster until, all of a sudden, you're done!

SKILL LEVEL: INTERMEDIATE

FINISHED MEASUREMENTS: **Width along Shaped Edge:** 48 ½" (123.2cm) / **Length at Center:** 25 ¼" (64.1cm)

YARN

626 yds (572m) #2 fine weight yarn

MATERIALS

US Size 7 (4.5mm) circular needles, or size required for gauge, in lengths of 24" (61cm) or 32" (81.3cm)

Stitch markers, optional

Scissors

Tapestry needle

YARN INFORMATION

Sample uses Ombré Sport from Freia Fibers (100% wool; 2.65oz [75g]; 217yds [198m]) in color Canyon—3 cakes

GAUGE

18 sts and 34 ½ rows = 4" (10.2cm) in Body of Shawl patt

PATTERN NOTES

This triangular shawl is worked in one piece from the wide end to the narrow end, beginning with the entrelac border. After reaching the tip at the far end of the triangle, do not fasten off the last stitch; instead, use it as the first stitch of the edging. When binding off the edging along the long shaped edge, do not fasten off the last stitch of the edging from the long edge; instead, use it as the first stitch of the short side edging.

The colors in this yarn fade from one shade to the next, with one cake being a full repeat of the color fade. To make sure that the fade continues seamlessly, make sure to begin the new cake with the same color that the old cake ended with.

SHAWL

■ ENTRELAC BORDER

CO 133 sts. Do not join.

Row 1 (RS, dec): Knit to the last 3 sts, ssk, k1—1 st dec.

Row 2 (WS): Knit.

Rep the last 2 rows 3 more times, then rep Row 1 again—128 sts rem. If desired, pm every 8 sts across the last row and leave them in place as you work the Base Triangles.

Base Triangles

Next Row (WS): P2, turn; *k2, turn; p3, turn; k3, turn; p4, turn; k4, turn; p5, turn; k5, turn; p6, turn; k6, turn; p7, turn; k7, turn*, then p10, turn; rep from * to the last 6 sts of the row, rep from * to * again, p8, then turn—128 sts, with 16 base triangles.

Right-Hand Triangle

K2, turn; p2, turn; k1fb, ssk (the last st of Right-Hand Triangle and first st of Base Triangle), turn; p3, turn; k1fb, k1, ssk, turn; p4, turn; k1fb, k2, ssk, turn; p5, turn; k1fb, k3, ssk, turn; p6, turn; k1fb, k4, ssk, turn; p7, turn; k1fb, k5, ssk, do not turn.

Right Side Rectangles

*Pick up and knit 8 sts along the side of the next Base Triangle, turn; p8, turn; [k7, ssk (the last st of RS Rectangle with the next st of Base Triangle), turn; p8, turn] 7 times, k7, ssk, do not turn; rep from * to the last 2 sts, sk2p, turn; BO 7 sts of the last rectangle worked but do not fasten off rem st—121 sts rem, with 14 rectangles and 1 triangle.

Wrong Side Rectangles

Using the rem st as the first st of the next rectangle, pick up and purl 7 sts along the side of the next RS Rectangle and turn, *[k8, turn; p7, p2tog (the last st of WS Rectangle with the next st of RS Rectangle), turn] 8 times, pick up and purl 8 sts along the side of the next RS Rectangle and turn; rep from * to the end of the row. Do not turn at the end of the last rectangle—120 sts rem, with 15 rectangles.

Rep the Right-Hand Triangle once more, working the last st of the Right-Hand Triangle with the next st of the WS Rectangle at the end of RS rows.

Rep the row of RS Rectangles again (working the last st of each RS Rectangle with the next st of the WS Rectangle), then turn and BO 7 sts at the end of the last rectangle—113 sts rem, with 14 rectangles and 1 triangle.

End Triangles

*Using the rem st as the first st of the End Triangle, pick up and knit 7 sts along the side of the RS Rectangle and turn, k8, turn; p2tog, p5, p2tog (the last st of the End Triangle with the next st of the RS Rectangle), turn; k7, turn; p2tog, p4, p2tog, turn; k6, turn; p2tog, p3, p2tog, turn; k5, turn; p2tog, p2, p2tog, turn; p4, turn; p2tog, p1, p2tog, turn; k3, turn; [p2tog] twice, turn, k2, turn; sl 1, p3tog, psso, turn; rep from * to the end of the row—1 st rem. Do not fasten off the rem st.

■ BODY OF SHAWL

With RS facing and using rem st as the first st, pick up and knit another 127 sts along the top edge of the end triangles (9 sts in each End Triangle, and 1 st in the last st)—128 sts.

Row 1 (WS): Knit.

Row 2 (RS, dec): Knit to the last 3 sts, ssk, k1—1 st dec.

Rows 3 and 4: Rep Rows 1 and 2 again—1 st dec.

Row 5: Purl.

Rows 6–8 (dec): Rep Rows 2 and 5 again, then rep Row 2—2 sts dec.

Row 9: Knit.

Row 10 (dec): Knit to the last 3 sts, ssk, k1—1 st dec.

Row 11: Knit.

Row 12 (eyelet, dec): K1, (k2tog, yo) to the last 4 sts, ssk, k2—1 st dec.

Rows 13–15: Rep Rows 9–11 again—1 st dec.

Row 16 (dec): Knit to the last 3 sts, ssk, k1—1 st dec.

Row 17: Purl.

Rows 18–22: Rep Rows 16 and 17 two more times, then rep Row 16 again—3 sts dec.

Rows 23–25: Rep Rows 9–11 again—1 st dec.

Row 26 (eyelet, dec): K1, (k2tog, yo) to the last 3 sts, ssk, k1—1 st dec.

Rows 27–29: Rep Rows 9–11 once more—1 st dec.

Rows 30–36: Rep Rows 16–22 again—4 sts dec.

Rep Rows 9–36 until 3 sts rem in work, ending with a WS row. *Note: The last time an eyelet row is worked, there may be too few stitches to work the (k2tog, yo) across the row. Instead, just knit those stitches.*

Dec Row: Sk2p—1 st rem. Do not fasten off.

Long Edging

With RS facing, pick up and knit approx 3 sts for every 4 rows along the long-shaped edge, and 1 st in each BO st of entrelac border.

Knit 2 rows.

BO knitwise but do not fasten off the rem st at end of the row.

Side Edging

With WS facing, pick up and purl approx 3 sts for every 4 rows along the straight side edge.

Purl 2 rows.

BO purlwise. Fasten off rem st.

■ FINISHING

Weave in ends. Block to measurements *(Fig. 1)*. The shawl will be pinned out larger than the finished measurements. After removing the pins, the shawl will relax to the dimensions listed at the beginning of the pattern.

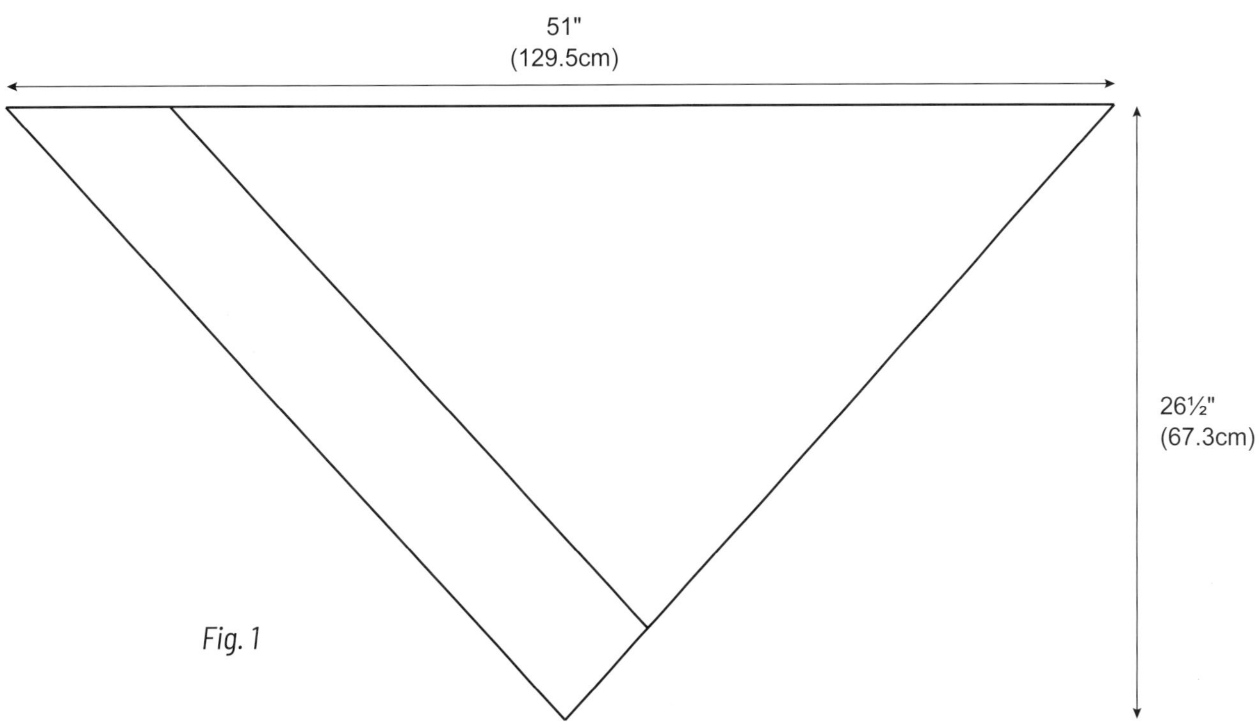

Fig. 1

CABIN FEVER *Tote*

Everyone needs a sturdy tote bag, whether you use it for carrying your books, knitting projects, or weekly shopping. This one is a quick-to-knit piece that's easy to customize with your favorite colors. Leather handles and decorative buttons add the perfect finishing touches to make your bag stand out.

SKILL LEVEL: INTERMEDIATE

FINISHED MEASUREMENTS: 12 ½" (31.8cm) long x 12 ½" (31.8cm) high x 4" (10.2cm) wide

YARN

385 yds (352m) #4 medium weight yarn in Main Color (MC)

21 yds (19m) #4 medium weight yarn in Contrast Color 1 (CC1)

13 ½ yds (12.5m) #4 medium weight yarn in Contrast Color 2 (CC2)

29 yds (26.5m) #4 medium weight yarn in Contrast Color 3 (CC3)

MATERIALS

US Size 7 (4.5mm) circular needle, or size required for gauge, in length of 32" (81.3cm)

US Size 7 (4.5mm) double-pointed needles, or size required for gauge

Stitch markers

Tapestry needle

Pair of leather handles

Scissors

Button thread

⅝ yd (57.2cm) cotton fabric, optional

Sewing needle and thread

Two large post buttons or decorative buttons

YARN INFORMATION

Sample uses Weekend Wool from Green Mountain Spinnery (100% American wool; 2.4oz [68g]; 140yds [128m]) in colors Natural Grey #10552 (MC—3 skeins), Blue Jay #10447 (CC1—1 skein), Pumpkin #7762 (CC2—1 skein), and Poppy #7706 (CC3—1 skein)

GAUGES

16 sts and 25 rnds = 4" (10.2cm) in stockinette stitch with stripes, blocked

16 sts and 40 rnds = 4" (10.2cm) in Mosaic Band patt, blocked

PATTERN NOTES

The lining in this bag is optional, but it will help the tote to retain its shape and prevent small items for falling through the knitted fabric.

Button thread was used to sew the handles to the tote because it's thicker and sturdier than regular sewing thread; other heavy-duty thread, such as beading thread, can be used in place of button thread.

Mosaic Band Chart

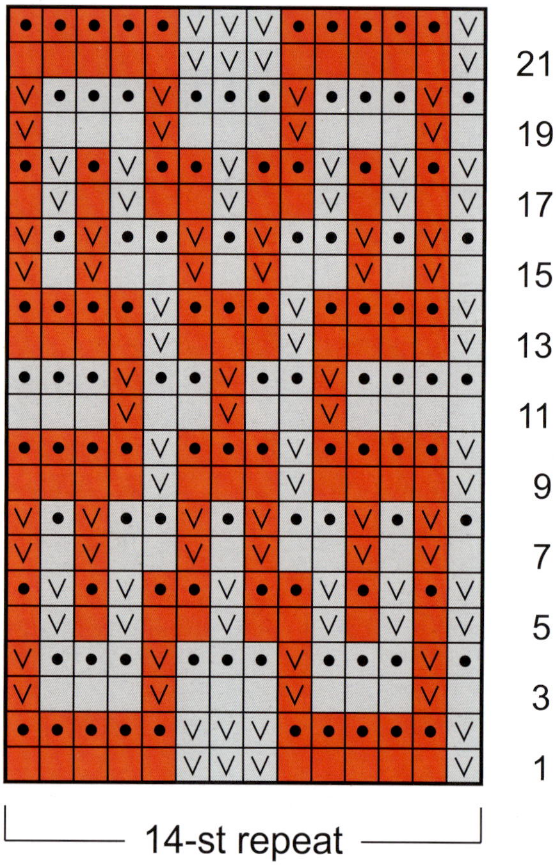

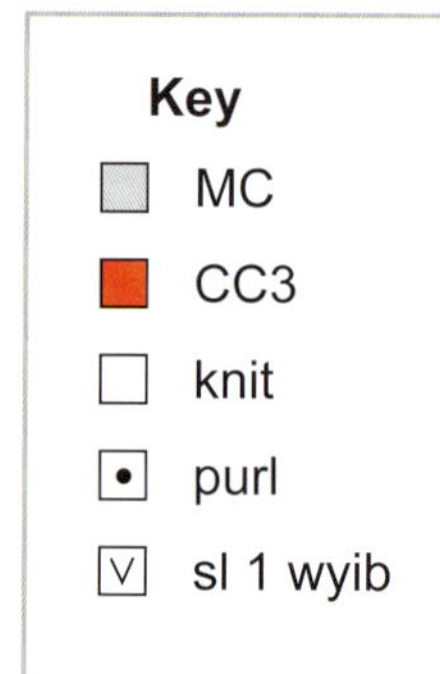

TOTE

■ BASE

Using the double-pointed needles and MC, CO 18 sts. Do not join.

Knit every row until base measures approx 13" (33cm).

BO all sts.

■ BODY

Using circular needle and MC, and with RS facing, beg at center of one short edge of base, pick up and knit 9 sts, 52 sts along one side edge, 18 sts along rem short edge, 52 sts along rem side edge, then 9 sts along remainder of short edge—140 sts. Pm and join to work in the rnd.

Knit 1 rnd. *Note: When working the contrast color stripes, there is no need to cut the main color. Simply carry it loosely up the WS.*

Join CC1. Knit 1 rnd, then purl 1 rnd. Cut CC1.

Using MC, knit 10 rnds.

Join CC2. Knit 1 rnd, then purl 1 rnd. Cut CC2.

Using MC, knit 10 rnds.

Join CC3. Knit 1 rnd, then purl 1 rnd. Cut CC2.

Using MC, knit 10 rnds.

Join CC1. Knit 1 rnd, then purl 1 rnd. Cut CC1.

Using MC, knit 10 rnds.

Join CC2. Knit 1 rnd, then purl 1 rnd. Cut CC2.

Using MC, knit 2 rnds.

Join CC3. Knit 1 rnd, then purl 1 rnd. Leave CC3 attached and carry it loosely up along the WS.

Using MC, knit 2 rnds.

Join CC1. Knit 1 rnd, then purl 1 rnd. Cut CC1.

Using MC, knit 2 rnds.

Work Rnds 1–22 of Mosaic Band Chart.

Cut CC3.

Using MC only, knit 2 rnds.

(Purl 1 rnd, knit 1 rnd) 4 times, then purl 1 rnd.

BO knitwise.

■ CORNER TABS

Using double-pointed needles and MC, and with RS facing, pick up and knit 17 sts along purl ridge at one short end of base.

Row 1 (WS): P1, k1, purl to the last 2 sts, k1, p1.

Row 2 (RS): K1, p1, knit to last 2 sts, p1, k1.

Row 3: Rep Row 1.

Row 4 (dec): K1, p1, ssk, knit to last 4 sts, k2tog, p1, k1—2 sts dec.

Rows 5–16: Rep Rows 1–4 three times—9 sts rem.

Row 17: Rep Row 1.

Row 18 (dec): K1, p1, ssk, k1, k2tog, p1, k1—7 sts rem.

Row 19: P1, k1, p3, k1, p1.

Row 20 (dec): K1, p1, sk2p, p1, k1—5 sts rem.

Row 21: (P1, k1) twice, p1.

Row 22 (dec): Ssk, k1, k2tog—3 sts rem.

Row 23 (dec): P3tog. Cut yarn and pull through the rem st.

Rep Corner Tab on other short end of base.

■ FINISHING

Weave in ends. Lightly block if desired.

OPTIONAL LINING

Cut fabric to 18" (45.7cm) wide x 28 ½" (72.4cm) long.

Fold fabric in half across the width *(Fig. 1)*, with RS together.

Place a marker about 10" (25.4cm) down from top edge along each side of lining.

Sew a ⅜" (1cm) wide seam along each side edge to the marker.

Sew a few backstitches to secure the opening, then cut the thread if sewing by hand. If sewing by machine, raise the needle out of the fabric, lift the presser foot, and move the lining so the needle will go back into the fabric to leave about a ½" (1.3cm) gap. Reinsert the needle and sew a couple of stitches, backstitch a few stitches to secure the opening, then sew to the bottom edge.

Press open each seam as far as possible. Lightly press the fold at the bottom edge of the lining. *Note: This will serve as a guide for the corner seams.*

Fold 1" (2.5cm) of the top edge to the WS and press.

With WS still facing, open out the lining, and align the seam with the pressed fold at the bottom of lining and place several pins to hold the layers together.

Measure down from the point about 2" (5.1cm); the width of the corner perpendicular to the seam should be 4" (10.2cm). Draw a line from edge to edge at this mark *(Fig. 2)*. Sew across the corner where marked.

Rep on the other corner of the lining.

With the WS of the lining still facing, open out the tote and slip the lining into the tote. Pin the top edge of the lining along the bottom of the garter band below the top edge, about 1" (2.5cm) in.

Sew the lining in place.

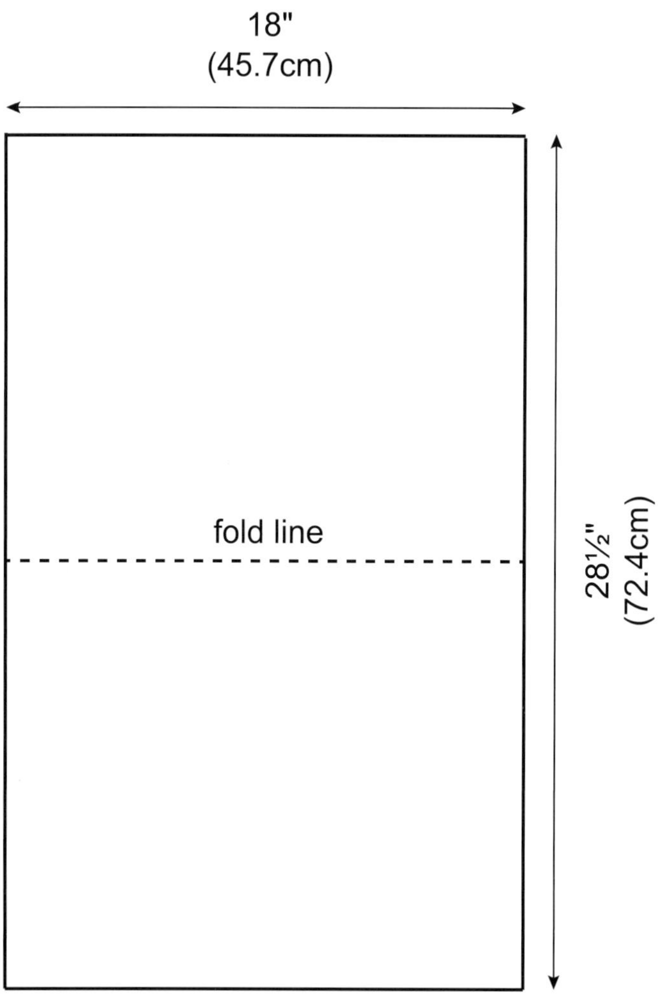

Fig. 1

■ FINISHING

Using a doubled strand of button thread, sew one handle to each side of the tote through all the layers.

Raise each tab up on the sides of the tote and insert a post button through the tab and the side of the tote. Working from the inside, push the post through the gap left when sewing the side seams, then push the stopper over the post to secure.

If you're using decorative buttons, sew a button near the tip of each tab, through all layers.

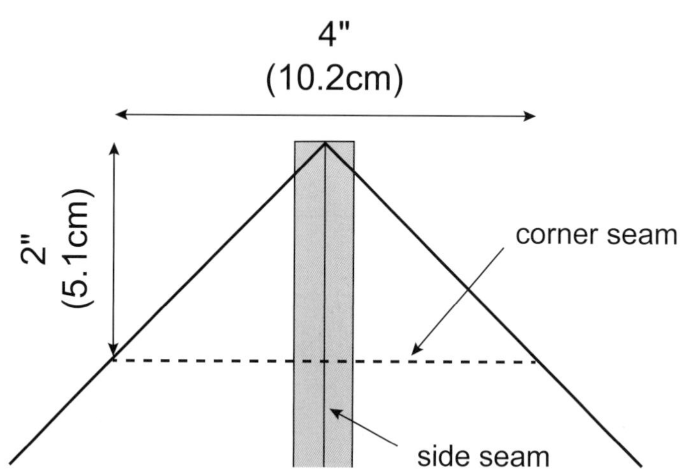

Fig. 2

CROSSHATCH *Tunic*

When the weather finally turns from the heat of summer to the cooler days and nights of autumn, we naturally begin to think of warm, comfy sweaters. Full of texture and varying stitches, and more fun than dragging around your favorite blanket, you'll love wearing this oversized tunic-length sweater indoors or out.

SKILL LEVEL: INTERMEDIATE

FINISHED MEASUREMENTS:
Chest: 63 ½ [72, 81, 90]" (161.3 [182.9, 205.7, 228.6]cm) / **Length:** 25 [26, 27, 28]" (63.5 [66, 68.6, 71.1]cm)

SIZES

XS/S [M/L, XL/2XL, 3XL/4XL]

YARN

1474 [1741, 1997, 2254] yds (1348 [1592, 1826, 2061]m) #4 medium weight yarn

MATERIALS

US Size 8 (5mm) circular needles, or size required for gauge, in lengths of 16" (40.6cm), 32" (81.3cm), and 40" (101.6cm)

Four or five US 8 (5mm) double-pointed needles, or size required for gauge

Stitch markers

Cable needle

Stitch holders or scrap yarn

Scissors

Tapestry needle

YARN INFORMATION

Sample uses Ultra Alpaca from Berroco (50% Peruvian wool/50% superfine alpaca; 3.5oz [100g]; 219yds [200m]) in color #6209 Moonshadow—7 (8, 10, 11) skeins

GAUGES

18 ½ sts and 28 rows = 4" (10.2cm) in Basket Weave patt

24 sts and 23 rnds = 4" (10.2cm) in K1, P1 Rib

74-st center panel measures approx 14 ½" (36.8cm) wide

PATTERN NOTES

The front and back are worked separately on long circular needle cables to accommodate the large number of stitches. The shoulders are sewn together to create more stable seams.

The sleeves are worked in the round from the cuff up. After picking up stitches along the armholes, the sleeves are then joined to the armholes using Three-Needle Bind Off (see page 9).

The sleeves are shorter for the larger sizes to adjust for the extra width across the body. Once complete, the sleeves should measure approximately 28 [30, 31 ½, 33]" (71.1 [76.2, 80, 83.8]cm) from the center of the back to the cast-on edge of the cuff.

cont. on page 112

Shown in size Medium/Large, with approximately 30" (76.2cm) of positive ease.

SPECIAL STITCHES

1/2 LC (1 over 2 left cross) = Sl 1 st to cable needle and hold in front, k2, then k1 from cable needle.

1/2 RC (1 over 2 right cross) = Sl 2 sts to cable needle and hold in back, k1, then k2 from cable needle.

3/2 LPC (3 over 2 left purl cross) = Sl 3 sts to cable needle and hold in front, p2, then k3 from cable needle.

3/2 RPC (3 over 2 right purl cross) = Sl 2 sts to cable needle and hold in back, k3, then p2 from cable needle.

3/3 LC (3 over 3 left cross) = Sl 3 sts to cable needle and hold in front, k3, then k3 from cable needle.

3/3 RC (3 over 3 right cross) = Sl 3 sts to cable needle and hold in back, k3, then k3 from cable needle.

TUNIC

BACK

Using the longer circular needle, CO 150 [170, 190, 210] sts. Do not join.

Row 1 (RS): Knit.

Row 2 (WS): K6 [4, 6, 4], *p2, k2; rep from * to last 8 [6, 8, 6] sts, p2, k6 [4, 6, 4].

Row 3: K6 [4, 6, 4], *k2, p2; rep from * to last 8 [6, 8, 6] sts, p2, k6 [4, 6, 4].

Rep last 2 rows until piece measures 1 ½" (3.8cm), ending with a RS row.

Inc Row (WS): Work 40 [50, 60, 70] sts in established patt, pm, (k2, p2) 5 times, k1, M1, k1, (p2, k2) 3 times, (M1p, p1) twice, (k2, p2) 3 times, k1, M1, k1, (p2, k2) 5 times, pm, work in patt to end of row—154 [174, 194, 214] sts.

Next Row (RS): K6 [4, 6, 4], beg at the right edge of Left Front/Right Back Basket Weave Chart for your size and work 4 [16, 4, 16] sts, work the 20-st rep 1 [1, 2, 2] time(s), then work 10 sts after the rep, sm, work Row 1 of Center Cable Panel over the next 74 sts, sm, beg at the right edge of Right Front & Left Back Basket Weave Chart, work 10 sts before rep, work the 20-st rep 1 [1, 2, 2] time(s), work 4 [16, 4, 16] sts after rep, then k6 [4, 6, 4].

Note: When working the chart, Right Back/Front and Left Back/Front refer to the corresponding side of the back and front (as worn) on each side of the center cable panel on RS rows.

Cont to knit the first 6 [4, 6, 4] sts and last 6 [4, 6, 4] sts of every row, work in established patt until piece measures 5" (12.7cm) from the beg, ending with a WS row. Pm in each end of last row for side slit.

Next Row (RS): Beg working the first 6 [4, 6, 4] sts and last 6 [4, 6, 4] sts in Basket Weave patt, work 40 [50, 60, 70] sts in patt, sm, work next row of Center Cable Panel over the next 74 sts, sm, then work in Basket Weave patt to end of row.

Cont in established patt until piece measures 18" (45.7cm). Pm in each end of last row for armholes.

Work even until piece measures 23 [24, 25, 26]" (58.4 [61, 63.5, 66]cm), ending with a WS row.

Shape Shoulders and Neck

Rows 1–8: BO 6 [7, 8, 9] sts at the beg of next 8 rows—106 [118, 130, 142] sts rem.

Pm 40 (45, 50, 55) sts from each end of row, with 26 [28, 30, 32] sts between markers for neck.

Row 9 (RS): BO 6 [7, 8, 9] sts, work to the marker, join a second ball of yarn and BO marked 26 [28, 30, 32] sts, then work to the end of row.

Row 10: BO 6 [7, 8, 9] sts, work to the neck edge; the other side, BO 3 sts, then work to the end of row.

Row 11: BO 6 [7, 8, 10] sts, work to the neck edge; the other side, BO 3 sts, then work to the end of row.

Row 12: BO 6 [7, 8, 10] sts, work to the neck edge; the other side, BO 2 sts, then work to the end of row.

Row 13: BO 5 [6, 9, 10] sts, work to the neck edge; the other side, BO 2 sts, then work to the end of row.

Row 14: BO 5 [6, 9, 10] sts, then work to the end of row—18 [20, 20, 21] sts rem for each shoulder. BO rem sts.

Basket Weave Chart, Left Front & Right Back

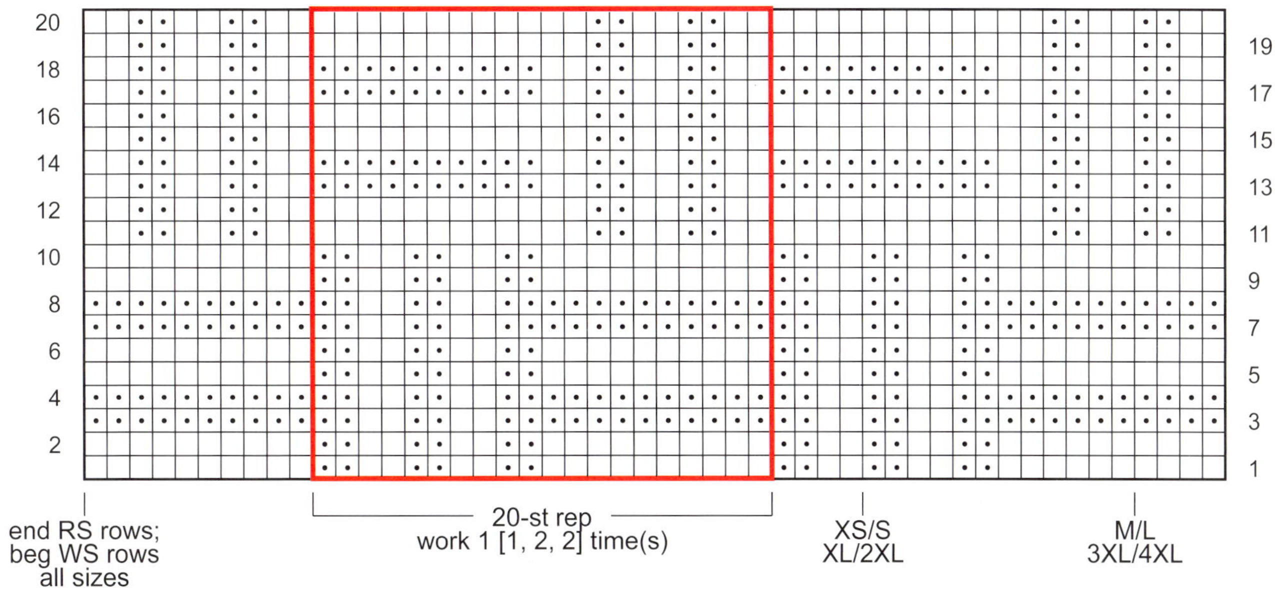

Basket Weave Chart, Right Front & Left Back

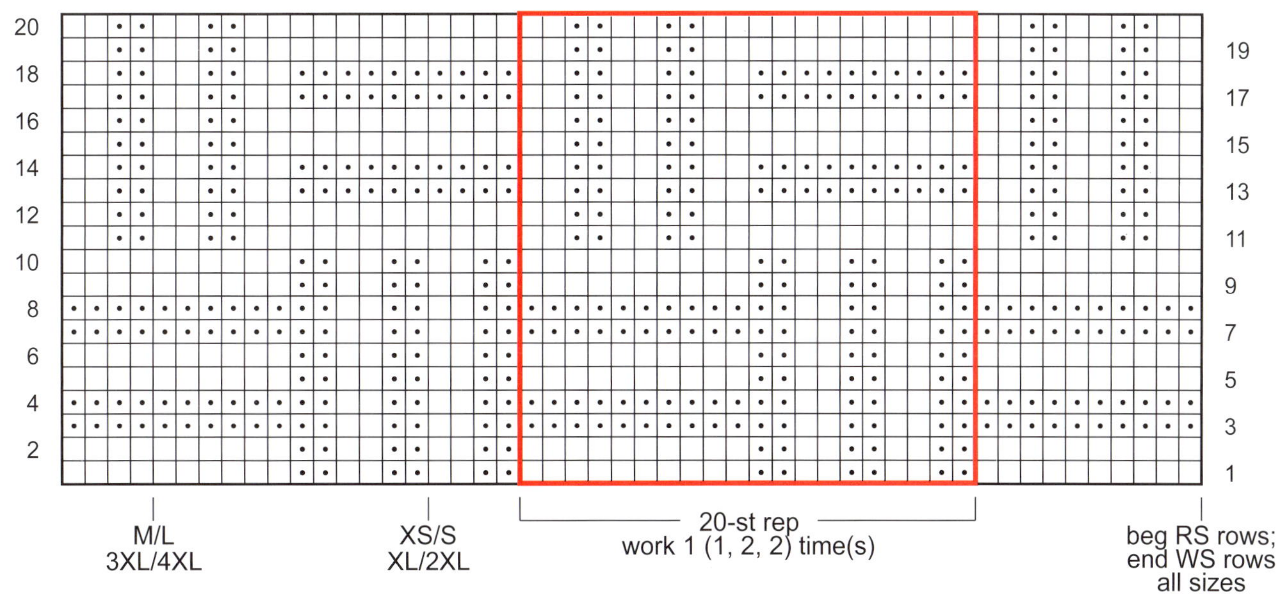

Key

- ☐ k on RS, p on WS
- ⊡ p on RS, k on WS
- ☐ (red) repeat

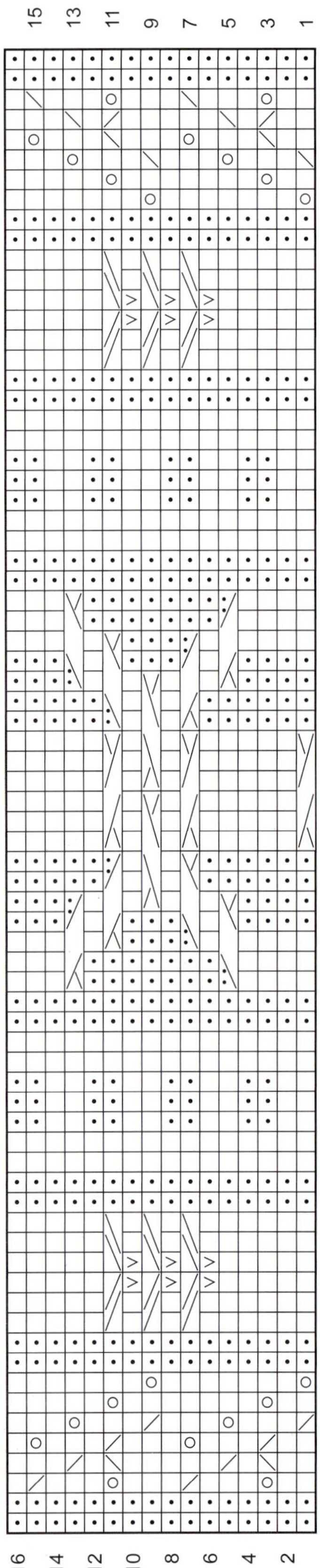

Center Cable Panel

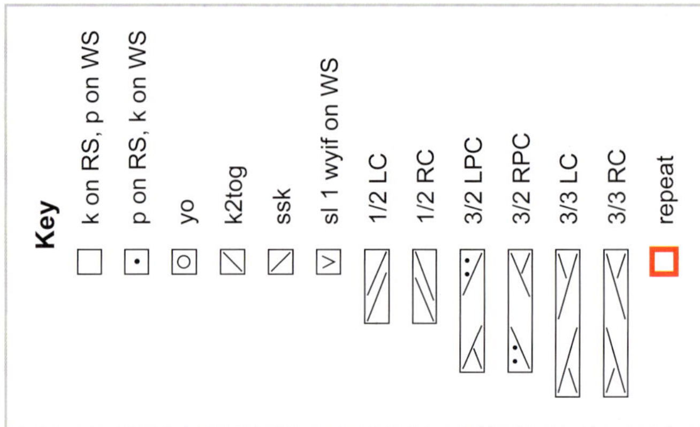

■ FRONT

Work the front same as the back until piece measures 22 [22 ¾, 23 ½, 24 ¼]" (55.9 [57.8, 59.7, 61.6]cm) from the beg, ending with a WS row.

Shape Neck and Shoulders

Pm 70 (80, 90, 100) sts from each end of row, with 14 sts between markers for the neck.

Next Row (RS): Work to the marker, join a second ball of yarn and BO center 14 sts, then work to the end of row—70 [80, 90, 100] sts rem for each shoulder.

Working both sides at the same time, BO at each neck edge 3 sts once, then 2 sts twice—63 [73, 83, 93] sts rem for each shoulder.

Work 1 WS row even.

Dec Row (RS): Work to 2 sts before the neck edge, k2tog; the other side, ssk, work to the end of row—1 st dec on each side.

Rep last 2 rows 0 [0, 1, 2] time(s) more—62 [72, 81, 90] sts rem for each shoulder.

Work 1 WS row even.

Cont to dec at each neck edge every RS row 3 [4, 4, 4] times more, and *at the same time*, BO 6 [7, 8, 9] sts at the beg of next 12 [12, 12, 10] rows, then 5 [6, 9, 10] sts at the beg of next 2 [2, 2, 4] rows—18 [20, 20, 21] sts rem for each shoulder. BO rem sts.

■ SLEEVES

Using double-pointed needles, CO 47 [51, 55, 61] sts. Join to work in the rnd, being careful not to twist the sts.

Rnd 1: P1, *k1, p1; rep from * to end of rnd.

Rep last rnd 7 [5, 3, 2] more times.

Inc Rnd 1: P1, M1p, *k1, p1; rep from * to last 2 sts, k1, M1p, p1—2 sts inc.

Work 7 [5, 3, 2] rnds even.

Inc Rnd 2: P1, M1, *p1, k1; rep from * to last 2 sts, p1, M1, p1—2 sts inc.

Cont inc every 8 [6, 4, 3] rnds 3 [4, 9, 15] times more, then every 10 [7, 5, 0] rnds 2 [4, 3, 0] times, alternating Inc Rnd 1, then Inc Rnd 2, and working inc sts into rib patt—61 [71, 83, 95] sts. *Note: Change to shorter circular needle when there are too many stitches to work on the double-pointed needles.*

Work even until piece measures 12 [12, 11 ¼, 10 ½]" (30.5 [30.5, 28.6, 26.7]cm). Place sts on holder or scrap yarn.

■ FINISHING

Weave in ends. Block pieces to measurements *(Fig. 1)*. Sew front and back together at the shoulders. Sew sides seams between markers.

Collar

Using the shorter circular needle and with RS facing, pick up and knit 68 [72, 76, 80] sts evenly along the front neck edge and 40 [42, 44, 46] sts along the back neck edge—108 [114, 120, 126] sts.

Pm and join to work in the rnd.

Rnd 1: *K1, p1; rep from * around.

Rep Rnd 1 until collar measures 7" (17.8cm). BO all sts loosely in ribbing.

Attach Sleeves

Return sts for one sleeve to the shorter circular needle.

Using the longer circular needle and with RS facing, beg at the bottom of the armhole, pick up and knit 30 [35, 41, 47] sts evenly along one side of armhole, 30 [35, 41, 47] sts along other side of armhole, then 1 st in the seam at the bottom of the armhole—61 [71, 83, 95] sts.

Turn the body with WS facing out, and insert the sleeve into the armhole so the RS of both pieces are held together, making sure the shaped edge of the sleeve is at the bottom of the armhole.

Join the sleeve to the body using Three-Needle Bind Off (see page 9).

Rep with the rem sleeve.

Weave in the rem ends.

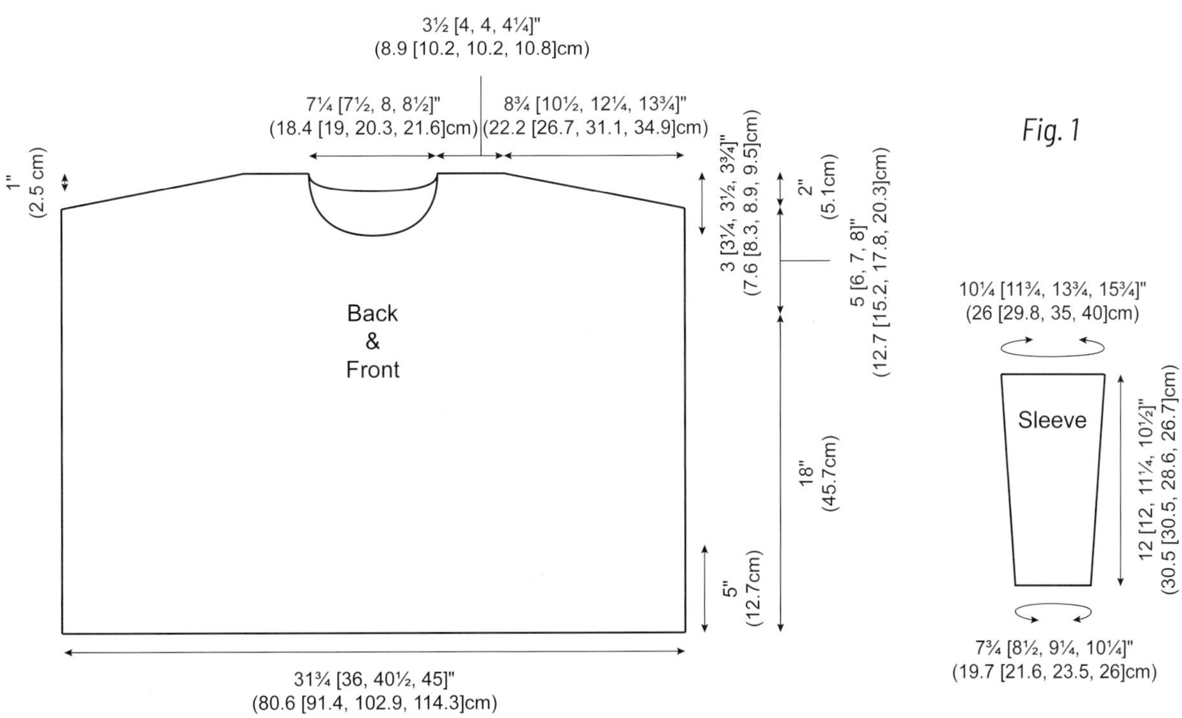

Fig. 1

HEDGEROW *Cardigan*

Ideal for both men and women, this cardigan is perfect for chilly autumn hikes. The two-color mosaic pattern across the yoke is easy to customize in your favorite color combinations, and it would look fantastic with a contrast color featuring a color fade. The body is worked in one piece from the bottom up, with the shoulders joined using Three-Needle Bind Off. The only seams are where you sew the sleeves into the body, so finishing is quick and easy.

SKILL LEVEL: INTERMEDIATE

FINISHED MEASUREMENTS:

Woman's Cardigan

Bust: 34 ¼ [38, 42 ½, 47 ¼, 50 ¾, 55, 58 ½, 62 ¾]" (87 [96.5, 108, 120, 128.9, 139.7, 148.6, 159.4]cm)

Length: 24 ½ [25, 25 ½, 26, 26 ½, 27, 27 ½, 28]" (62.2 [63.5, 64.8, 66, 67.3, 68.6, 69.9, 71.1]cm)

Man's Cardigan

Chest: 40 [44, 48 ¼, 51 ¾, 56, 60]" (101.6 [111.8, 122.6, 131.4, 142.2, 152.4]cm)

Length: 25 ½ [26, 26 ½, 27, 27 ½, 28]" (64.8 [66, 67.3, 68.6, 69.9, 71.1]cm)

SIZES

Woman's: XS [S, M, L, XL, 2XL, 3XL, 4XL]

Man's: S [M, L, XL, 2XL, 3XL]

YARN

Woman's Cardigan

965 [1068, 1159, 1272, 1365, 1494, 1588, 1763] yds (882 [977, 1060, 1163, 1248, 1366, 1452, 1612]m) #4 medium weight yarn in Main Color (MC)

92 [101, 115, 125, 136, 146, 159, 170] yds (84 [92, 105, 114, 124, 134, 145, 155] m) #4 medium weight yarn in Contrast Color (CC)

Man's Cardigan

1220 [1357, 1487, 1593, 1706, 1842] yds (1116 [1241, 1360, 1457, 1560, 1684]m) #4 medium weight yarn in Main Color (MC)

239 [265, 291, 311, 334, 359] yds (219 [242, 266, 284, 305, 328]m) #4 medium weight yarn in Contrast Color (CC)

MATERIALS

US 8 (5mm) circular needles in lengths of 16" (40.6cm), 32" (81.3cm), and 40" (101.6cm)

Four or five US 8 (5mm) double-pointed needles

Stitch markers

Stitch holders or scrap yarn

Tapestry needle

Scissors

⅞" (23mm) diameter buttons, seven for Woman's Cardigan or six for Man's Cardigan

Sewing needle and thread

YARN INFORMATION

Sample uses Cozy Cotton from Green Mountain Spinnery (20% organic cotton/80% fine wool; 2oz [56.7g]; 140yds [128m]), in colors #10199 Echo (MC—7 [8, 9, 10, 10, 11, 12, 13] skeins for Woman's Cardigan, and 9 [10, 11, 12, 13, 14] skeins for Man's Cardigan), and #10200 Pomelo (CC—1 [1, 1, 1, 2, 2, 2] skeins for Woman's Cardigan, and 2 [2, 3, 3, 3, 3] skeins for Man's Cardigan)

GAUGES

15 ½ sts and 22 rows/rnds = 4" (10.2cm) in stockinette stitch, blocked

16 sts and 40 rows = 4" (10.2cm) in Rough Diamond patt, blocked

SPECIAL STITCH

St st (stockinette stitch) = Knit RS rows and purl WS rows.

Shown in size Woman's Small, with 4" to 6" (10.2 to 15.2cm) of positive ease.

WOMAN'S CARDIGAN

■ BODY

Using longer circular needle and MC, CO 132 [144, 164, 180, 196, 212, 224, 240] sts. Do not join.

Row 1 (WS): K1, *p2, k2; rep from * to last 3 sts, p2, k1.

Row 2 (RS): Sl 1 wyif, *k2, p2; rep from * to last 3 sts, k3.

Row 3: Sl 1 wyif, *p2, k2; rep from * to last 3 sts, p2, k1.

Rep last 2 rows until ribbing measures approx 1 ¾" (4.4cm), ending with a WS row.

Dec Row (RS): Knit and dec 3 [1, 3, 1, 3, 3, 1, 1] st(s) evenly across row—129 [143, 161, 179, 193, 209, 223, 239] sts rem.

Knitting the first st and last st of every row, work in St st until piece measures 15 ¾" (40cm) from beg, ending with a WS row.

Pm 31 [34, 39, 44, 47, 51, 55, 59] sts from beg and end of row, with 67 [75, 83, 91, 99, 107, 113, 121] sts between markers for back.

Set-Up Row (RS): Join CC, k1, beg at right side of chart as marked for your size and working Row 1 of Rough Diamond Mosaic Chart, work 8 [3, 12, 9, 4, 12, 7, 3] sts before rep, work 12-st rep 9 [11, 12, 13, 15, 16, 17, 19] times, work 11 [6, 3, 12, 7, 3, 10, 6] sts after rep, then k1.

Next Row (WS): With CC, k1, beg at left side of chart as marked for your size and working Row 2 of Rough Diamond Mosaic Chart, work 11 [6, 3, 12, 7, 3, 10, 6] sts before rep, work 12-st rep 9 [11, 12, 13, 15, 16, 17, 19] times, work 8 [3, 12, 9, 4, 12, 7, 3] sts after rep, then k1.

Divide Front and Back

Next Row (RS): With MC, k1, ssk, *work in patt to 2 [3, 4, 5, 6, 7, 8, 9] sts before marker, BO 4 [6, 8, 10, 12, 14, 16, 18] sts; rep from * once more, then work to last 3 sts, k2tog, k1—28 [30, 34, 38, 40, 43, 46, 49] sts rem for each front, and 63 [69, 75, 81, 87, 93, 97, 103] sts rem for back.

Place sts for right front and back on holders or scrap yarn.

■ LEFT FRONT

Shape Armhole and Neck

Cont in established patt, BO at beg of RS rows 4 sts 0 [0, 0, 0, 0, 1, 1, 1] time, 3 sts 0 [0, 0, 1, 1, 1, 1, 1] time, 2 sts 1 [1, 1, 1, 2, 1, 1, 2] time(s), then 1 st 1 [3, 4, 3, 3, 3, 4, 4] time(s). *At the same time*, cont dec 1 st at neck edge every 6 rows 10 [10, 11, 13, 12, 10, 10, 10] more times, then every 0 [0, 0, 0, 0, 8, 8, 8] rows 0 [0, 0, 0, 0, 3, 4, 5] times—15 [15, 17, 17, 18, 18, 19, 19] sts rem when all shaping is complete.

Work even until armhole measures 7 ½ [8, 8 ½, 9, 9 ½, 10, 10 ½, 11]" (19 [20.3, 21.6, 22.9, 24.1, 25.4, 26.7, 28]cm), ending with an RS row in MC.

Key

- MC
- CC
- k on RS, p on WS
- p on RS, k on WS
- sl 1 wyib on RS, sl 1 wyif on WS
- repeat

Rough Diamond Mosaic Chart, Woman's

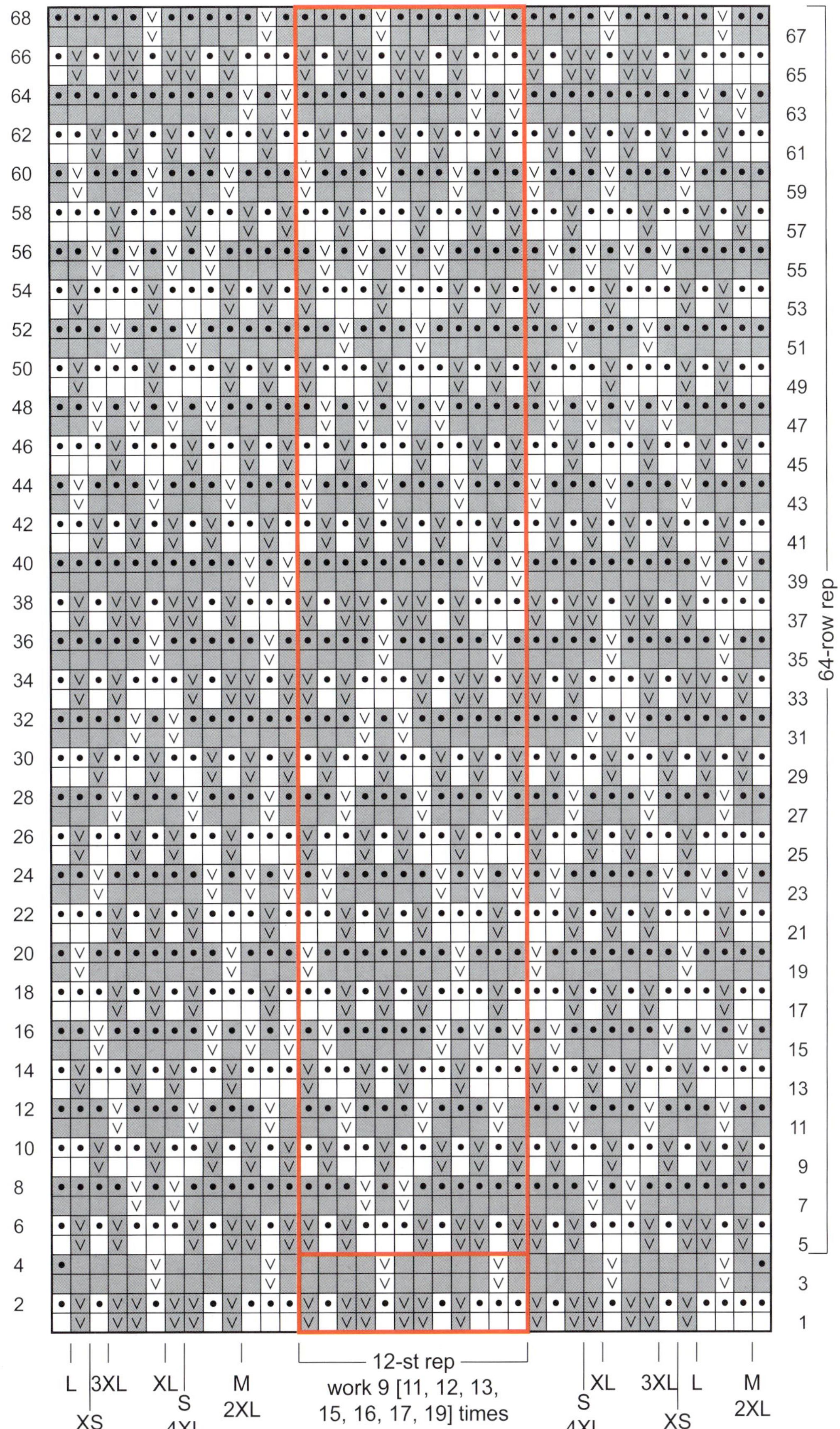

Shape Shoulder

Short Row 1 (WS): Cont in established patt and work to last 3 sts, w&t.

Short Rows 2, 4, 6, and 8 (RS): Work to neck edge.

Short Row 3: Work to 2 [2, 2, 2, 2, 2, 3, 3] sts before wrapped st, w&t.

Short Row 5: Work to 2 [2, 2, 2, 3, 3, 3, 3] sts before wrapped st, w&t.

Short Row 7: Work to 2 [2, 3, 3, 3, 3, 3, 3] sts before wrapped st, w&t.

Next Row (WS): With MC, work to end of row and hide wraps as you come to them. Place rem sts on holder or scrap yarn.

■ RIGHT FRONT

Return held 28 [30, 34, 38, 40, 43, 46, 49] sts to shorter circular needle. Rejoin appropriate color to beg with a WS row.

Shape Armhole and Neck

Cont in patt, BO at beg of WS rows 4 sts 0 [0, 0, 0, 0, 1, 1, 1] time, 3 sts 0 [0, 0, 1, 1, 1, 1, 1] time, 2 sts 1 [1, 1, 1, 2, 1, 1, 2] time(s), then 1 st 1 [3, 4, 3, 3, 3, 4, 4] time(s). *At the same time*, cont dec 1 st at neck edge every 6 rows 10 [10, 11, 13, 12, 10, 10, 10] more times, then every 0 [0, 0, 0, 0, 8, 8, 8] rows 0 [0, 0, 0, 0, 3, 4, 5] times—15 [15, 17, 17, 18, 18, 19, 19] sts rem when all shaping is complete.

Work even until armhole measures 7 ½ [8, 8 ½, 9, 9 ½, 10, 10 ½, 11]" (19 [20.3, 21.6, 22.9, 24.1, 25.4, 26.7, 28]cm), ending with a WS row in MC.

Shape Shoulder

Short Row 1 (RS): Cont in established patt and work to last 3 sts, w&t.

Short Rows 2, 4, 6, and 8 (WS): Work to neck edge.

Short Row 3: Work to 2 [2, 2, 2, 2, 2, 3, 3] sts before wrapped st, w&t.

Short Row 5: Work to 2 [2, 2, 2, 3, 3, 3, 3] sts before wrapped st, w&t.

Short Row 7: Work to 2 [2, 3, 3, 3, 3, 3, 3] sts before wrapped st, w&t.

Next Row (RS): With MC, work to end of row and hide wraps as you come to them. Place rem sts on holder or scrap yarn.

■ BACK

Return held 63 [69, 75, 81, 87, 93, 97, 103] sts to shorter circular needle. Rejoin appropriate color to beg with a WS row.

Cont in established patt, BO 4 sts at beg of next 0 [0, 0, 0, 0, 2, 2, 2] rows, 3 sts at beg of next 0 [0, 0, 2, 2, 2, 2, 2] rows, 2 sts at beg of next 2 [2, 2, 2, 4, 2, 2, 4] rows, then dec 1 st at each end of every RS row 1 [3, 4, 3, 3, 3, 4, 4] time(s)—57 [59, 63, 65, 67, 69, 71, 73] sts rem.

Work even until armholes measure 7 ½ [8, 8 ½, 9, 9 ½, 10, 10 ½, 11]" (19 [20.3, 21.6, 22.9, 24.1, 25.4, 26.7, 28]cm), ending with a WS row in MC.

Pm each side of center 21 (23, 23, 25, 25, 27, 27, 29) sts.

Shape Neck and Shoulders

Short Rows 1 and 2: Work to last 3 sts, w&t.

Short Row 3: Work to marker, join a second ball of yarn and BO marked sts, then work to 2 [2, 2, 2, 2, 2, 3, 3] sts before wrapped st, w&t.

Short Row 4: Work to neck edge; other side, BO 3 sts, work to 2 [2, 2, 2, 2, 2, 3, 3] sts before wrapped st, w&t.

Short Row 5: Work to neck edge; other side, BO 3 sts, work to 2 [2, 2, 2, 3, 3, 3, 3] sts before wrapped st, w&t.

Short Row 6: Work to neck edge; other side, work to 2 [2, 2, 2, 3, 3, 3, 3] sts before wrapped st, w&t.

Short Rows 7 and 8: Work to neck edge; other side, work to 2 [2, 3, 3, 3, 3, 3, 3] sts before wrapped st, w&t.

Short Row 9: With MC, work to neck edge; other side, work to end of row and hide wraps as you come to them. Place these 15 [15, 17, 17, 18, 18, 19, 19] sts on holder or scrap yarn.

Next Row: With MC, work to end of row and hide wraps as you come to them. Place rem 15 [15, 17, 17, 18, 18, 19, 19] sts on holder or scrap yarn.

■ SLEEVES

Using double-pointed needles and MC, CO 32 [36, 36, 40, 40, 44, 44, 48] sts. Join to work in the rnd, being careful not to twist sts.

Rnd 1: *K2, p2; rep from * around.

Rep last rnd until ribbing measures 2" (5.1cm) and dec 0 [2, 0, 2, 0, 2, 2, 4] sts evenly spaced across the last rnd—32 [34, 36, 38, 40, 42, 42, 44] sts rem.

Beg St st and work 3 [3, 3, 3, 1, 1, 1, 1] rnd(s) even.

Inc Rnd: K1, M1L, knit to last st, M1R, k1—2 sts inc.

Rep Inc Rnd every 6 [4, 4, 4, 4, 4, 2, 2] rnds 11 [4, 4, 3, 10, 15, 6, 7] more times, every 0 [6, 6, 6, 6, 6, 4, 4] rnds 0 [4, 4, 10, 5, 3, 15, 15] times, then every 0 [8, 8, 0, 0, 0, 0, 0] rnds 0 [4, 4, 0, 0, 0, 0, 0] times—56 [60, 62, 66, 72, 80, 86, 90] sts. Change to shorter circular needle when there are too many sts to work on double-pointed needles.

Cont even until piece measures 17 ¼ [17 ¾, 17 ¾, 18 ¼, 18 ¼, 18 ¾, 18 ¾, 19 ¼]" (43.8 [45, 45, 46.4, 46.4, 47.6, 47.6, 48.9]cm) from beg, ending last rnd 2 [3, 4, 5, 6, 7, 8, 9] sts before end of rnd.

Shape Cap

BO 4 [6, 8, 10, 12, 14, 16, 18] sts, then knit to end of rnd—52 [54, 54, 56, 60, 66, 70, 72] sts rem.

Working back and forth, BO 3 sts at beg of next 2 [2, 2, 2, 2, 4, 4, 4] rows, then 2 sts at beg of next 4 [4, 4, 4, 4, 2, 2, 2] rows—38 [40, 40, 42, 46, 50, 54, 56] sts rem.

Dec 1 st at each end of every RS row 5 [5, 6, 6, 7, 7, 9, 9] times as follows: k1, k2tog, knit to last 3 sts, ssk, k1—28 [30, 28, 30, 32, 36, 36, 38] sts rem.

BO 2 sts at beg of next 4 [4, 6, 6, 4, 2, 2, 2] rows, then 3 sts at beg of next 2 [2, 0, 0, 2, 4, 4, 4] rows—14 [16, 16, 18, 18, 20, 20, 22] sts rem.

BO rem sts.

■ FINISHING

Weave in ends. Block pieces to measurements *(Fig. 1)*.

Using MC, join shoulders using Three-Needle Bind Off (see page 9).

Collar and Front Bands

Using longer circular needle and MC, and with RS facing, pick up and knit 64 sts evenly spaced along right front edge to beg of neck shaping, pm, 47 [50, 52, 55, 57, 58, 60, 61] sts along right front neck, pm, 34 [36, 36, 38, 38, 40, 40, 42] sts along back neck, pm, 47 [50, 52, 55, 57, 58, 60, 61] sts along left front neck, pm, then 64 sts along left front edge—256 [264, 268, 276, 280, 284, 288, 292] sts. Do not join.

Short Row 1 (WS): Sl 1 wyif, (p2, k2) to 7 [8, 8, 9, 9, 10, 10, 11] sts past right shoulder marker, w&t.

Short Row 2 (RS): Work in established ribbing to 7 [8, 8, 9, 9, 10, 10, 11] sts past left shoulder marker, w&t.

Short Rows 3 and 4: Work to wrapped st, work next st and hide wrap, then work 5 [5, 5, 5, 6, 6, 6, 6] more sts, w&t.

Short Rows 5 and 6: Rep Short Rows 3 and 4.

Short Rows 7 and 8: Work to wrapped st, work next st and hide wrap, then work 3 [5, 5, 5, 5, 5, 5, 5] more sts, w&t.

Short Rows 9 and 10: Work to wrapped st, work next st and hide wrap, then work 3 [3, 3, 5, 5, 5, 5, 5] more sts, w&t.

Short Rows 11 and 12: Work to wrapped st, work next st and hide wrap, then work 3 [3, 3, 3, 3, 3, 5, 5] more sts, w&t.

Short Rows 13 and 14: Work to wrapped st, work next st and hide wrap, then work 3 more sts, w&t.

Short Rows 15 and 16: Work to wrapped st, work next st and hide wrap, then work 2 [2, 3, 3, 3, 3, 3, 3] more sts, w&t.

Short Rows 17 and 18: Work to wrapped st, work next st and hide wrap, then work 2 [2, 3, 3, 3, 3, 3, 3] more sts, w&t.

Woman's Cardigan

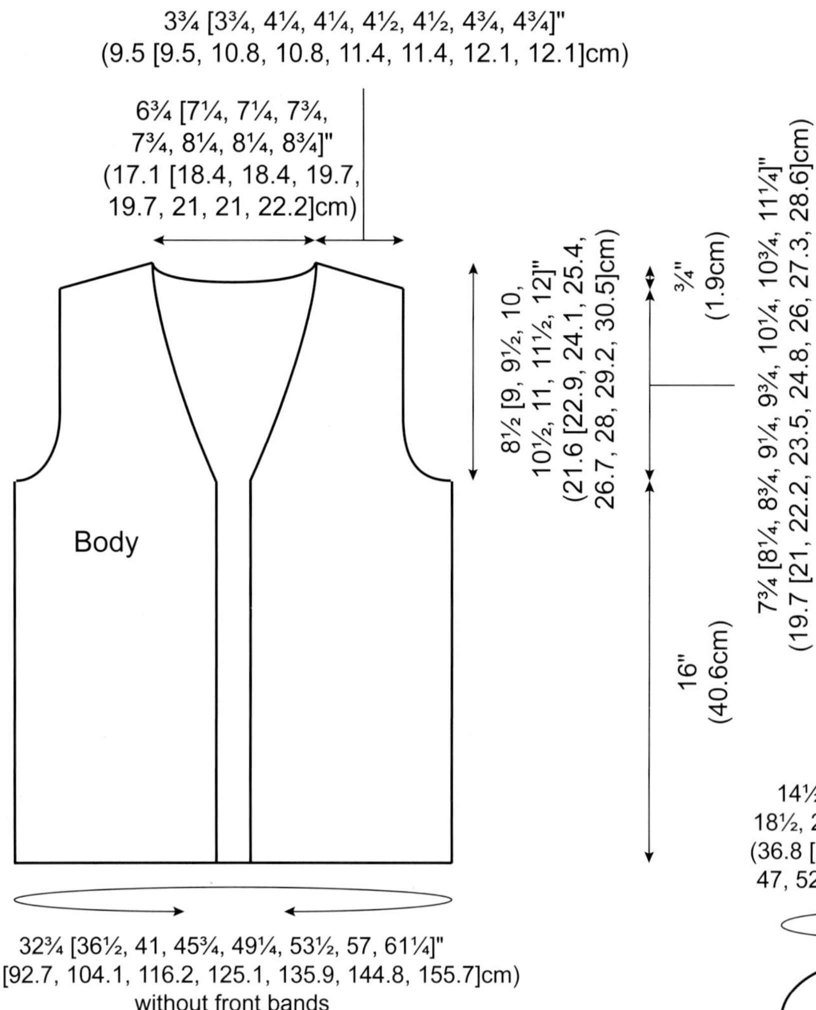

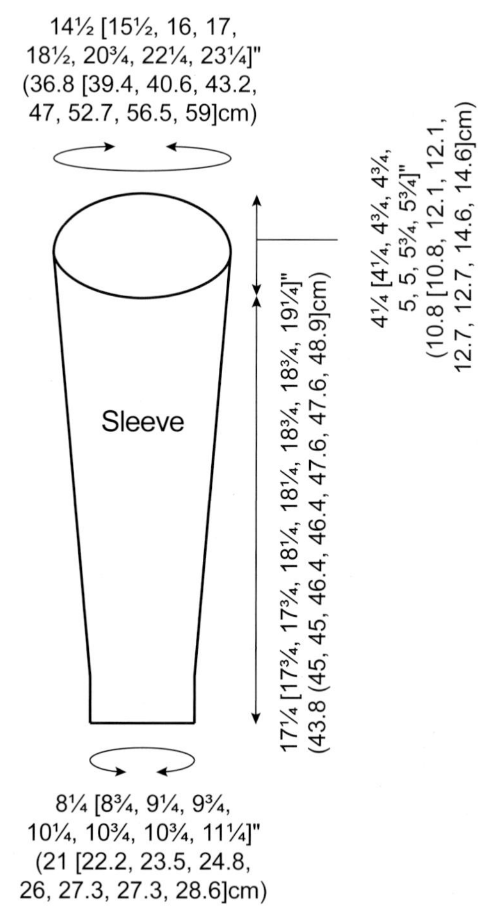

Fig. 1

Short Rows 19–24: Work to wrapped st, work next st and hide wrap, then work 1 more st, w&t. *Note: Short Rows 23 and 24 should end at the markers that were placed at the beginning of the neck shaping on both sides of the front.*

Short Row 25: Work to wrapped st, work next st and hide wrap, then work to last st, k1.

Row 1 (RS): Removing all markers, sl 1 wyif, (k2, p2) to last 3 sts, k3.

Row 2 (WS): Sl 1 wyif, (p2, k2) to last 3 sts, p3.

Row 3 (buttonholes): Sl 1 wyif, k2, (work One-Row Buttonhole [see page 9] over next 2 sts, work 8 sts) 6 times, work One-Row Buttonhole over next 2 sts, then work to end of row.

Work 4 more rows in established rib.

BO in ribbing.

Sew in sleeves. Weave in rem ends.

Sew buttons to button band opposite buttonholes.

MAN'S CARDIGAN

■ BODY

Using longer circular needle and MC, CO 152 [168, 184, 196, 212, 228] sts. Do not join.

Row 1 (WS): K1, *p2, k2; rep from * to last 3 sts, p2, k1.

Row 2 (RS): Sl 1 wyif, *k2, p2; rep from * to last 3 sts, k3.

Row 3: Sl 1 wyif, *p2, k2; rep from * to last 3 sts, p2, k1.

Rep last 2 rows until ribbing measures approx 2" (5.1cm), ending with a WS row.

Dec Row (RS): Knit and dec 3 [3, 3, 1, 1, 1] st(s) evenly across row—149 [165, 181, 195, 211, 227] sts rem.

Knitting the first st and last st of every row, work in St st until piece measures 15 ½" (39.4cm) from beg, ending with a WS row.

Pm 36 [40, 44, 47, 51, 55] sts from beg and end of row, with 77 [85, 93, 101, 109, 117] sts between markers for back.

Set-Up Row (RS): Join CC, k1, beg at right side of chart as marked for your size and working Row 1 of Rough Diamond Mosaic Chart, work 6 [2, 4, 5, 1, 3] st(s) before rep, work 12-st rep 11 [13, 14, 15, 17, 18] times, work 9 [5, 7, 8, 4, 6] sts after the rep, then k1.

Next Row (WS): With CC, k1, beg at left side of chart as marked for your size and working Row 2 of Rough Diamond Mosaic Chart, work 9 [5, 7, 8, 4, 6] sts before rep, work 12-st rep 11 [13, 14, 15, 17, 18] times, work 6 [2, 4, 5, 1, 3] st(s) after the rep, then k1.

Divide Front and Back

Next Row (RS): With MC, k1, ssk, *work in patt to 3 [4, 5, 6, 7, 8] sts before marker, BO 6 [8, 10, 12, 14, 16] sts; rep from * once more, then work to last 3 sts, k2tog, k1—32 [35, 38, 40, 43, 46] sts rem for each front, and 71 [77, 83, 89, 95, 101] sts rem for back.

Place sts for right front and back on holders or scrap yarn.

■ LEFT FRONT

Shape Armhole and Neck

Cont in established patt, BO at beg of RS rows 4 sts 0 [0, 0, 0, 1, 1] time, 3 sts 0 [0, 1, 1, 1, 1] time, 2 sts 1 [2, 1, 2, 1, 1] time(s), then 1 st 3 [2, 2, 2, 2, 3] times. *At the same time*, cont dec 1 st at neck edge every 6 [6, 6, 0, 0, 0] rows 5 [4, 3, 0, 0, 0] more times, then every 8 rows 7 [9, 10, 13, 13, 14] times—15 [16, 18, 18, 19, 20] sts rem when all shaping is complete.

Work even until armhole measures 9 [9 ½, 10, 10 ½, 11, 11 ½]" (22.9 [24.1, 25.4, 26.7, 28, 29.2]cm), ending with a RS row in MC.

Shape Shoulder

Short Row 1 (WS): Cont in established patt and work to last 3 [3, 3, 3, 3, 4] sts, w&t.

Short Rows 2, 4, 6, and 8 (RS): Work to neck edge.

Short Row 3: Work to 2 [2, 2, 2, 3, 3] sts before wrapped st, w&t.

Rough Diamond Mosaic Chart, Man's

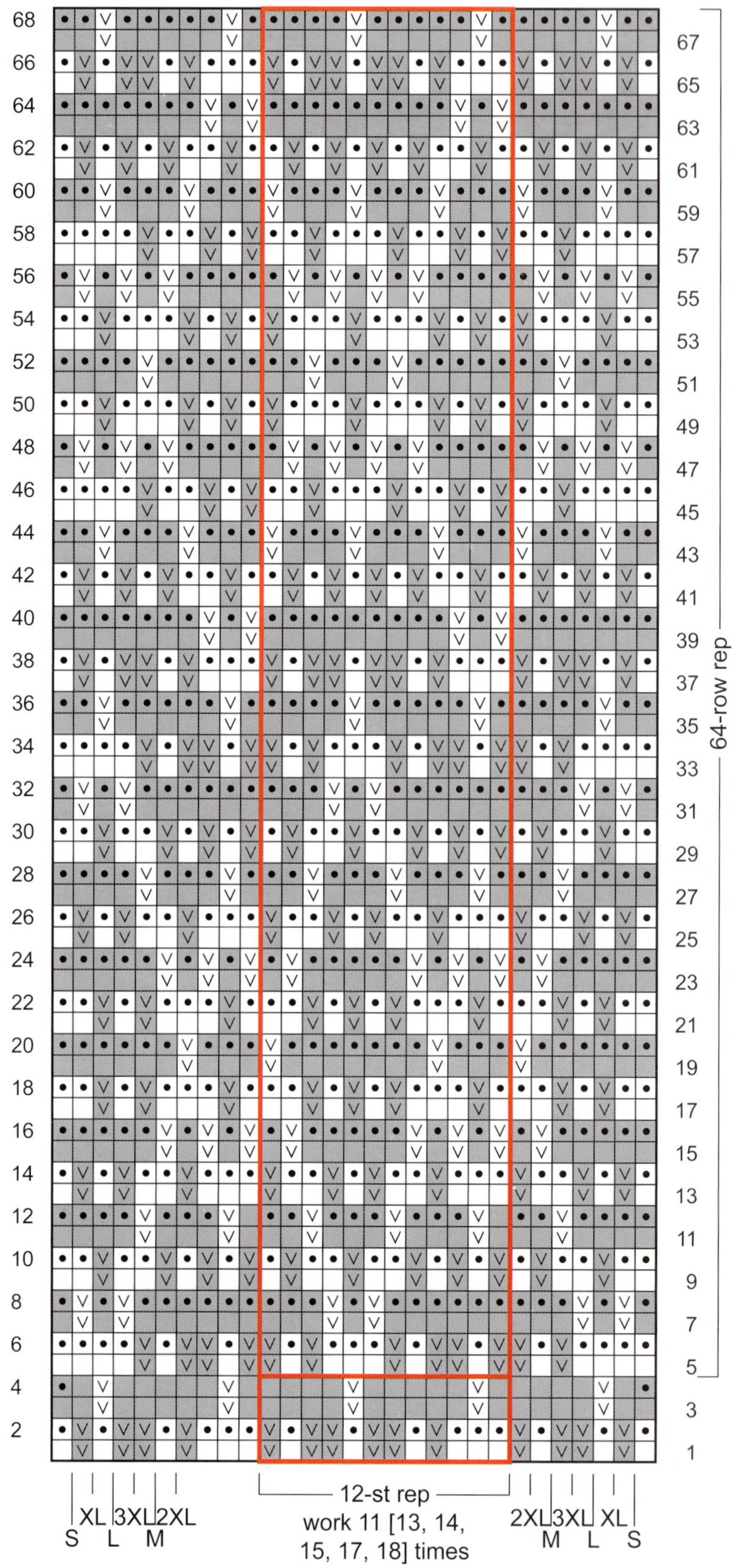

Key

- MC
- CC
- k on RS, p on WS
- p on RS, k on WS
- sl 1 wyib on RS, sl 1 wyif on WS
- repeat

Short Row 5: Work to 2 [2, 3, 3, 3, 3] sts before wrapped st, w&t.

Short Row 7: Work to 2 [2, 3, 3, 3, 3] sts before wrapped st, w&t.

Next Row (WS): With MC, work to end of row and hide wraps as you come to them. Place rem sts on holder or scrap yarn.

■ RIGHT FRONT

Return held 32 [35, 38, 40, 43, 46] sts to shorter circular needle. Rejoin appropriate color to beg with a WS row.

Shape Armhole and Neck

Cont in established patt, BO at beg of WS rows 4 sts 0 [0, 0, 0, 1, 1] time, 3 sts 0 [0, 1, 1, 1, 1] time, 2 sts 1 [2, 1, 2, 1, 1] time(s), then 1 st 3 [2, 2, 2, 2, 3] times. *At the same time*, cont dec 1 st at neck edge every 6 [6, 6, 0, 0, 0] rows 5 [4, 3, 0, 0, 0] more times, then every 8 rows 7 [9, 10, 13, 13, 14] times—15 [16, 18, 18, 19, 20] sts rem when all shaping is complete.

Work even until armhole measures 9 [9 ½, 10, 10 ½, 11, 11 ½]" (22.9 [24.1, 25.4, 26.7, 28, 29.2]cm), ending with a WS row in MC.

Shape Shoulder

Short Row 1 (RS): Cont in established patt and work to last 3 [3, 3, 3, 3, 4] sts, w&t.

Short Rows 2, 4, 6, and 8 (WS): Work to neck edge.

Short Row 3: Work to 2 [2, 2, 2, 3, 3] sts before wrapped st, w&t.

Short Row 5: Work to 2 [2, 3, 3, 3, 3] sts before wrapped st, w&t.

Short Row 7: Work to 2 [2, 3, 3, 3, 3] sts before wrapped st, w&t.

Next Row (RS): With MC, work to end of row and hide wraps as you come to them. Place rem sts on holder or scrap yarn.

■ BACK

Return held 71 [77, 83, 89, 95, 101] sts to shorter circular needle. Rejoin appropriate color to beg with a WS row.

Cont in established patt, BO 4 sts at beg of next 0 [0, 0, 0, 2, 2] rows, 3 sts at beg of next 0 [0, 2, 2, 2, 2] rows, 2 sts at beg of next 2 [4, 2, 4, 2, 2] rows, then dec 1 st at each end of every RS row 3 [2, 2, 2, 2, 3] times—61 [65, 69, 71, 73, 77] sts rem.

Work even until armholes measure 9 [9 ½, 10, 10 ½, 11, 11 ½]" (22.9 [24.1, 25.4, 26.7, 28, 29.2]cm), ending with a WS row in MC.

Pm 18 [19, 21, 21, 22, 23] sts from each end of the needle, with 25 [27, 27, 29, 29, 31] sts between markers for neck.

Shape Neck and Shoulders

Short Rows 1 and 2: Work to last 3 [3, 3, 3, 3, 4] sts, w&t.

Short Row 3: Work to marker, join a second ball of yarn and BO marked sts, then work to 2 [2, 2, 2, 3, 3] sts before wrapped st, w&t.

Short Row 4: Work to neck edge; other side, BO 3 sts, work to 2 [2, 2, 2, 3, 3] sts before wrapped st, w&t.

Short Row 5: Work to neck edge; other side, BO 3 sts, work to 2 [2, 3, 3, 3, 3] sts before wrapped st, w&t.

Short Row 6: Work to neck edge; other side, work to 2 [2, 3, 3, 3, 3] sts before wrapped st, w&t.

Short Rows 7 and 8: Work to neck edge; other side, work to 2 [2, 3, 3, 3, 3] sts before wrapped st, w&t.

Short Row 9: With MC, work to neck edge; other side, work to end of row and hide wraps as you come to them. Place these 15 [16, 18, 18, 19, 20] sts on holder or scrap yarn.

Next Row: With MC, work to end of row and hide wraps as you come to them. Place rem 15 [16, 18, 18, 19, 20] sts on holder or scrap yarn.

SLEEVES

Using double-pointed needles and MC, CO 36 [36, 36, 40, 40, 40] sts. Join to work in the rnd, being careful not to twist sts.

Rnd 1: *K2, p2; rep from * around.

Rep last rnd until ribbing measures 2" (5.1cm) and inc 0 [2, 4, 2, 4, 6] sts evenly spaced across the last rnd—36 [38, 40, 42, 44, 46] sts.

Beg St st and work 7 [5, 5, 5, 3, 3] rnds even.

Inc Rnd: K1, M1L, knit to last st, M1R, k1—2 sts inc.

Rep Inc Rnd every 8 [6, 6, 6, 4, 4] rnds 3 [3, 9, 11, 4, 6] more times, then every 10 [8, 8, 8, 6, 6] rnds 5 [7, 3, 2, 10, 9] times—54 [60, 66, 70, 74, 78] sts. Change to shorter circular needle when there are too many sts to work on double-pointed needles.

Cont even until piece measures 19 ½ [19 ½, 19 ¾, 20, 20, 20]" (49.5 [49.5, 50.2, 50.8, 50.8, 50.8]cm) from beg, ending last rnd 3 [4, 5, 6, 7, 8] sts before end of rnd.

Shape Cap

BO 6 [8, 10, 12, 14, 16] sts, then knit to end of rnd—48 [52, 56, 58, 60, 62] sts rem.

Working back and forth, BO 3 sts at beg of next 0 [0, 0, 0, 2, 2] rows, then 2 sts at beg of next 4 [4, 4, 4, 2, 2] rows—40 [44, 48, 50, 50, 52] sts rem.

Dec 1 st at each end of the next RS row, every 4 rows 4 [4, 4, 4, 6, 7] times, then every RS row 2 [4, 5, 6, 4, 4] times as follows; k1, k2tog, knit to last 3 sts, ssk, k1—26 [26, 28, 28, 28, 28] sts rem.

BO 2 sts at beg of next 2 [2, 2, 2, 4, 4] rows, then 3 [3, 3, 3, 0, 0] sts at beg of next 2 [2, 2, 2, 0, 0] rows—16 [16, 18, 18, 20, 20] sts rem.

BO rem sts.

■ FINISHING

Weave in ends. Block pieces to measurements *(Fig. 2)*.

Using MC, join shoulders using Three-Needle Bind Off (see page 9).

Collar and Front Bands

Using longer circular needle and MC, and with RS facing, pick up and knit 63 sts evenly spaced along right front edge to beg of neck shaping, pm, 53 [56, 58, 59, 61, 62] sts along right front neck, pm, 36 [38, 38, 40, 40, 42] sts along back neck, pm, 53 [56, 58, 59, 61, 62] sts along left front neck, pm, then 63 sts along left front edge—268 [276, 280, 284, 288, 292] sts. Do not join.

Short Row 1 (WS): Sl 1 wyif, (p2, k2) to 8 [9, 9, 10, 10, 11] sts past right shoulder marker, w&t.

Short Row 2 (RS): Work in established ribbing to 8 [9, 9, 10, 10, 11] sts past left shoulder marker, w&t.

Short Rows 3 and 4: Work to wrapped st, work next st and hide wrap, then work 5 [5, 6, 6, 6, 6] more sts, w&t.

Short Rows 5 and 6: Rep Short Rows 3 and 4.

Short Rows 7 and 8: Work to wrapped st, work next st and hide wrap, then work 5 more sts, w&t.

Short Rows 9 and 10: Work to wrapped st, work next st and hide wrap, then work 3 [5, 5, 5, 5, 5] more sts, w&t.

Short Rows 11 and 12: Work to wrapped st, work next st and hide wrap, then work 3 [3, 3, 3, 5, 5] more sts, w&t.

Short Rows 13–18: Work to wrapped st, work next st and hide wrap, then work 3 more sts, w&t.

Short Rows 19–22: Work to wrapped st, work next st and hide wrap, then work 1 more st, w&t.

Short Rows 23 and 24: Work to wrapped st, work next st and hide wrap, then work 2 more sts, w&t. *Note: Short Rows 23 and 24 should end at the markers that were placed at the beginning of the neck shaping on both sides of the front.*

Short Row 25: Work to wrapped st, work next st and hide wrap, then work to last st, k1.

Row 1 (RS): Sl 1 wyif, (k2, p2) to last 3 sts, k3.

Row 2 (WS): Sl 1 wyif, work in established ribbing to marker, sm, (work to marker, remove marker) 3 times, work to last 3 sts, p3.

Row 3 (buttonholes): Sl 1 wyif, work in ribbing to marker, sm, work 2 sts, (work One-Row Buttonhole [see page 9] over next 2 sts, work 9 sts) 5 times, work One-Row Buttonhole over next 2 sts, then work to end of row.

Work 4 more rows in established rib.

BO in ribbing.

Sew in sleeves. Weave in rem ends.

Sew buttons to button band opposite buttonholes.

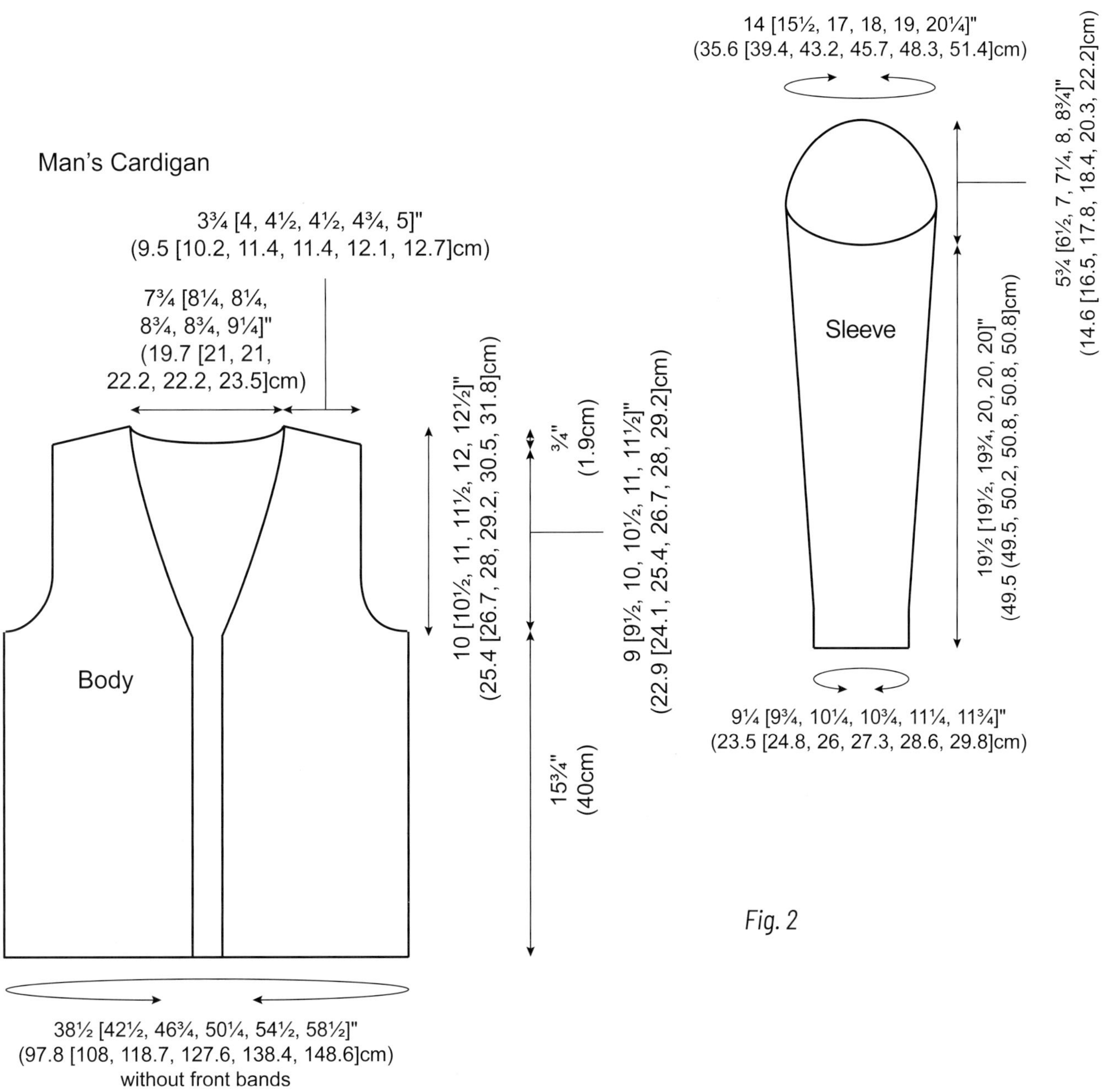

Fig. 2

BACKCOUNTRY TRAILS *Pullover*

Everyone needs a comfy sweater for their autumn adventures. The easy-to-knit garter rib is causal enough for outdoor activities, and the massive cable at the center of the front and back give this design enough panache to take you from casual evenings by the fire to gatherings with family and friends.

SKILL LEVEL: INTERMEDIATE

FINISHED MEASUREMENTS:

Woman's Pullover

Bust: 37 ½ [41 ¾, 45 ¾, 50, 54, 58 ¼, 62 ¼]" (95.3 [106, 116.2, 127, 137.2, 148, 158.1]cm)

Length: 25 [25 ½, 26, 26 ½, 27, 27 ½, 28]" (63.5 [64.8, 66, 67.3, 68.6, 69.9, 71.1]cm)

Man's Pullover

Chest: 39 ½ [43 ¾, 47 ¾, 52, 56, 60 ¼]" (100.3 [111.1, 121.3, 132.1, 142.2, 153]cm)

Length: 26 [26 ½, 27, 27 ½, 28, 28 ½]" (66 [67.3, 68.6, 69.9, 71.1, 72.4]cm)

SIZES

Woman's: XS [S, M, L, XL, 2XL, 3XL, 4XL]

Man's: S [M, L, XL, 2XL, 3XL]

YARN

Note: These yarn amounts are for a mock-neck pullover; if you make a crewneck version, you will need slightly less yarn.

Woman's: 920 [1013, 1110, 1203, 1300, 1399, 1513] yds (841 [926, 1015, 1100, 1189, 1279, 1383]m) #4 medium weight yarn

Man's: 1037 [1150, 1290, 1403, 1514, 1645] yds (948 [1052, 1180, 1283, 1384, 1504]m) #4 medium weight yarn

MATERIALS

US Size 9 (5.5mm) circular needles, or size required for gauge, in lengths of 16" (40.6cm) and 32" (81.3cm)

Four or five US 9 (5.5mm) double-pointed needles, or size required for gauge

Stitch markers

Two cable needles

Stitch holders or scrap yarn

Scissors

Tapestry needle

cont. on page 130

Shown in sizes Woman's Small and Man's Medium, with 4" to 6" (10.2 to 15.2cm) of positive ease.

YARN INFORMATION

Samples shown in Becket from Valley Yarns (50% superfine alpaca/50% wool; 3.5oz [100g]; 141yds [129m]) in colors #25 Storm Cloud (7 [8, 8, 9, 10, 10, 11] balls for Woman's Pullover), and #05 Moose (8 [9, 10, 11, 11, 12] balls for Man's Pullover)

GAUGES

15 ½ sts and 21 rnds/rows = 4" (10.2cm) in Garter Rib

14-st cable panel measures approx 2 ¾" (7cm) wide

PATTERN NOTES

The body is worked in the round from the bottom up to the armholes, then divided to work the front and back separately. The shoulder slope is worked by binding off stitches rather than using short rows to create a more stable shoulder seam. The sleeves are worked in the round from the cuff to the armhole, then the sleeve cap is worked back and forth.

Yarn overs are added before and after the second cable needle when crossing cables. On the following row or round, the yarn overs are dropped so the cable will relax slightly and won't pull in too much.

SPECIAL STITCHES

6/2/6 LC (6 over 2 over 6 left cross) = Sl 6 sts to first cable needle and hold in front, sl next 2 sts to second cable needle and hold in front, k6, yo, k2 from second cable needle, yo, then k6 from first cable needle. Drop the yarn overs on next round/row.

Garter Rib (multiple of 4 sts)

Rnd 1: Knit.

Rnd 2: *K2, p2; rep from * around.

Rep Rnds 1 and 2 for patt.

Woman's Body Chart

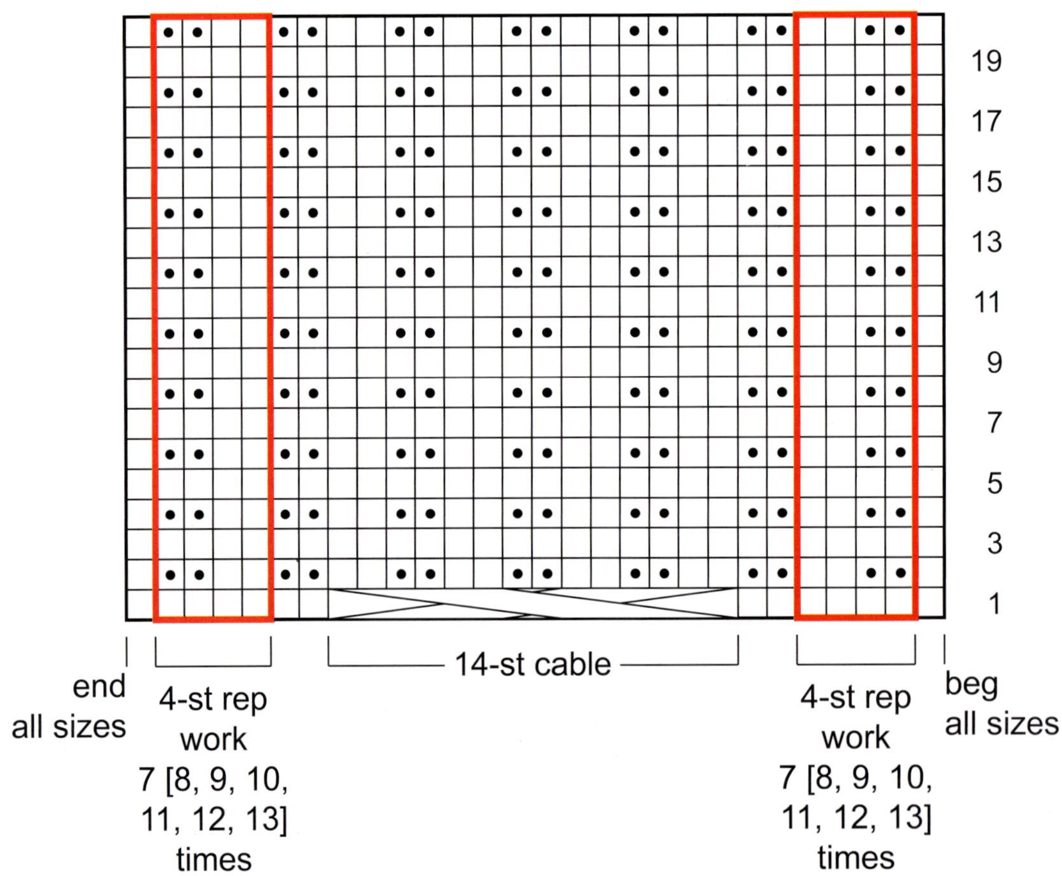

WOMAN'S PULLOVER

■ BODY

Using longer circular needle, CO 152 [168, 184, 200, 216, 232, 248] sts. Pm and join to work in the rnd, taking care not to twist sts.

Set-Up Rnd 1: Knit.

Set-Up Rnd 2: K1, (p2, k2) 7 [8, 9, 10, 11, 12, 13] times, p2, pm, (k2, p2) 3 times, k2, pm, (p2, k2) 15 [17, 19, 21, 23, 25, 27] times, p2, pm, (k2, p2) 3 times, k2, pm, (p2, k2) 7 [8, 9, 10, 11, 12, 13] times, p2, k1.

Sm as you come to them, work 8 more rnds in established Garter Rib, ending with Rnd 2 of patt.

Pm 76 [84, 92, 100, 108, 116, 124] sts from beg of rnd for side of body.

Next Rnd: Working Row 1 of Woman's Body Chart, *work 1 st before rep at RH side of chart, work 4-st rep 7 [8, 9, 10, 11, 12, 13] times, work next 2 sts, sm, work next 14 sts, sm, work next 2 sts, work 4-st rep 7 [8, 9, 10, 11, 12, 13] times, work 1 st at LH side of chart, sm; rep from * once more.

Cont in established patt and work until piece measures 16" (40.6cm) from beg, ending with a Rnd 2 of Garter Rib, and end last rnd 3 [4, 6, 7, 8, 10, 11] sts before end of rnd.

Key

□ k on RS, p on WS

⊡ p on RS, k on WS

6/2/6 LC

□ repeat

Note: When working in the round, read all chart rows from right to left. When working back and forth, read all RS (odd-numbered) rows from right to left, and all WS (even-numbered) rows from left to right.

Divide Front and Back

BO 6 [8, 12, 14, 16, 20, 22] sts, work to 3 [4, 6, 7, 8, 10, 11] sts before side marker, BO 6 [8, 12, 14, 16, 20, 22] sts, then work to end of rnd—70 [76, 80, 86, 92, 96, 102] sts rem each for front and back.

Place front sts on holder or scrap yarn.

■ BACK

Working back and forth, beg with a WS row and BO 2 sts at beg of next 2 [2, 2, 4, 6, 6, 6] rows, then dec 1 st at each end of every RS row 1 [3, 4, 4, 4, 5, 7] time(s)—64 [66, 68, 70, 72, 74, 76] sts rem.

Cont even until armholes measure 8 [8 ½, 9, 9 ½, 10, 10 ½, 11]" (20.3 [21.6, 22.9, 24.1, 25.4, 26.7, 28]cm), ending with a WS row.

Pm 22 [22, 23, 23, 24, 24, 25] sts from each end of row, with 20 [22, 22, 24, 24, 26, 26] sts between markers for neck.

Shape Neck and Shoulders

Row 1 (RS): BO 5 [5, 6, 6, 6, 6, 6] sts, knit to marker, join a second ball of yarn and BO marked 20 [22, 22, 24, 24, 26, 26] sts, then knit to end of row.

Row 2 (WS): BO 5 [5, 6, 6, 6, 6, 6] sts, work in established patt to neck edge; the other side, BO 3 sts, then work to end of row.

Row 3: BO 6 [6, 6, 6, 6, 6, 7] sts, work to neck edge; the other side, BO 3 sts, then work to end of row.

Row 4: BO 6 [6, 6, 6, 6, 6, 7] sts, work to neck edge; the other side BO 2 sts, then work to end of row.

Row 5: BO rem 6 [6, 6, 6, 7, 7, 7] sts; the other side, BO 2 sts, then work to end of row.

Row 6: BO rem 6 [6, 6, 6, 7, 7, 7] sts.

■ FRONT

Return held sts to longer circular needle and join yarn to beg with a WS row.

Shape armholes same as back—64 [66, 68, 70, 72, 74, 76] sts rem.

Cont even until armholes measure 6 [6 ½, 6 ½, 7, 7 ¼, 7 ¾, 7 ¾]" (15.2 [16.5, 16.5, 17.8, 18.4, 19.7, 19.7]cm), ending with a WS row.

Pm 27 [28, 29, 29, 30, 31, 32] sts from each end of row, with 10 [10, 10, 12, 12, 12, 12] sts between markers for neck.

Shape Neck and Shoulders

Next Row (RS): Knit to marker, join a second ball of yarn and BO marked sts, then knit to end of row—27 [28, 29, 29, 30, 31 32] sts rem for each side.

Working both sides at the same time with separate balls of yarn, BO at each neck edge 4 sts once, 2 sts twice, then 1 st 2 [3, 3, 3, 3, 4, 4] times. *At the same time*, when armholes measure 8 [8 ½, 9, 9 ½, 10, 10 ½, 11]" (20.3 [21.6, 22.9, 24.1, 25.4, 26.7, 28]cm), end with a WS row.

Cont any rem neck shaping and BO 5 [5, 6, 6, 6, 6, 6] sts at beg of next 2 [2, 6, 6, 4, 4, 2] rows, then 6 [6, 0, 0, 7, 7, 7] sts at beg of next 4 [4, 0, 0, 2, 2, 4] rows.

■ SLEEVES

Using double-pointed needles, CO 32 [34, 36, 38, 40, 42, 44] sts. Distribute sts evenly over 3 or 4 needles. Join to work in the rnd, being careful not to twist sts.

Set-Up Rnd 1: Knit.

Set-Up Rnd 2: Working Row 2 of Woman's Sleeve Chart, beg at RH side of chart for your size and work 3 [4, 1, 2, 3, 4, 1] st(s) before rep, work 4-st rep 6 [7, 8, 8, 8, 9, 10] times, then work 5 [2, 3, 4, 5, 2, 3] sts after rep at LH side of chart.

Work 3 more rnds even.

Inc Rnd: Work 1 st, M1R, work in established patt to last st, M1L, work 1 st—2 sts inc.

Working new sts into patt, rep Inc Rnd every 6 [6, 6, 6, 4, 4, 4] rnds 3 [6, 9, 13, 2, 8, 13] more times, then every 8 [8, 8, 0, 6, 6, 6] rnds 7 [5, 3, 0, 12, 8, 5] times—54 [58, 62, 66, 70, 76, 82] sts. Change to shorter circular needle when there are too many sts to work on double-pointed needles.

Cont even until piece measures 17 [17, 17 ½, 17 ½, 18, 18, 18 ½]" (43.2 [43.2, 44.5, 44.5, 45.7, 45.7, 47]cm) from beg, ending with Rnd 2 of patt, and ending last rnd 3 [4, 6, 7, 8, 10, 11] sts before end of rnd.

Shape Cap

BO 6 [8, 12, 14, 16, 20, 22] sts, then work to end of rnd—48 [50, 50, 52, 54, 56, 60] sts rem.

Working back and forth, BO 2 sts at beg of next 4 [4, 4, 6, 6, 6, 8] rows—40 [42, 42, 40, 42, 44, 44] sts rem.

Dec 1 st at each end of every RS row 4 [6, 6, 6, 6, 7, 7] times—32 [30, 30, 28, 30, 30, 30] sts rem.

BO 2 sts at beg of next 2 rows, 3 sts at beg of next 2 [4, 4, 4, 4, 4, 4] rows, then 4 sts at beg of next 2 [0, 0, 0, 0, 0, 0] rows—14 [14, 14, 12, 14, 14, 14] sts rem.

BO the rem sts.

Key

☐ k on RS, p on WS

⊡ p on RS, k on WS

☐ repeat

Note: When working in the round, read all chart rows from right to left. When working back and forth, read all RS (odd-numbered) rows from right to left, and all WS (even-numbered) rows from left to right.

Woman's Sleeve Chart

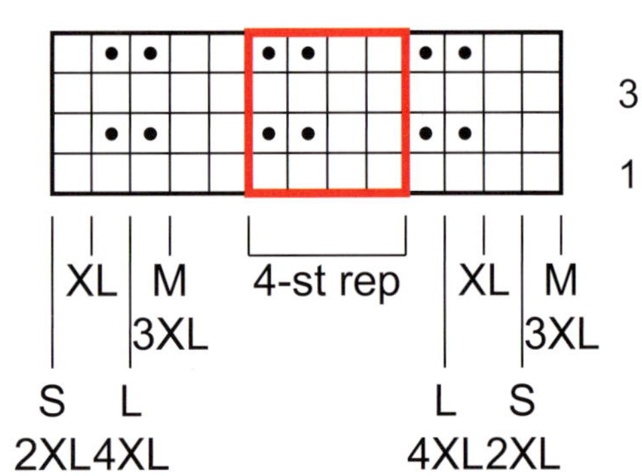

■ FINISHING

Weave in ends. Block pieces to measurements *(Fig. 1)*.

Sew front and back together at shoulders.

Neckband

Note: When picking up stitches along the neck edge, make sure to line up the stitches so the knit and garter stitches line up along both the center front and back neck edges.

Using shorter circular needle and with RS facing, pick up and knit 40 [42, 42, 44, 44, 46, 46] sts along front neck edge and 32 [34, 34, 36, 36, 38, 38] sts along back neck edge—72 [76, 76, 80, 80, 84, 84] sts. Pm and join to work in the rnd.

Beg with Rnd 2 of Garter Rib, making sure knit and purl sts line up with body. For a mock-neck pullover, work in Garter Rib for approx 3" (7.6cm); for a crewneck pullover, work in Garter Rib for 5 rnds. BO in patt. *Note: It doesn't matter which round you end with, though a knit bind-off edge will have a slightly different look than one worked in rib.*

Sew in sleeves.

Woman's Pullover

Fig. 1

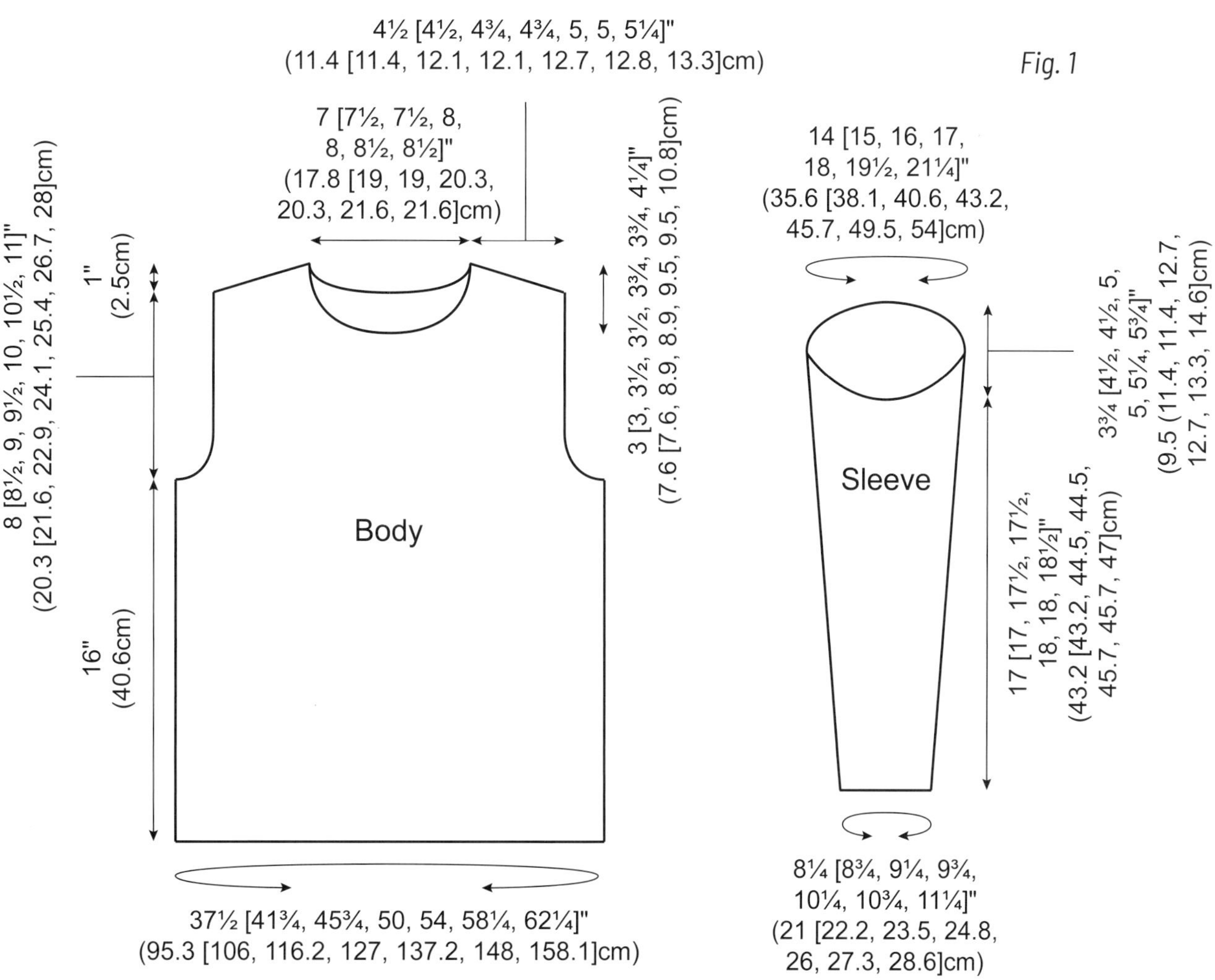

Man's Body Chart

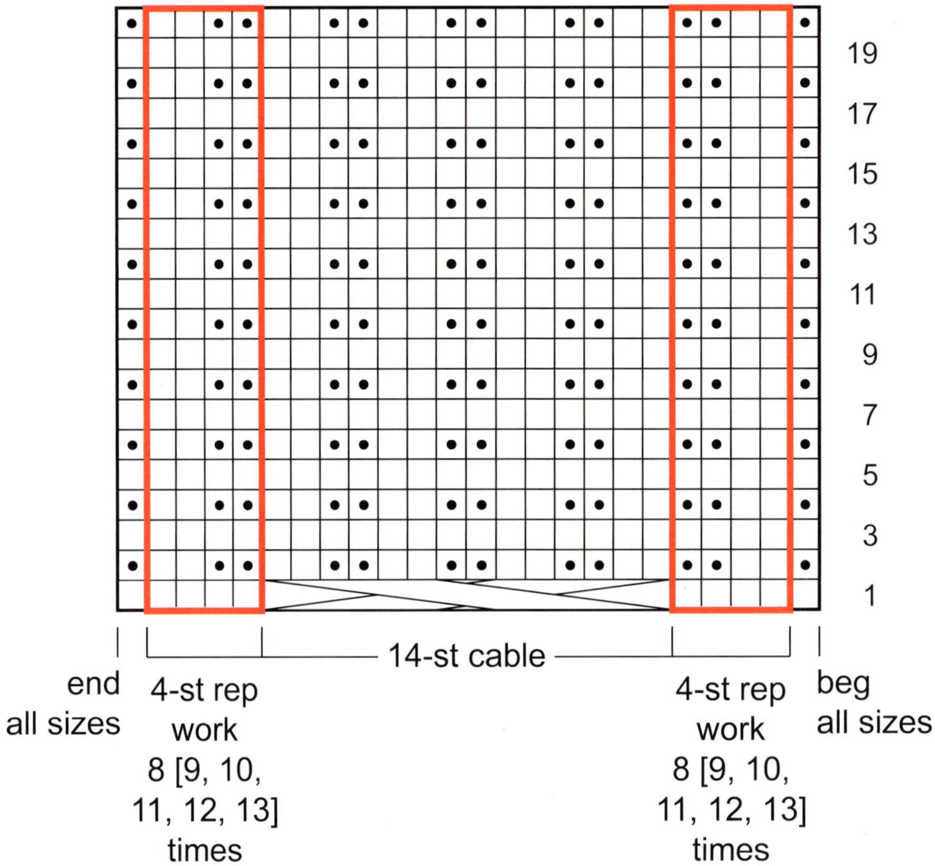

Key

- k on RS, p on WS
- p on RS, k on WS
- 6/2/6 LC
- repeat

Note: When working in the round, read all chart rows from right to left. When working back and forth, read all RS (odd-numbered) rows from right to left, and all WS (even-numbered) rows from left to right.

MAN'S PULLOVER

■ BODY

Using longer circular needle, CO 160 [176, 192, 208, 224, 240] sts. Pm and join to work in the rnd, taking care not to twist sts.

Set-Up Rnd 1: Knit.

Set-Up Rnd 2: P1, (k2, p2) 8 [9, 10, 11, 12, 13] times, pm, (k2, p2) 3 times, k2, pm, (p2, k2) 16 [18, 20, 22, 24, 26] times, p2, pm, (k2, p2) 3 times, k2, pm, (p2, k2) 8 [9, 10, 11, 12, 13] times, p1.

Sm as you come to them, work 8 more rnds in established Garter Rib, ending with Rnd 2 of patt.

Pm 80 [88, 96, 104, 112, 120] sts from the beg of rnd for the side of body.

Next Rnd: Working Row 1 of Man's Body Chart, *work 1 st before rep at RH side of chart, work 4-st rep 8 [9, 10, 11, 12, 13] times, sm, work next 14 sts of chart, sm, work 4-st rep 8 [9, 10, 11, 12, 13] times, work 1 st at LH side of chart, sm; rep from * once more.

Cont in established patt until piece measures 16" (40.6cm) from beg, ending with a Rnd 2 of Garter Rib, and end last rnd 3 [4, 4, 5, 6, 8] sts before end of rnd.

Divide Front and Back

BO 6 [8, 8, 10, 12, 16] sts, work to 3 [4, 4, 5, 6, 8] sts before side marker, BO 6 [8, 8, 10, 12, 16] sts, then work to end of rnd—74 [80, 88, 94, 100, 104] sts rem each for front and back.

Place front sts on holder or scrap yarn.

■ BACK

Working back and forth, beg with a WS row and BO 2 sts at beg of next 2 [2, 4, 4, 4, 4] rows, then dec 1 st at each end of every RS row 1 [2, 2, 3, 4, 4] time(s)—68 [72, 76, 80, 84, 88] sts rem.

Work even until armholes measure 9 [9 ½, 10, 10 ½, 11, 11 ½]" (22.9 [24.1, 25.4, 26.7, 28, 29.2]cm), ending with a WS row.

Pm 23 [24, 25, 26, 27, 28] sts from each end of needle, with 22 [24, 26, 28, 30, 32] sts between markers for neck.

Shape Neck and Shoulders

Row 1 (RS): BO 6 [6, 6, 7, 7, 7] sts, knit to marker, join a second ball of yarn and BO marked 22 [24, 26, 28, 30, 32] sts, then knit to end of row.

Row 2 (WS): BO 6 [6, 6, 7, 7, 7] sts, work in established patt to neck edge; the other side, BO 3 sts, then work to end of row.

Row 3: BO 6 [6, 7, 7, 7, 8] sts, work to neck edge; the other side, BO 3 sts, then work to end of row.

Row 4: BO 6 [6, 7, 7, 7, 8] sts, work to neck edge; the other side BO 2 sts, then work to end of row.

Row 5: BO rem 6 [7, 7, 7, 8, 8] sts; the other side, BO 2 sts, then work to end of row.

Row 6: BO rem 6 [7, 7, 7, 8, 8] sts.

■ FRONT

Return held sts to longer circular needle and join yarn to beg with a WS row.

Shape armholes same as back—68 [72, 76, 80, 84, 88] sts rem.

Cont even until armholes measure 7 ½ [7 ¾, 8 ¼, 8 ¼, 8 ¾, 8 ¾]" (19 [19.7, 21, 21, 22.2, 22.2]cm), ending with a WS row.

Pm 28 [30, 31, 32, 33, 35] sts from each end of row, with 12 [12, 14, 16, 18, 18] sts between markers for neck.

Shape Neck and Shoulders

Next Row (RS): Knit to marker, join a second ball of yarn and BO marked 12 [12, 14, 16, 18, 18] sts, then knit to end of row—28 [30, 31, 32, 33, 35] sts rem for each side.

Working both sides at the same time with separate balls of yarn, BO at each neck edge 4 sts once, 2 sts twice, then 1 st 2 [3, 3, 3, 3, 4] times. *At the same time*, when armholes measure 9 [9 ½, 10, 10 ½, 11, 11 ½]" (22.9 [24.1, 25.4, 26.7, 28, 29.2]cm), end with a WS row.

BO 6 [6, 6, 7, 7, 7] sts at beg of next 6 [4, 2, 6, 4, 2] rows, then 0 [7, 7, 0, 8, 8] sts at beg of next 0 [2, 4, 0, 2, 4] rows.

■ SLEEVES

Using double-pointed needles, CO 34 [36, 40, 42, 44, 46] sts. Distribute sts evenly over 3 or 4 needles. Join to work in the rnd.

Rnd 1: Knit.

Rnd 2: Working Row 2 of Man's Sleeve Chart, beg at RH side of chart for your size and work 4 [1, 3, 4, 1, 2] st(s) before rep, work 4-st rep 7 [8, 8, 9, 10, 10] times, then work 2 [3, 5, 2, 3, 4] sts after rep at LH side of chart.

Work 3 more rnds even.

Inc Rnd: Work 1 st, M1R, work in established patt to last st, M1L, work 1 st—2 sts inc.

Working new sts into patt, rep Inc Rnd every 6 rnds 0 [7, 9, 10, 15, 15] more times, then every 8 rnds 10 [5, 4, 4, 0, 0] times—56 [62, 68, 72, 76, 78] sts. Change to shorter circular needle when there are too many sts to work on double-pointed needles.

Cont even until piece measures 18 [18 ½, 19 ½, 20, 20 ½, 20 ½]" (45.7 [47, 49.5, 50.8, 52, 52]cm) from beg, ending with a Rnd 2 of patt, and end last rnd 3 [4, 4, 5, 6, 8] sts before end of rnd.

Shape Cap

BO 6 (8, 8, 10, 12, 16) sts, then work to end of rnd—50 [54, 60, 62, 64, 62] sts rem.

Working back and forth, BO 2 sts at beg of next 4 [4, 6, 6, 6, 6] rows—42 [46, 48, 50, 52, 50] sts rem.

Dec 1 st at each end of every RS row 10 [10, 9, 9, 9, 9] times—22 [26, 30, 32, 34, 32] sts rem.

BO 2 sts at beg of next 6 [4, 2, 2, 2, 2] rows, 3 sts at beg of next 0 [2, 4, 2, 2, 4] rows, then 4 sts at beg of next 0 [0, 0, 2, 2, 0] rows—10 [12, 14, 14, 16, 16] sts rem.

BO the rem sts.

■ FINISHING

Weave in ends. Block pieces to measurements *(Fig. 2)*.

Sew front and back together at shoulders.

Neckband

Note: When picking up stitches along the neck edge, make sure to line up the stitches so knit and garter stitches line up along both the center front and back neck edges.

Key

- ☐ k on RS, p on WS
- ⊡ p on RS, k on WS
- ☐ (red) repeat

Note: When working in the round, read all chart rows from right to left. When working back and forth, read all RS (odd-numbered) rows from right to left, and all WS (even-numbered) rows from left to right.

Man's Sleeve Chart

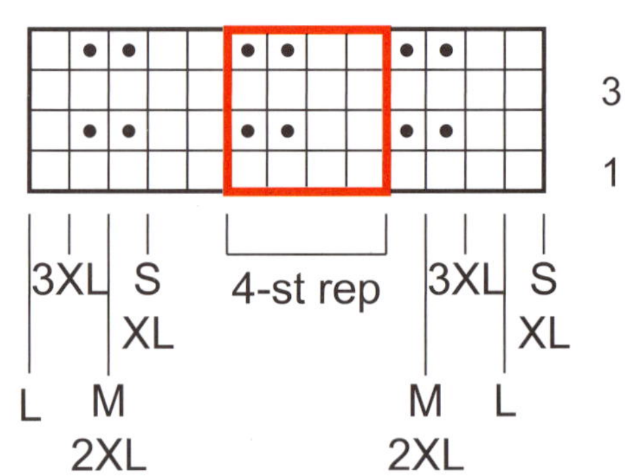

Using shorter circular needle and with RS facing, pick up and knit 36 [40, 42, 46, 48, 52] sts along front neck edge and 36 [36, 38, 38, 40, 40] sts along back neck edge—72 [76, 80, 84, 88, 92] sts. Pm and join to work in the rnd.

Beg with Rnd 2 of Garter Rib, making sure knit and purl sts line up with body. For a mock-neck pullover, work in Garter Rib for approx 3" (7.6cm); for a crewneck pullover, work in Garter Rib for 5 rnds. BO in patt. *Note: It doesn't matter which round you end with, though a knit bind-off edge will have slightly different look than one worked in rib.*

Sew in sleeves.

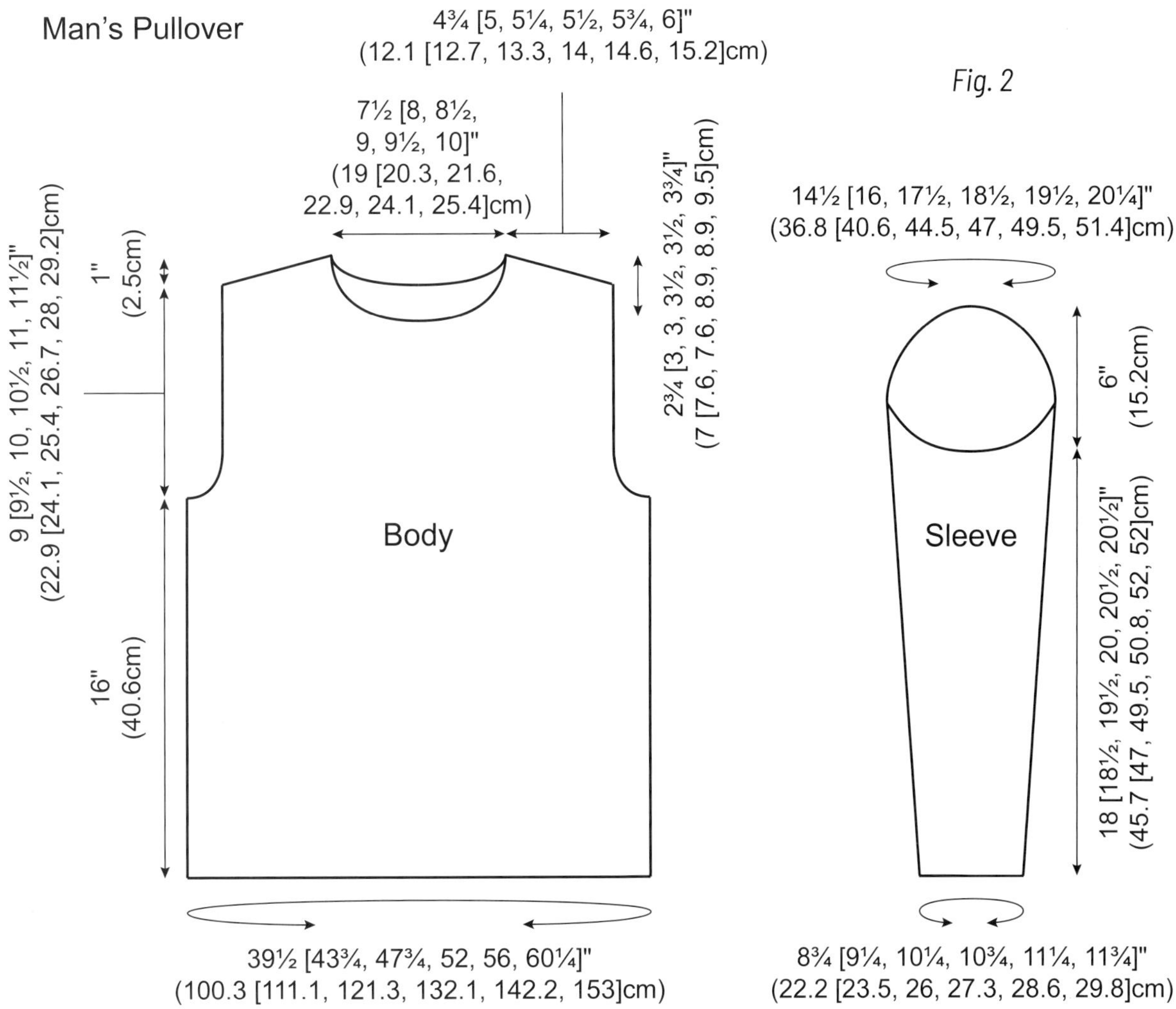

Fig. 2

THE WANDERER *Pullover*

Loose fitting and not too difficult to knit, this sweater is a perfect layering piece that's sized for both men and women. Stay warm and comfy while wandering, whether it's to get away from crazy everyday life, find yourself, rediscover nature, or perhaps all three. Though the skill level is labelled as "advanced," this is a perfect pattern for an intermediate-level knitter to try if they want to level up their skill set.

SKILL LEVEL: ADVANCED

FINISHED MEASUREMENTS:

Woman's Pullover

Bust: 34 [38 ½, 42 ¼, 46, 50, 54 ½, 58 ¼, 62]" (86.4 [97.8, 107.3, 116.8, 127, 138.4, 148, 157.5] cm)

Length: 24 [24 ½, 25, 25 ½, 26, 26 ½, 27, 27 ½]" (61 [62.2, 63.5, 64.8, 66, 67.3, 68.6, 69.9] cm)

Man's Pullover

Chest: 40 ½ [44 ¼, 48, 51 ¾, 56 ½, 60 ¼]" (102.9 [112.4, 122, 131.4, 143.5, 153] cm)

Length: 25 ¼ [26, 26 ¾, 27 ½, 28 ¼, 29]" (64.1 [66, 67.9, 69.9, 71.8, 73.7] cm)

SIZES

Woman's: XS [S, M, L, XL, 2XL, 3XL, 4XL]

Man's: S [M, L, XL, 2XL, 3XL]

YARN

Woman's Pullover

790 [879, 960, 1046, 1148, 1266, 1363, 1444] yds (722 [804, 878, 956, 1050, 1158, 1246, 1320] m) #4 medium weight yarn in Main Color (MC)

83 [92, 102, 111, 122, 134, 146, 152] yds (76 [84, 93, 101, 112, 123, 134, 139] m) #4 medium weight yarn in Contrast Color 1 (CC1)

95 [106, 116, 127, 139, 152, 164, 173] yds (87 [97, 106, 116, 127, 139, 150, 158] m) #4 medium weight yarn in Contrast Color 2 (CC2)

58 [62, 69, 76, 83, 92, 99, 104] yds (53 [57, 63, 69, 76, 84, 91, 95] m) #4 medium weight yarn in Contrast Color 3 (CC3)

37 [42, 46, 51, 55, 60, 65, 69] yds (34 [38, 42, 47, 50, 55, 59, 63] m) #4 medium weight yarn in Contrast Color 4 (CC4)

Man's Pullover

1126 [1241, 1355, 1482, 1607, 1745] yds (1030 [1135, 1239, 1355, 1469, 1596] m) #4 medium weight yarn in Main Color (MC)

108 [119, 130, 143, 155, 168] yds (99 [109, 119, 131, 142, 154] m) #4 medium weight yarn in Contrast Color 1 (CC1)

123 [136, 148, 162, 176, 191] yds (112 [124, 135, 148, 161, 175] m) #4 medium weight yarn in Contrast Color 2 (CC2)

74 [81, 89, 97, 106, 115] yds (68 [74, 81, 89, 97, 105] m) #4 medium weight yarn in Contrast Color 3 (CC3)

cont. on page 140

Shown in size Woman's Medium, with 4" to 6" (10.2 to 15.2cm) *of positive ease.*

49 [54, 59, 65, 70, 76] yds (45 [49, 54, 59, 64, 69]m) #4 medium weight yarn in Contrast Color 4 (CC4)

MATERIALS

US Size 8 (5mm) circular needles, or size required for gauge, in lengths of 16" (40.6cm) and 32" (81.3cm)

US Size 8 (5mm) double-pointed needles, or size required for gauge

Stitch markers

Stitch holders or scrap yarn

Scissor

Tapestry needle

YARN INFORMATION

Sample uses Soft Donegal from Studio Donegal (100% Merino wool; 3.5oz [100g]; 210yds [190m]) in colors #5509 Oatmeal (MC—4 [5, 5, 5, 6, 7, 7, 7] skeins for Woman's Pullover, and 6 [6, 7, 8, 8, 9] skeins for Man's Pullover), #5538 Burgundy (CC1—1 skein), #5525 Sedge (CC2—1 skein), #5528 Irish Emerald (CC3—1 skein), and #5534 Ripe Wheat (CC4—1 skein)

GAUGES

17 sts and 20 rnds = 4" (10.2cm) in stranded colorwork, blocked

15 sts and 25 rnds/rows = 4" (10.2cm) in texture patts, blocked

PATTERN NOTES

Because the stranded color pattern and the texture pattern have different stitch gauges, you'll decrease stitches when transitioning from the stranded color pattern to the texture pattern. Make sure to check your gauge over both patterns and adjust your needle sizes accordingly.

A faux side-seam stitch on each side of the body is purled along the length of the body to the armholes to ensure that the charts are centered on the front and back, since they do not create a continuous repeat around the body.

WOMAN'S PULLOVER

■ BODY

Using the longer circular needle and MC, CO 144 [164, 180, 196, 212, 232, 248, 264] sts. Pm and join to work in the rnd, being careful not to twist the sts.

Rnd 1: *K2, p2; rep from * around.

Rep Rnd 1 until the ribbing measures 2" (5.1cm).

Set-Up Rnd: P1, k71 [81, 89, 97, 105, 115, 123, 131], pm, p1, k71 [81, 89, 97, 105, 115, 123, 131].

Next Rnd: *P1, working Row 1 of Chart A, work 6 [11, 3, 7, 11, 4, 8, 0] sts before the rep, work the 12-st rep 5 [5, 7, 7, 7, 9, 9, 10] times, then work the 5 [10, 2, 6, 10, 3, 7, 11] sts after the rep, sm; rep from * once more.

Work Rnds 2–7 of Chart A as established.

Next Rnd: *P1, working Row 1 of Chart B, work 4 [9, 13, 1, 5, 10, 14, 2] st(s) before the rep, work the 16-st rep 4 [4, 4, 6, 6, 6, 6, 8] times, then work the 3 [8, 12, 0, 4, 9, 13, 1] st(s) after the rep, sm; rep from * once more.

Work Rnds 2–10 of Chart B as established.

Next Rnd: *P1, working Row 1 of Chart C, work 0 [1, 1, 1, 1, 2, 2, 2] st(s) before the rep, work the 4-st rep 17 [20, 22, 24, 26, 28, 30, 32] times, then work 3 [0, 0, 0, 0, 1, 1, 1] st(s) after the rep, sm; rep from * once more.

Work Rnds 2–8 of Chart C as established.

Next Rnd: *P1, working Row 1 of Chart D, work 5 [10, 14, 18, 22, 27, 1, 5] st(s) before the rep, work the 30-st rep 2 [2, 2, 2, 2, 2, 4, 4] times, then work the 6 [11, 15, 19, 23, 28, 2, 6] sts after the rep, sm; rep from * once more.

Work Rnds 2–20 of Chart D as established.

Chart A

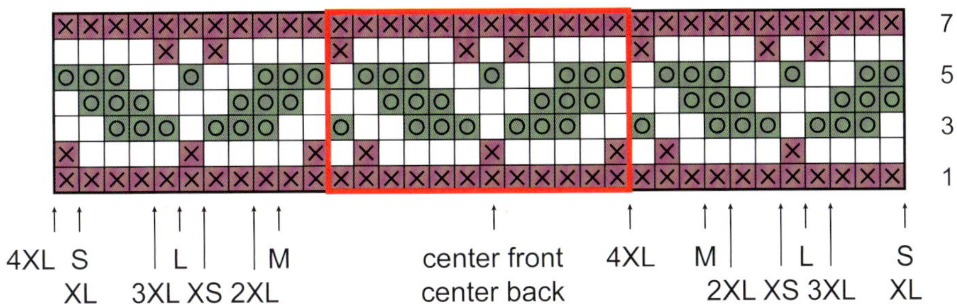

Chart B

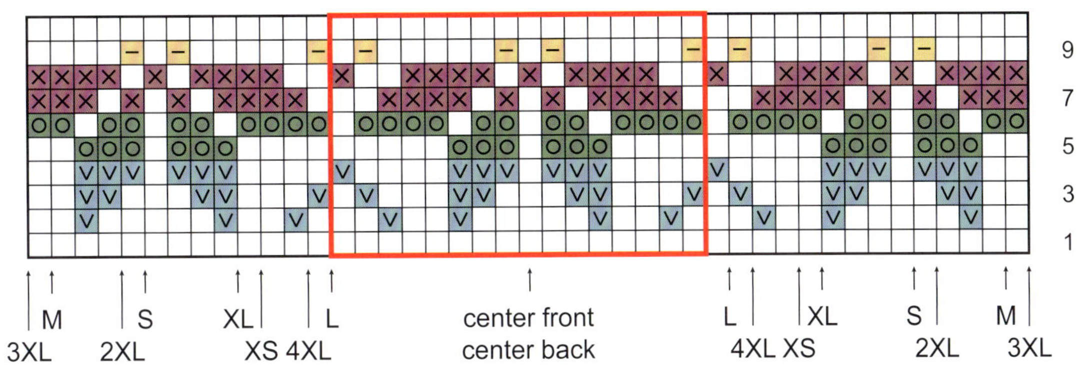

Chart C

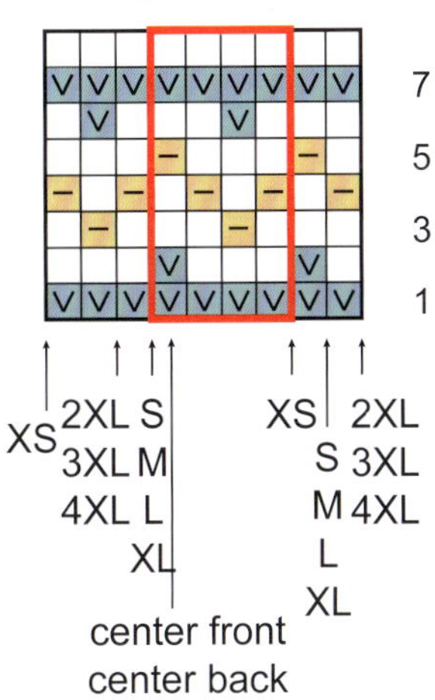

Chart E

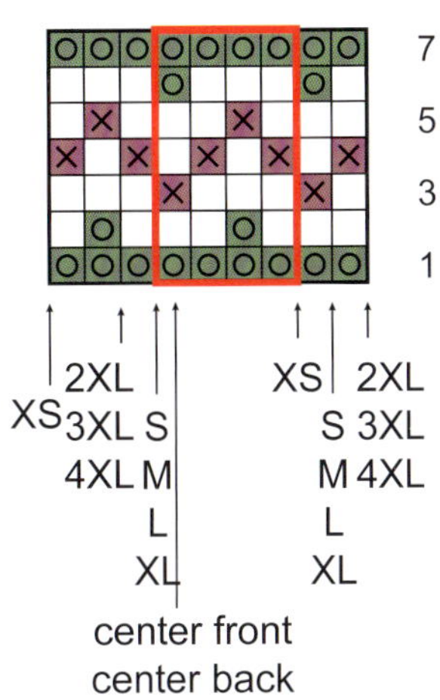

Key

- MC
- CC1
- CC2
- CC3
- CC4
- k on RS, p on WS
- p on RS, k on WS
- repeat

Chart D

Next Rnd: *P1, working Row 1 of Chart E, work 0 [1, 1, 1, 1, 2, 2, 2] st(s) before the rep, work the 4-st rep 17 [20, 22, 24, 26, 28, 30, 32] times, then work the 3 [0, 0, 0, 0, 1, 1, 1] st(s) after the rep, sm; rep from * once more.

Work Rnds 2–7 of Chart E as established. Cut CC.

Next Rnd: With MC only, *p1, knit to marker, sm; rep from * once more.

Dec Rnd: *P1, knit to marker and dec 8 [10, 10, 12, 12, 14, 14, 16] sts evenly spaced, sm; rep from * once more—128 [144, 160, 172, 188, 204, 220, 232] sts rem.

†**Next Rnd:** *P1, working Row 1 of Chart F, work 5 [3, 1, 4, 2, 0, 4, 1] st(s) before the rep, work the 6-st rep 9 [11, 13, 13, 15, 16, 17, 19] times, then work 4 [2, 0, 3, 1, 5, 3, 0] st(s) after the rep, sm; rep from * once more.

Work Rnds 2–21 of Chart F as established.

Next Rnd: *P1, working Row 1 of Chart G, work 10 [0, 4, 7, 11, 1, 5, 8] st(s) before the rep, work the 14-st rep 3 [5, 5, 5, 5, 7, 7, 7] times, then work the 11 [1, 5, 8, 12, 2, 6, 9] st(s) after the rep, sm; rep from * once more.

Work Rnds 2–12 of Chart G as established.

Rep the 33 rows from † to the end. *At the same time*, when piece measures 16" (40.6cm), end last rnd 2 [3, 4, 5, 5, 6, 7, 8] sts before the end of the rnd.

Divide Front and Back

BO 5 [7, 9, 11, 11, 13, 15, 17] sts, work to 2 [3, 4, 5, 5, 6, 7, 8] sts before the side marker, BO 5 [7, 9, 11, 11, 13, 15, 17] sts, then work to the end of rnd—59 [65, 71, 75, 83, 89, 95, 99] sts rem each for front and back.

Place the front sts on holder or scrap yarn.

■ BACK

Working back and forth, cont patt and BO 4 sts at the beg of next 0 [0, 0, 0, 0, 2, 2, 2] rows, 3 sts at the beg of next 0 [0, 2, 2, 2, 2, 2, 2] rows, then 2 sts at the beg of next 2 [4, 2, 2, 4, 2, 4, 4] rows—55 [57, 61, 65, 69, 71, 73, 77] sts rem.

Work 1 WS row even.

Dec 1 st at each end of every RS row 1 [1, 2, 3, 4, 4, 4, 5] time(s)—53 (55, 57, 59, 61, 63, 65, 67) sts rem.

Cont even until armholes measure approx 6 ¾ [7 ¼, 7 ¾, 8 ¼, 8 ¾, 9 ¼, 9 ¾, 10 ¼]" (17.1 [18.4, 19.7, 21, 22.2, 23.5, 24.8, 26]cm), ending with a WS row.

Chart F

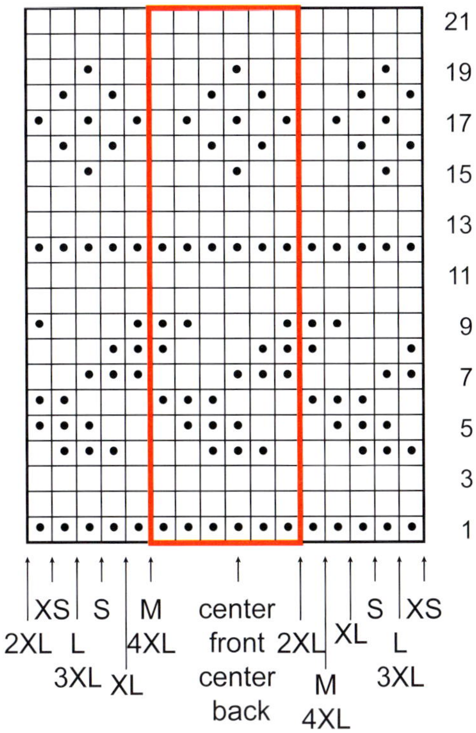

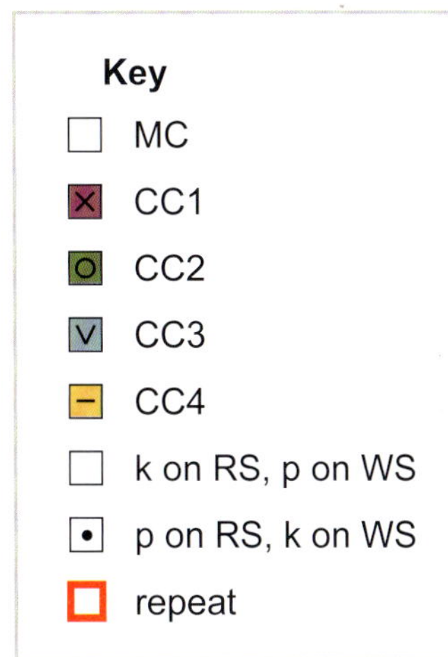

Chart G

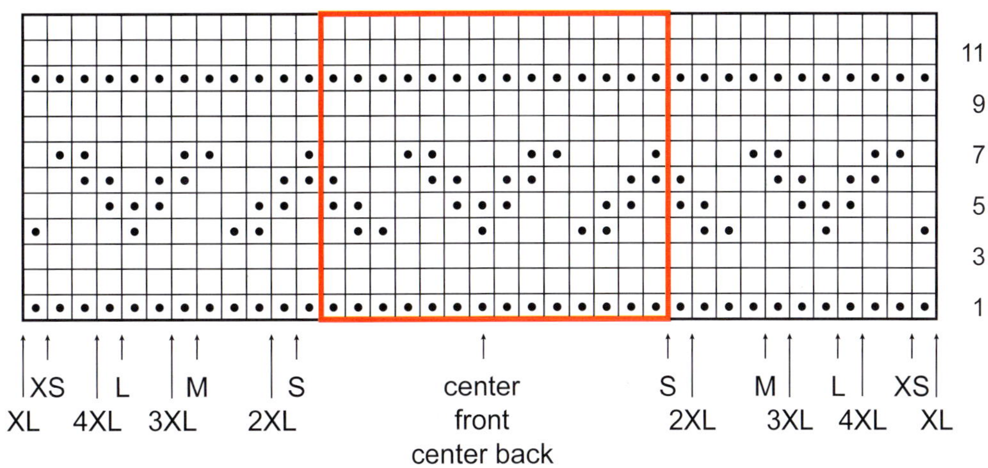

Pm 18 [18, 19, 19, 20, 20, 21, 21] sts from each end of row, with 17 [19, 19, 21, 21, 23, 23, 25] sts between markers for the neck.

Shape Shoulders and Neck

Short Row 1 (RS): Work to the last 3 [3, 3, 3, 3, 3, 4, 4] sts, turn.

Short Row 2 (WS): DS, work to the marker, join a second ball of yarn and BO marked sts, then work to the last 3 [3, 3, 3, 3, 3, 4, 4] sts, turn.

Short Rows 3 and 4: DS, work to the neck edge; the other side, BO 3 sts, then work to 2 [2, 2, 2, 3, 3, 3, 3] sts before DS, turn.

Short Rows 5 and 6: DS, work to the neck edge; the other side, BO 2 sts, work to 2 [2, 3, 3, 3, 3, 3, 3] sts before DS, turn.

Short Row 7: DS, work to the neck edge; the other side, work to the end of row and work both legs of each DS together. Place these 13 [13, 14, 14, 15, 15, 16, 16] sts on a holder.

Next Row: Work to the end of row and work both legs of each DS together. Place these 13 [13, 14, 14, 15, 15, 16, 16] sts on a holder.

■ FRONT

Return the held 59 [65, 71, 75, 83, 89, 95, 99] front sts to the circular needle, and working back and forth, shape the armholes same as the back—53 [55, 57, 59, 61, 63, 65, 67] sts rem.

Cont even until the armholes measure 5 [5 ½, 5 ¾, 6 ¼, 6 ¼, 6 ¾, 7, 7 ½]" (12.7 [14, 14.6, 15.9, 15.9, 17.1, 17.8, 19] cm), ending with a WS row.

Pm 21 [22, 23, 23, 24, 25, 26, 26] sts from each end of row, with 11 [11, 11, 13, 13, 13, 13, 15] sts between markers for the neck.

Shape Shoulders and Neck

Next Row (RS): Work to the neck marker, join a second ball of yarn and BO marked sts, then work to the end of row—21 [22, 23, 23, 24, 25, 26, 26] sts rem for each side.

Working both sides at the same time, BO each neck edge 3 sts once, 2 sts once, then dec 1 st every RS row 3 [4, 4, 4, 4, 5, 5, 5] times—13 [13, 14, 14, 15, 15, 16, 16] sts rem for each side.

Cont even until the armholes measure approx 6 ¾ [7 ¼, 7 ¾, 8 ¼, 8 ¾, 9 ¼, 9 ¾, 10 ¼]" (17.1 [18.4, 19.7, 21, 22.2, 23.5, 24.8, 26]cm), ending with a WS row.

Short Row 1 (RS): Work to the neck edge; the other side, work to the last 3 [3, 3, 3, 3, 3, 4, 4] sts, turn.

Short Row 2 (WS): DS, work to the neck edge; the other side, work to the last 3 [3, 3, 3, 3, 3, 4, 4] sts, turn.

Short Rows 3 and 4: DS, work to the neck edge; the other side, work to 2 [2, 2, 2, 3, 3, 3, 3] sts before DS, turn.

Short Rows 5 and 6: DS, work to the neck edge; the other side, work to 2 [2, 3, 3, 3, 3, 3, 3] sts before DS, turn.

Short Row 7: DS, work to the neck edge; the other side, work to the end of row and work both legs of each DS together. Place these 13 [13, 14, 14, 15, 15, 16, 16] sts on a holder.

Next Row: Work to the end of row and work both legs of each DS together. Place these 13 [13, 14, 14, 15, 15, 16, 16] sts on a holder.

■ SLEEVES

Using the double-pointed needles and MC, CO 32 [32, 36, 36, 40, 40, 44, 44] sts. Divide the sts evenly over 3 or 4 needles. Join to work in the rnd, being careful not to twist the sts.

Rnd 1: *K2, p2; rep from * around.

Rep Rnd 1 until the ribbing measures 2" (5.1cm).

Inc Rnd: Knit and inc 1 st at the end of rnd—33 [33, 37, 37, 41, 41, 45, 45] sts.

Work Chart H, beg and end as shown for your size, and *at the same time*, inc 1 st at each end of every 6 [4, 4, 4, 4, 2, 2, 2] rnds 4 [3, 3, 9, 12, 6, 10, 16] times, then every 8 [6, 6, 6, 0, 4, 4, 4] rnds 3 [6, 6, 2, 0, 9, 7, 4] times, working new sts into the patt—47 [51, 55, 59, 65, 71, 79, 85] sts. *Note: Change to the shorter circular needle when there are too many stitches to work on the double-pointed needles.*

> ***Note***
> To make reading the charts easier as you add stitches, additional width has been added to Charts H and I.

Key

- MC
- CC1
- CC2
- CC3
- CC4
- k on RS, p on WS
- p on RS, k on WS
- repeat

Chart H

51
49
47
45
43
41
39
37
35
33
31
29
27
25
23
21
19
17
15
13
11
9
7
5
3
1
XS S
M L
XL 2XL
3XL 4XL
center
XS S
M L
XL 2XL
3XL 4XL

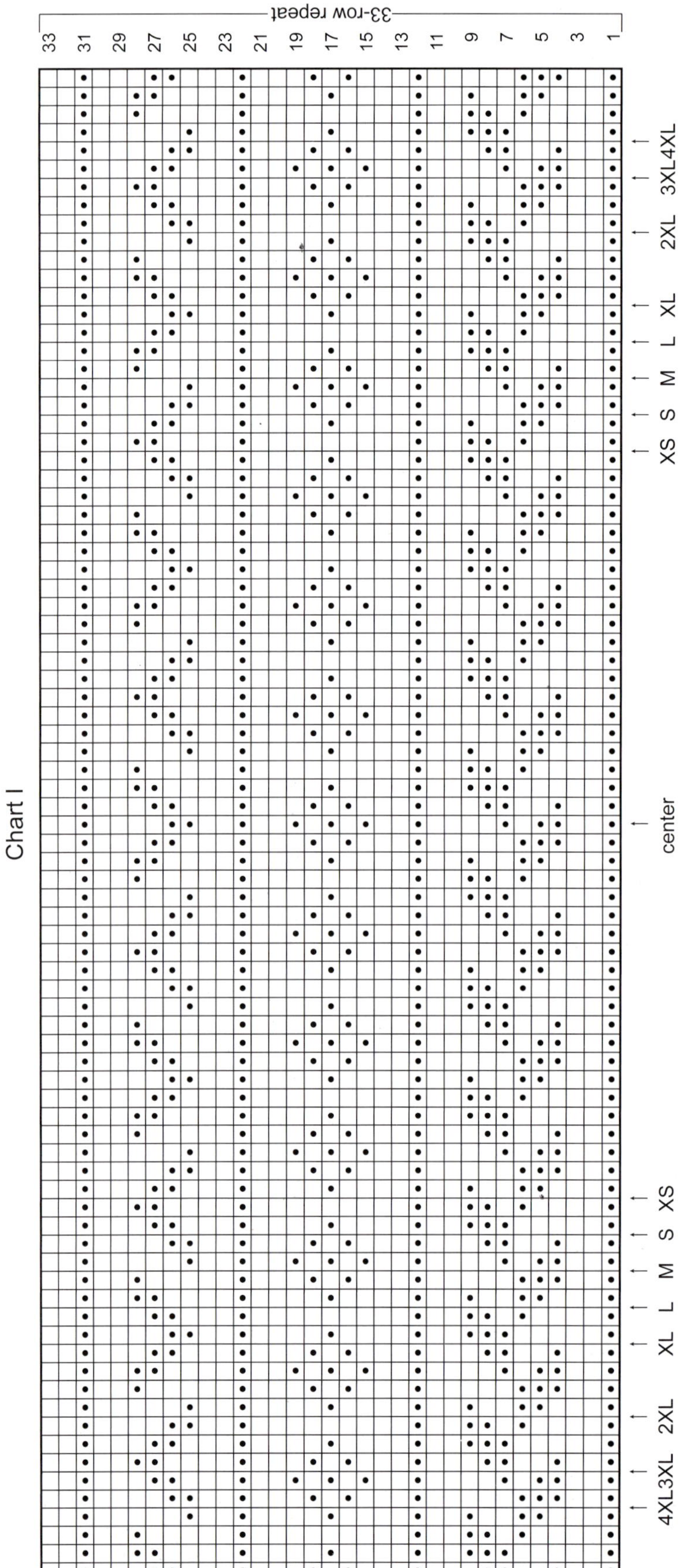

When Chart H is complete, cut CC. Piece should measure approx 12 ½" (31.8cm) from the beg.

Next Rnd: With MC only, knit.

Set-Up (Dec) Rnd: Knit and dec 6 [6, 6, 6, 8, 6, 8, 10] sts evenly spaced—41 [45, 49, 53, 57, 65, 71, 75] sts rem.

Work Chart I, beg and end as shown for your size, and rep Rows 1–33 to the end. *At the same time*, cont to inc 1 st at each end of the second rnd, then every 6 [6, 8, 8, 6, 6, 6, 6] rnds 3 [3, 2, 2, 3, 3, 3, 3] more times, working new sts into the patt—49 [53, 55, 59, 65, 73, 79, 83] sts.

Cont even until the piece measures 16 ½ [17, 17, 17 ½, 17 ½, 18, 18, 18]" (41.9 [43.2, 43.2, 44.5, 44.5, 45.7, 45.7, 45.7]cm), ending the last rnd 2 [3, 4, 5, 5, 6, 7, 8] sts before the end of rnd.

Shape Cap

BO 4 [6, 8, 10, 10, 12, 14, 16] sts, then work to the end of rnd—45 [47, 47, 49, 55, 61, 65, 67] sts rem.

Working back and forth, cont in the patt and BO 3 sts at the beg of next 2 [2, 0, 0, 0, 0, 2, 0] rows, then 2 sts at the beg of next 4 [4, 4, 2, 4, 6, 4, 6] rows—31 [33, 39, 45, 47, 49, 51, 55] sts rem.

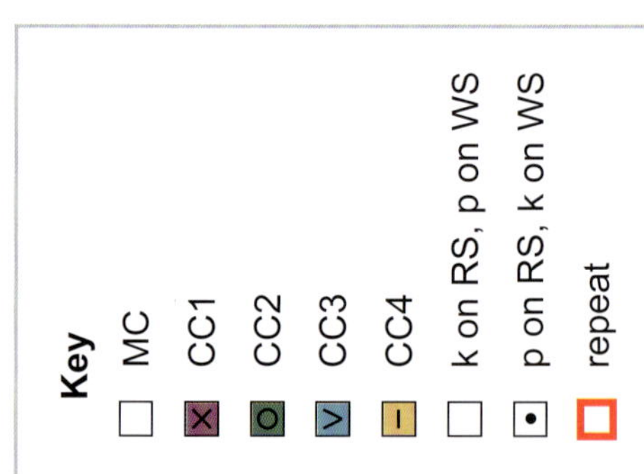

Dec 1 st at each end of every RS row 7 [8, 11, 13, 14, 14, 15, 15] times—17 [17, 17, 19, 19, 21, 21, 25] sts rem.

BO 2 sts at the beg of next 4 [4, 4, 4, 4, 4, 4, 6] rows—9 [9, 9, 11, 11, 13, 13, 13] sts rem.

BO the rem sts.

FINISHING

Weave in the ends. Block the pieces to measurements *(Fig. 1)*.

Join the shoulders using Three-Needle Bind Off (see page 9), making sure to work the BO on the RS.

Neckband

Using the shorter circular needle and MC, and with the RS facing, pick up and knit 41 [43, 45, 47, 51, 53, 53, 55] sts evenly along the front neck edge, and 31 [33, 35, 37, 37, 39, 39, 41] sts evenly along the back neck edge—72 [76, 80, 84, 88, 92, 92, 96] sts. Pm and join to work in the rnd.

Rnd 1: *K2, p2; rep from * around.

Rep Rnd 1 until the neckband measures 1" (2.5cm).

BO in ribbing.

Sew in the sleeves.

Woman's Schematic

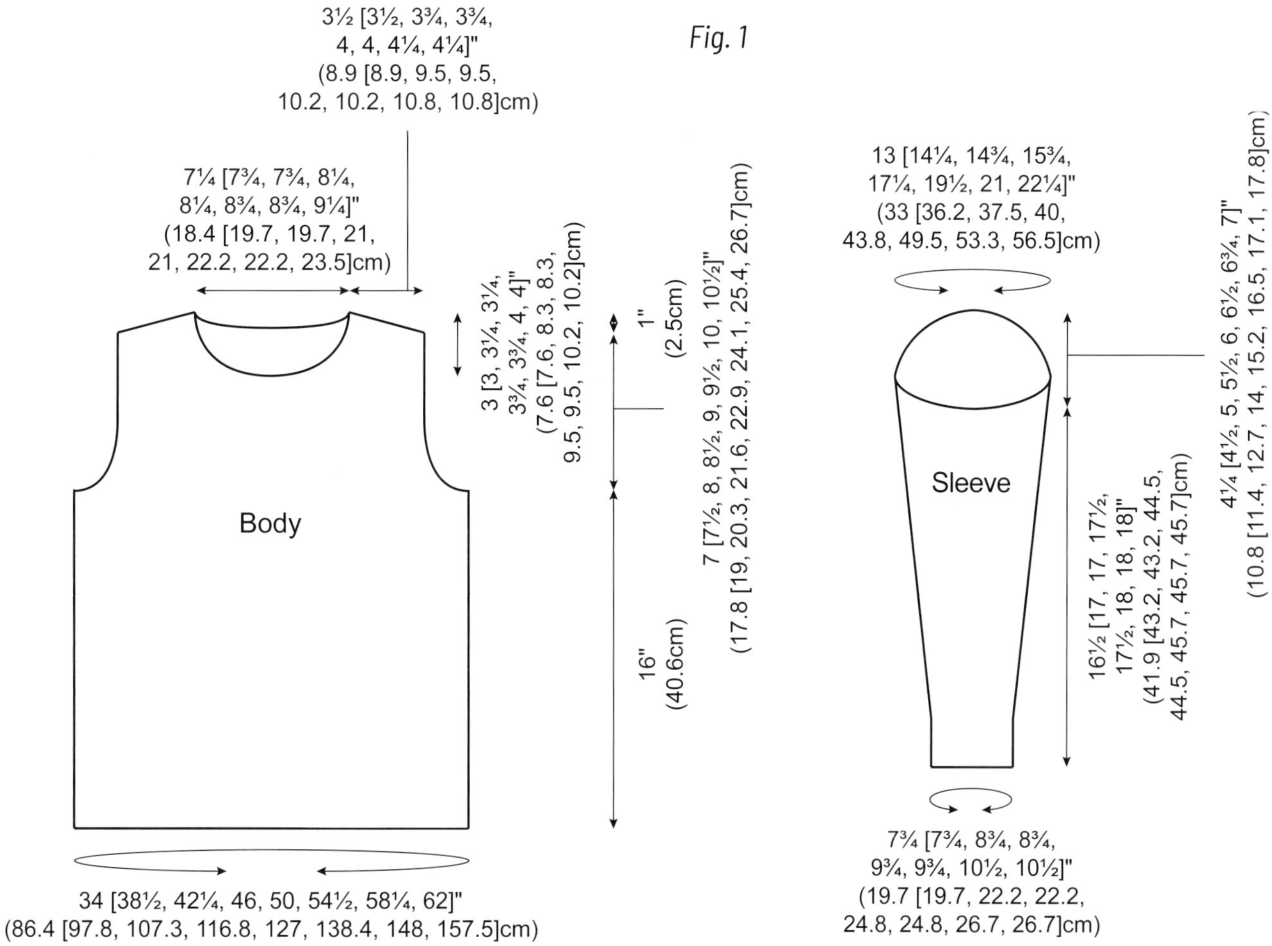

Fig. 1

MAN'S PULLOVER

■ BODY

Using the longer circular needle and MC, CO 172 [188, 204, 220, 240, 256] sts. Pm and join to work in the rnd, being careful not to twist the sts.

Rnd 1: *K2, p2; rep from * around.

Rep Rnd 1 until the ribbing measures 2" (5.1cm).

Set-Up Rnd: P1, k85 [93, 101, 109, 119, 127], pm, p1, k85 [93, 101, 109, 119, 127].

Next Rnd: *P1, working Row 1 of Chart A2, work 1 [5, 9, 1, 6, 10] st(s) before the rep, work the 12-st rep 7 [7, 7, 9, 9, 9] times, then work 0 [4, 8, 0, 5, 9] sts after the rep, sm; rep from * once more.

Work Rnds 2–7 of Chart A2 as established.

Next Rnd: *P1, working Row 1 of Chart B2, work 11 [15, 3, 7, 12, 0] sts before the rep, work the 16-st rep 4 [4, 6, 6, 6, 7] times, then work 10 [14, 2, 6, 11, 15] sts after the rep, sm; rep from * once more.

Work Rnds 2–10 of Chart B2 as established.

Next Rnd: *P1, working Row 1 of Chart C2, work 3 [3, 3, 3, 0, 0] sts before the rep, work the 4-st rep 20 [22, 24, 26, 29, 31] times, then work 2 [2, 2, 2, 3, 3] sts after the rep, sm; rep from * once more.

Work Rnds 2–8 of Chart C2 as established.

Next Rnd: *P1, working Row 1 of Chart D2, work 12 [16, 20, 24, 29, 3] sts before the rep, work the 30-st rep 2 [2, 2, 2, 3, 4] times, then work 13 [17, 21, 25, 0, 4] sts after the rep, sm; rep from * once more.

Work Rnds 2–20 of Chart D2 as established.

Next Rnd: *P1, working Row 1 of Chart E2, work 3 [3, 3, 3, 0, 0] sts before the rep, work the 4-st rep 20 [22, 24, 26, 29, 31] times, then work 2 [2, 2, 2, 3, 3] sts after the rep, sm; rep from * once more.

Work Rnds 2–7 of Chart E2 as established. Cut CC.

Next Rnd: With MC only, *p1, knit to the marker, sm; rep from * once more.

Dec Rnd: *P1, knit to the marker and dec 10 [12, 12, 12, 14, 16] sts evenly spaced, sm; rep from * once more—152 [164, 180, 196, 212, 224] sts rem.

†Next Rnd: *P1, working Row 1 of Chart F2, work 5 [2, 0, 4, 2, 5] sts before the rep, work the 6-st rep 11 [13, 14, 15, 17, 17] times, then work 4 [1, 5, 3, 1, 4] st(s) after the rep, sm; rep from * once more.

Work Rnds 2–21 of Chart F2 as established.

Next Rnd: *P1, working Row 1 of Chart G2, work 2 [5, 9, 13, 3, 6] sts before the rep, work the 14-st rep 5 [5, 5, 6, 7, 7] times, then work 3 [6, 10, 0, 4, 7] st(s) after the rep, sm; rep from * once more.

Work Rnds 2–12 of Chart G2 as established.

Rep the 33 rows from † to the end, work even until the piece measures 14 ¾ [15, 15 ¼, 15 ½, 15 ¾, 16]" (37.5 [38.1, 38.7, 39.4, 40, 40.6]cm), ending the last rnd 3 [4, 5, 6, 7, 8] sts before the end of the rnd.

Divide Front and Back

BO 7 [9, 11, 13, 15, 17] sts, work to 3 [4, 5, 6, 7, 8] sts before the side marker, BO 7 [9, 11, 13, 15, 17] sts, then work to end of rnd—69 [73, 79, 85, 91, 95] sts rem each for front and back.

Place the front sts on holder or scrap yarn.

■ BACK

Working back and forth, cont patt and BO 3 sts at the beg of next 0 [0, 2, 2, 2, 2] rows, then 2 sts at the beg of next 2 [4, 2, 2, 4, 4] rows—65 [65, 69, 75, 77, 81] sts rem.

Work 1 WS row even.

Dec 1 st at each end of every RS row 2 [1, 1, 3, 2, 3] time(s)—61 [63, 67, 69, 73, 75] sts rem.

Cont even until the armholes measure approx 9 ¼ [9 ¾, 10 ¼, 10 ¾, 11 ¼, 11 ¾]" (23.5 [24.8, 26, 27.3, 28.6, 29.8]cm), ending with a WS row.

Pm 20 [21, 22, 23, 24, 25] sts from end of row, with 21 [21, 23, 23, 25, 25] sts between markers for the neck.

Chart A2

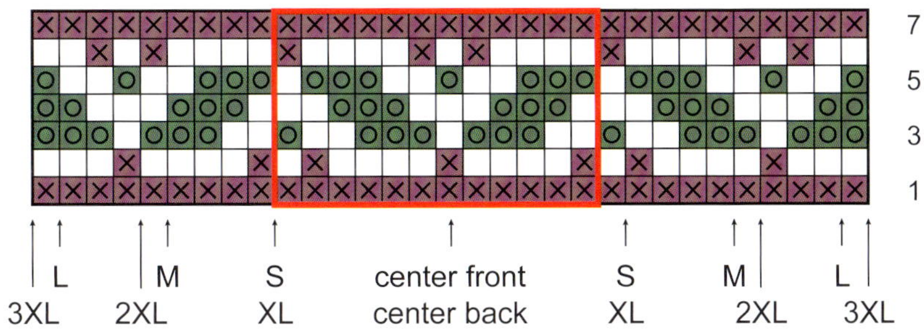

Chart B2

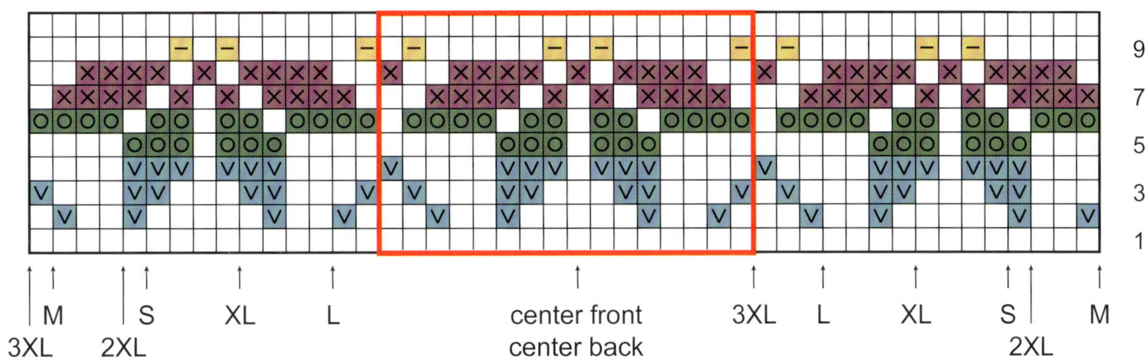

Chart C2

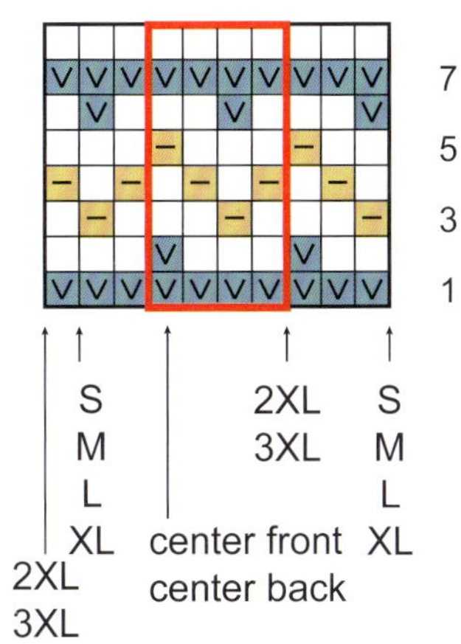

Chart E2

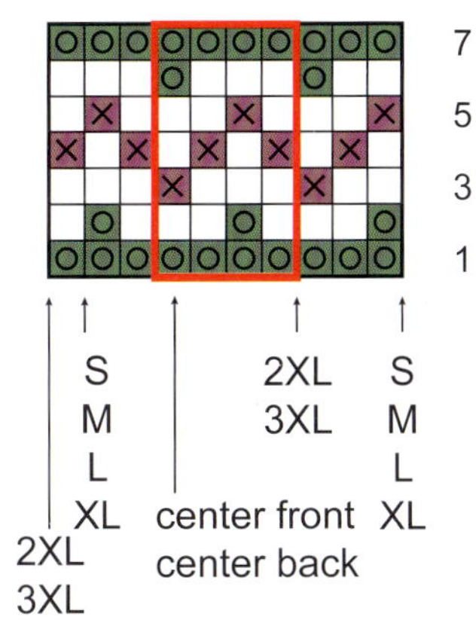

Key

- MC
- CC1
- CC2
- CC3
- CC4
- k on RS, p on WS
- p on RS, k on WS
- repeat

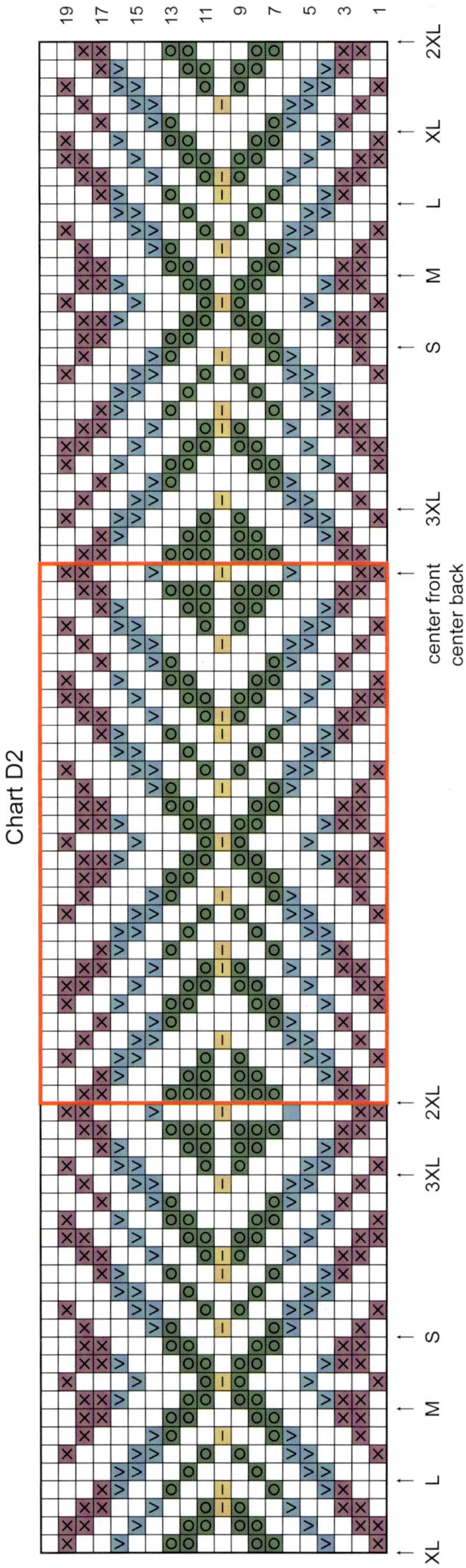

Shape Shoulders and Neck

Short Row 1 (RS): Work to the last 3 [4, 4, 4, 4, 5] sts, turn.

Short Row 2 (WS): DS, work to the marker, join a second ball of yarn and BO marked sts, then work to the last 3 [4, 4, 4, 4, 5] sts, turn.

Short Rows 3 and 4: DS, work to the neck edge; the other side, BO 3 sts, then work to 3 [3, 3, 3, 4, 4] sts before DS, turn.

Short Rows 5 and 6: DS, work to the neck edge; the other side, BO 2 sts, work to 3 [3, 3, 4, 4, 4] sts before DS, turn.

Short Row 7: DS, work to the neck edge; the other side, work to the end of row and work both legs of each DS together. Place these 15 [16, 17, 18, 19, 20] sts on a holder.

Next Row: Work to the end of row and work both legs of each DS together. Place these 15 [16, 17, 18, 19, 20] sts on a holder.

■ FRONT

Return the held 69 [73, 79, 85, 91, 95] front sts to the circular needle, and working back and forth, shape the armholes same as the back—61 [63, 67, 69, 73, 75] sts rem.

Cont even until armholes measure 7 ½ [8, 8, 8 ½, 8 ½, 9]" (19 [20.3, 20.3, 21.6, 21.6, 22.9]cm), ending with a WS row.

Pm 25 [26, 28, 29, 30, 31] sts from each end of row, with 11 [11, 11, 11, 13, 13] sts between markers for neck.

Shape Shoulders and Neck

Next Row (RS): Work to the marker, join a second ball of yarn and BO marked sts, then work to the end of row—25 [26, 28, 29, 30, 31] sts rem for each side.

Working both sides at the same time, BO at each neck edge 3 sts twice, 2 sts once, then dec 1 st every RS row 2 [2, 3, 3, 3, 3] times—15 [16, 17, 18, 19, 20] sts rem for each side.

Chart F2

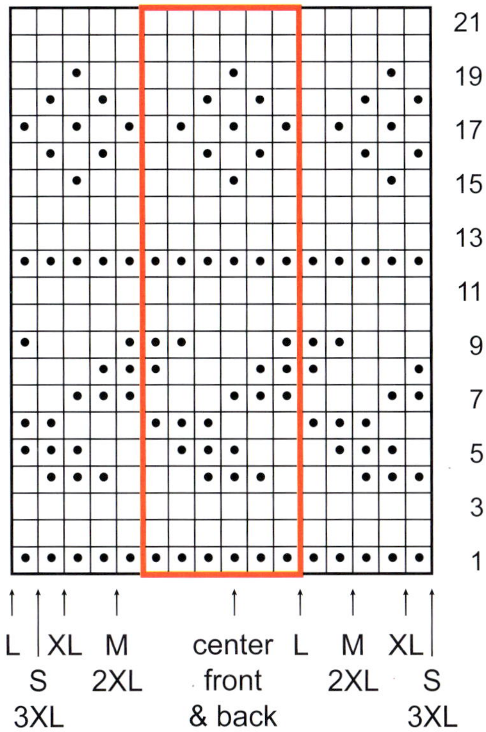

Key

- MC
- CC1
- CC2
- CC3
- CC4
- k on RS, p on WS
- p on RS, k on WS
- repeat

Chart G2

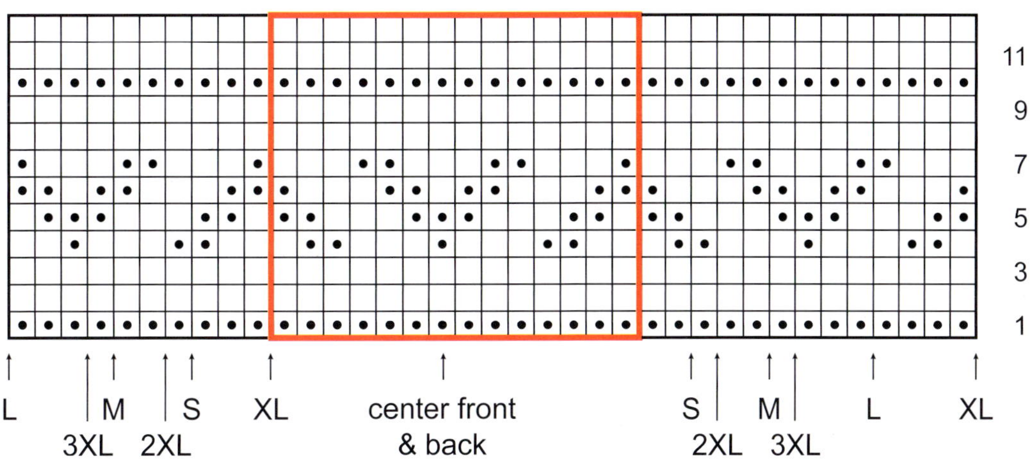

Chart H2

51
49
47
45
43
41
39
37
35
33
31
29
27
25
23
21
19
17
15
13
11
9
7
5
3
1
S M L XL 2XL 3XL
center
3XL XL 2XL L M S

Chart I2

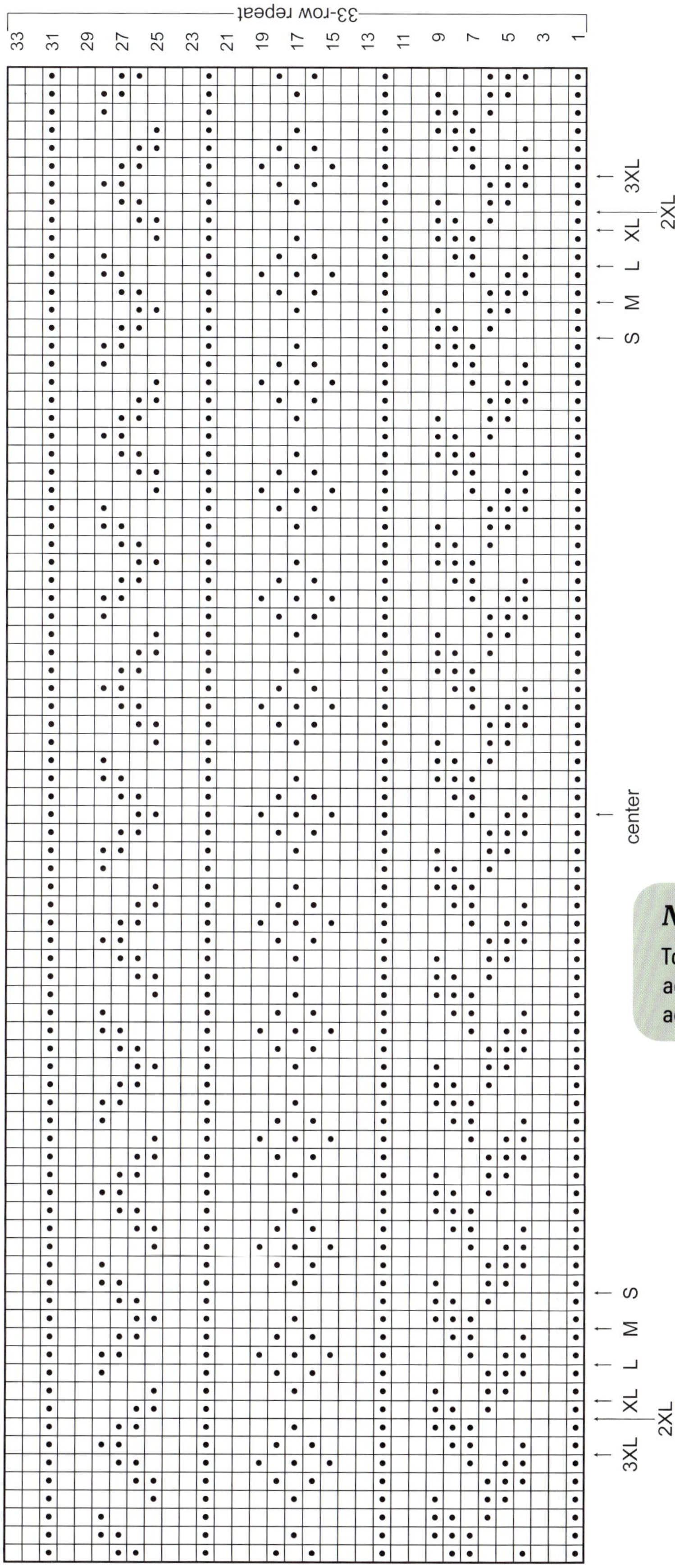

Key

- MC
- CC1
- CC2
- CC3
- CC4
- k on RS, p on WS
- p on RS, k on WS
- repeat

> ***Note***
>
> To make reading the charts easier as you add stitches, additional width has been added to Charts H2 and I2.

Cont even until the armholes measure approx 9 ¼ [9 ¾, 10 ¼, 10 ¾, 11 ¼, 11 ¾]" (23.5 [24.8, 26, 27.3, 28.6, 29.8]cm), ending with a WS row.

Short Row 1 (RS): Work to the neck edge; the other side, work to the last 3 [4, 4, 4, 4, 5] sts, turn.

Short Row 2 (WS): DS, work to the neck edge; the other side, work to the last 3 [4, 4, 4, 4, 5] sts, turn.

Short Rows 3 and 4: DS, work to the neck edge; the other side, work to 3 [3, 3, 3, 4, 4] sts before DS, turn.

Short Rows 5 and 6: DS, work to the neck edge; the other side, work to 3 [3, 3, 4, 4, 4] sts before DS, turn.

Short Row 7: DS, work to the neck edge; the other side, work to the end of row and work both legs of each DS together. Place these 15 [16, 17, 18, 19, 20] sts on a holder.

Next Row: Work to the end of row and work both legs of each DS together. Place these 15 [16, 17, 18, 19, 20] sts on a holder.

■ SLEEVES

Using the double-pointed needles and MC, CO 40 [44, 44, 48, 48, 52] sts. Divide the sts evenly over 3 or 4 needles. Join to work in the rnd, being careful not to twist the sts.

Rnd 1: *K2, p2; rep from * around.

Rep Rnd 1 until the ribbing measures 2" (5.1cm).

Inc Rnd: Knit and inc 1 st at the end of rnd—41 [45, 45, 49, 49, 53] sts.

Work Chart H2, beg and end as shown for your size, and *at the same time*, inc 1 st at each end of every 4 [4, 4, 4, 2, 2] rnds 6 [6, 12, 12, 2, 4] times, then every 6 [6, 0, 0, 4, 4] rnds 4 [4, 0, 0, 11, 10] times, working new sts into patt—61 [65, 69, 73, 75, 81] sts.

When Chart H2 is complete, cut CC. Piece should measure approx 12 ½" (31.8cm) from the beg.

Next Rnd: With MC only, knit.

Set-Up (Dec) Rnd: Knit and dec 8 [8, 8, 8, 8, 10] sts evenly spaced—53 [57, 61, 65, 67, 71] sts rem.

Work Chart I2, beg and end as shown for your size, and rep Rows 1–33 to the end. *At the same time*, cont inc 1 st at each end of the fourth rnd, then every 4 [6, 6, 6, 6, 6] rnds 1 [4, 4, 1, 3, 3] more time(s), then every 6 [0, 0, 8, 8, 8] rnds 3 [0, 0, 3, 2, 2] times, working new sts into patt—63 [67, 71, 75, 79, 83] sts. *Note: Change to the shorter circular needle when there are too many stitches to work on the double-pointed needles.*

Cont even until the piece measures 18 [18 ½, 19, 19 ½, 20, 20 ½]" (45.7 [47, 48.3, 49.5, 50.8, 52]cm), ending the last rnd 3 [4, 5, 6, 7, 8] sts before the end of rnd.

Shape Cap

BO 6 [8, 10, 12, 14, 16] sts, then work to end of rnd—57 [59, 61, 63, 65, 67] sts rem.

Working back and forth, cont in patt and BO 3 sts at the beg of next 2 rows, then 2 sts at the beg of next 2 [2, 2, 2, 4, 4] rows—47 [49, 51, 53, 51, 53] sts rem.

Dec 1 st at each end of every RS row 2 [2, 4, 4, 3, 2] times, every 4 rows 2 [2, 2, 2, 2, 3] times, then every RS row 8 [9, 7, 8, 8, 8] times—23 [23, 25, 25, 25, 27] sts rem.

BO 2 sts at the beg of next 2 rows, then 3 sts at the beg of next 2 rows—13 [13, 15, 15, 15, 17] sts rem.

BO the rem sts.

■ FINISHING

Weave in the ends. Block the pieces to measurements *(Fig. 2)*.

Join the shoulders using Three-Needle Bind Off (see page 9), making sure to work the BO on the RS.

Neckband

Using the shorter circular needle and MC, with the RS facing, pick up and knit 47 [47, 53, 53, 59, 59] sts evenly along the front neck edge, and 37 [37, 39, 39, 41, 41] sts evenly along the back neck edge—84 [84, 92, 92, 100, 100] sts. Pm and join to work in the rnd.

Rnd 1: *K2, p2; rep from * around.

Rep Rnd 1 until the neckband measures 1" (2.5cm).

BO in ribbing.

Sew in the sleeves.

Man's Schematic

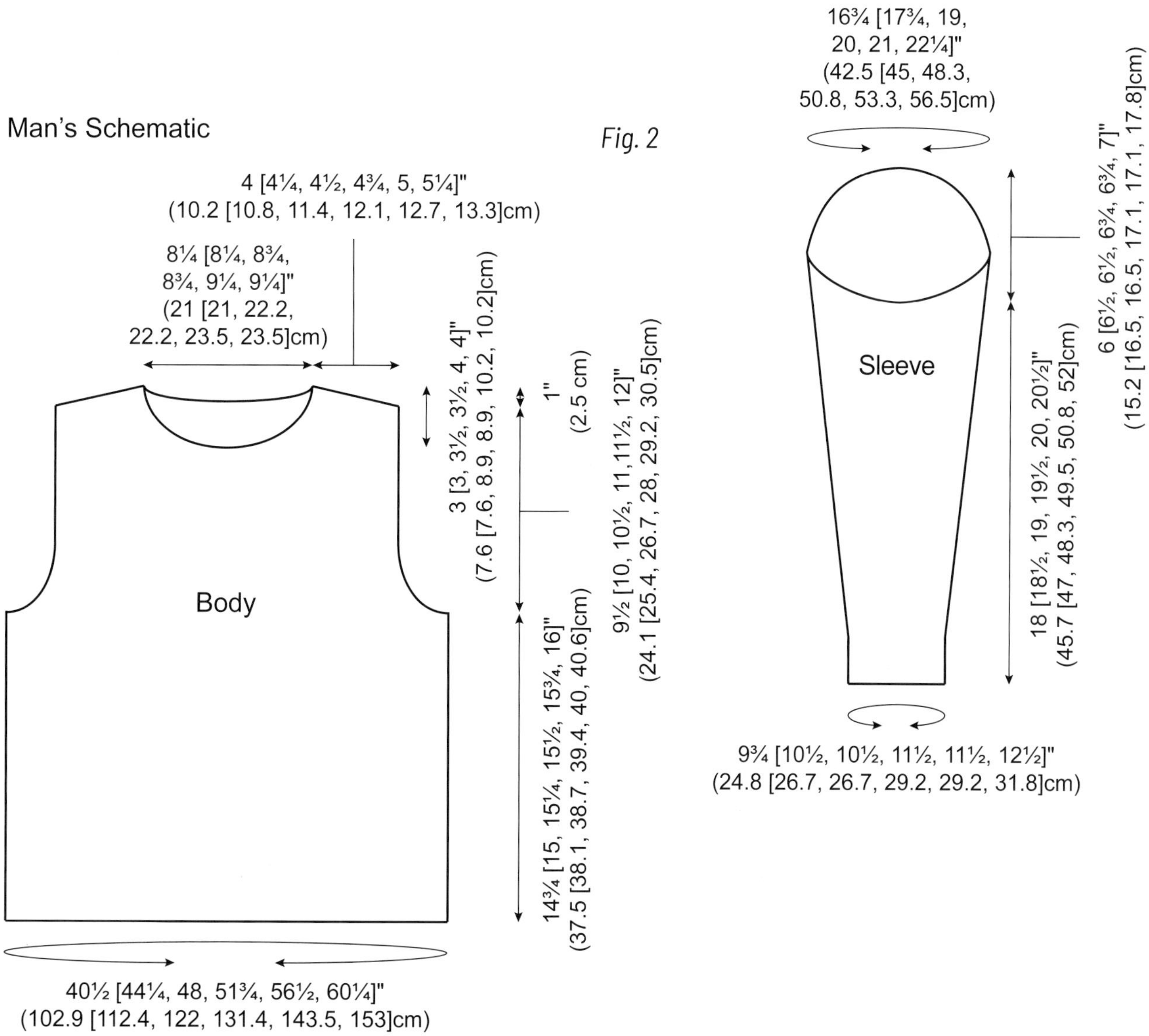

Fig. 2

COTTONWOOD *Cowl*

A quick-to-knit accessory piece, this cowl is ideal for gift giving or even to keep as a great addition to any wardrobe. Make one or several; the colors are so easy to customize that this charming cowl will suit any mood or outfit.

SKILL LEVEL: ADVANCED

FINISHED MEASUREMENTS: 19 ½" (49.5cm) circumference x 8 ¼" (21cm) high

YARN

175 yds (160m) #3 light weight yarn in Main Color (MC)

30 yds (27m) #3 light weight yarn in Contrast Color (CC)

MATERIALS

US Size 4 (3.5mm) circular needle, or size required for gauge, in length of 16" (40.6cm)

US Size 5 (3.75mm) circular needle, or size required for gauge, in length of 16" (40.6cm)

Stitch marker

Scissors

Tapestry needle

YARN INFORMATION

Sample uses Batiste (MC) and Handpainted Batiste (CC) from Knit One Crochet Too (50% Merino wool/30% linen/20% silk; 1.75oz [50g]; 208yds [190m]), in colors #156 Linen (MC—1 skein) and #6520 Sprout (CC—1 skein)

GAUGES

24 ½ sts and 30 rnds = 4" (10.2cm) in stockinette stitch using smaller needles, blocked

24 ½ sts and 28 rnds = 4" (10.2cm) in chart patt using larger needles, blocked

PATTERN NOTES

The larger needle size is used to work the charts because most knitters tend to knit stranded colorwork more tightly than plain stockinette. Make sure to check your gauges over both and adjust your needle sizes accordingly.

When working the two rounds between charts, it's not necessary to cut the contrast color; just float it loosely up along the wrong side.

SPECIAL STITCH

St st (stockinette stitch) = Knit RS rows and purl WS rows.

COWL

Using the smaller circular needle and MC, CO 120 sts. Pm and join to work in the rnd, being careful not to twist the sts.

Rnds 1 and 2: *K1, p1; rep from * around.

Rnd 3: Purl.

Rnd 4: Knit.

Rep Rnds 1–4 once more.

Cont in St st until piece measures approx 3 ¼" (8.3cm) from the beg.

Change to larger circular needle.

Join CC.

Next Rnd: Working Row 1 of Chart A, work the 4-st rep 13 times, work the next 5 sts of the chart, work the next 4-st rep 13 times, then work last 11 sts after the rep.

Rows 2–5 of the chart as established.

Using MC only, knit 2 rnds.

Next Rnd: Working Row 1 of Chart B, work the 20 sts before the rep, then work the 20-st rep 5 times.

Work Rows 2–15 of the chart as established.

Using MC only, knit 2 rnds.

Next Rnd: Working Row 1 of Chart A, work the 4-st rep 13 times, work the next 5 sts of the chart, work the next 4-st rep 13 times, then work last 11 sts after the rep.

Work Rows 2–5 of the chart as established.

Cut CC.

Change to smaller circular needle.

Using MC only, knit 2 rnds.

Next Rnd: Purl.

Next 2 Rnds: *K1, p1; rep from * around.

Next Rnd: Knit.

Next Rnd: Purl.

Next Rnd: *K1, p1; rep from * around.

BO in ribbing.

■ FINISHING

Weave in ends. Block to measurements.

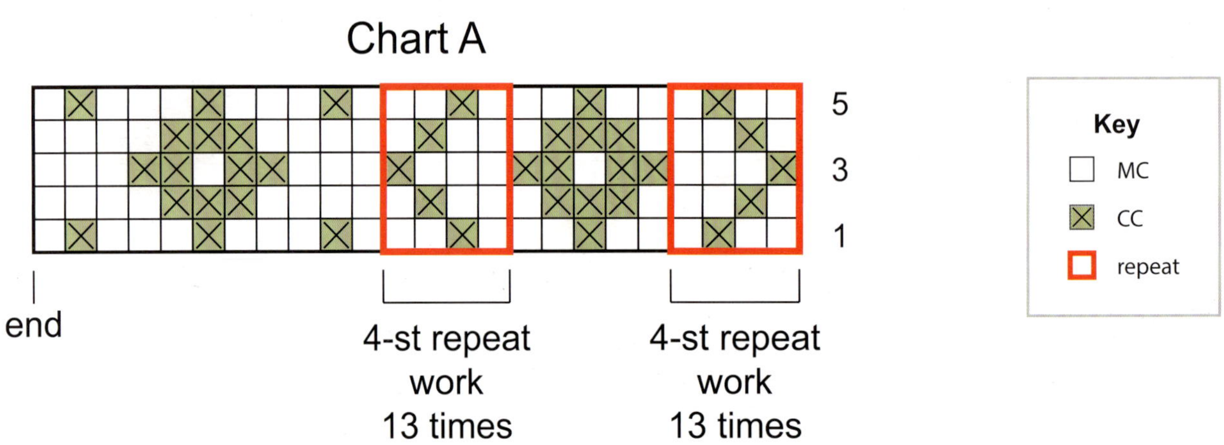

Chart B

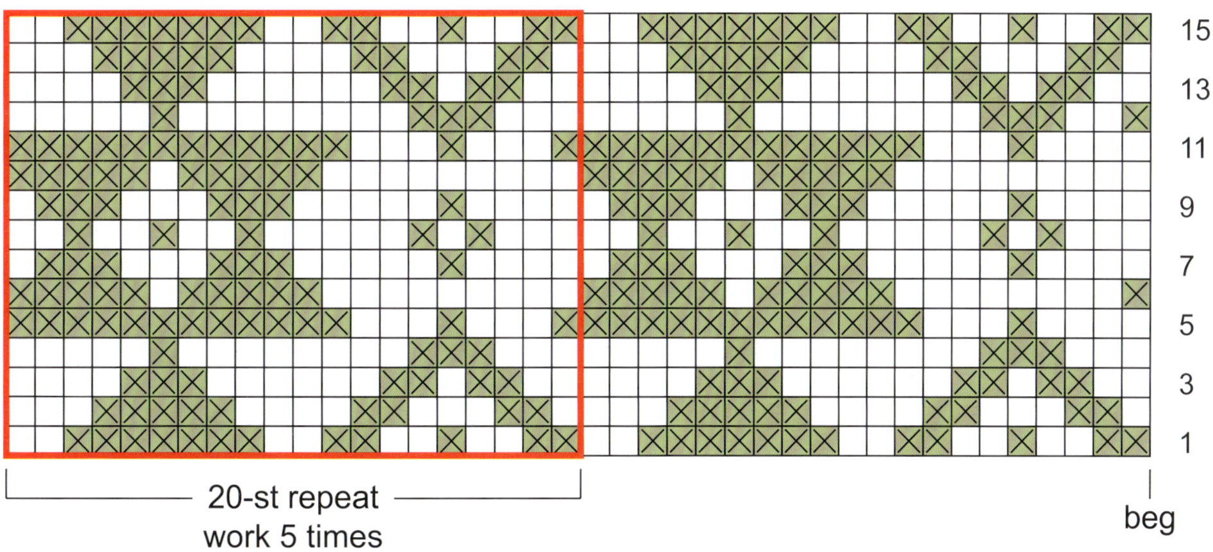

BOREAS PASS *Pullover*

Perfect for any outdoor adventures, this top-down raglan pullover is ideal for both men and women. Whether you choose to knit it in rustic-inspired colors, as shown here, select bold graphic shades, or use the latest fashion colors, you're sure to be a hit wherever you wear it!

SKILL LEVEL: ADVANCED

FINISHED MEASUREMENTS

Chest: 32 ½ [36 ½, 39 ¾, 44, 48, 52, 56 ¼, 60 ¼]" (82.6 [92.7, 101, 111.8, 121.9, 132.1, 142.9, 153]cm)

Length: 24 ½ [25 ¼, 26, 26 ¾, 27 ½, 28 ¼, 29, 29 ¾]" (62.2 [64.1, 66, 67.9, 69.9, 71.8, 73.7, 75.6]cm)

SIZES

XS [S, M, L, XL, 2XL, 3XL, 4XL]

YARN

Man's Pullover: 1091 [1223, 1331, 1486, 1637, 1777, 1946, 2121] yds (998 [1118, 1217, 1359, 1497, 1625, 1779, 1939]m) #3 light weight yarn in Main Color (MC)

Woman's Pullover: 1012 [1138, 1241, 1388, 1532, 1667, 1829, 1998] yds (925 [1041, 1135, 1269, 1401, 1524, 1672, 1827]m) #3 light weight yarn in Main Color (MC)

Both: 29 [32, 35, 39, 43, 47, 51, 56] yds (26.5 [29.3, 32, 35.7, 39.3, 43, 46.6, 51.2]m) #3 light weight yarn in Contrast Color 1 (CC1)

Both: 16 [18, 20, 22, 24, 26, 29, 31] yds (14.6 [16.5, 18.3, 20.1, 21.9, 23.8, 26.5, 28.3]m) #3 light weight yarn in Contrast Color 2 (CC2)

Both: 20 [22, 24, 27, 30, 32, 35, 39] yds (18.3 [20.1, 22, 24.7, 27.4, 29.3, 32, 35.7]m) #3 light weight yarn in Contrast Color 3 (CC3)

MATERIALS

US Size 7 (4.5mm) circular needles, or size required for gauge, in lengths of 16" (40.6cm), 32" (81.3cm), and 40" (101.6cm)

Four or five US 7 (4.5mm) double-pointed needles, or size required for gauge

Stitch markers

Stitch holders or scrap yarn

Scissors

Tapestry needle

cont. on page 162

ABOUT THE AUTHOR

A lifelong knitter always involved in creative pursuits of one kind or another, Therese Chynoweth has extensive experience as a knit technical editor and knitwear designer. After 10 years at Dale of Norway's North American office, where she edited the translated patterns for the North American market, she's been tech editing and designing for a number of clients both at home and abroad. Her design goal is to create pieces you want to keep in your wardrobe forever with clear and easy-to-follow pattern instructions.

When not knitting, she can be found walking around her neighborhood, gardening, reading, or baking.

ACKNOWLEDGMENTS

Every creative work is produced with the help, support, and hard work of many people. Without them, this book would not have happened.

Firstly, I'd like to thank Amelia Johanson and all the people at Fox Chapel Publishing for believing in and helping to shape this idea.

Next, I'm very grateful to all the yarn companies and other suppliers who generously provided yarn and various items to complete the samples shown in this book. I've known some of you for years, while others are new friends. Although at times I joked about feeling like I was chasing an entire herd of unicorns, you all came through for me! In fact, I really enjoyed the irony of finding a yarn called Unicorn for one of the pieces included here.

Then, there are the friends and their friends who helped along the way. I want to give special thanks to Elizabeth Lamb, Jill Ditlefsen, Karen Anderson, and Tina and Mike Farmer.

Most importantly, I'd like to thank my sisters and other friends for putting up with my obsession over the progress of this project and who, from time to time, even bravely asked how things were going.

Shown in size Medium, with approximately 2" to 4" (5.1 to 10.2cm) of positive ease.

YARN INFORMATION

Sample uses Merino Del Sol from Plymouth Yarn (100% Merino wool; 3.5oz [100g]; 246yds [225m]) in colors #201 Bark Heather (MC—5 [5, 6, 7, 7, 8, 8, 9] skeins for Man's Pullover, and 5 [5, 6, 6, 7, 7, 8, 9] skeins for Woman's Pullover), #207 Terracotta Heather (CC1—1 skein), #208 Indigo Heather (CC2—1 skein) and #206 Barn Red Heather (CC3—1 skein)

GAUGES

19 ½ sts and 29 rnds = 4" (10.2cm) in Chart A

21 sts = 4" (10.2cm) in Chart B

PATTERN NOTES

This raglan pullover is worked from the top down, using short rows to shape the neck. The stranded color pattern is worked on the lower yoke a short distance above the bottom of the yoke. Make sure to keep the charted patterns centered on the front, back, and sleeves. Different lengths are listed for the man's and woman's sleeves.

PULLOVER

■ YOKE

Using shortest circular needle and MC, CO 88 [88, 96, 96, 100, 104, 108, 108] sts. Pm and join to work in the rnd, being careful not to twist sts.

Rnd 1: *K2, p2; rep from * around.

Rep last rnd until ribbing measures 1" (2.5cm).

Turn with WS facing.

Shape Neck and Begin Raglan

Short Row 1 (WS, inc): M1p, p1, pm for raglan, p15 [15, 17, 17, 17, 19, 19, 19] sts for sleeve, pm for raglan, p1, M1p, p27 [27, 29, 29, 31, 31, 33, 33] sts for back, M1p, p1, pm for raglan, p15 [15, 17, 17, 17, 19, 19, 19] sts for sleeve, pm for raglan, p1, M1p, then turn—4 sts inc.

Short Row 2 (RS, inc): Sl 1, M1, k1, sm, k1, M1, working Row 2 of Chart A, k1 [1, 2, 2, 2, 3, 3, 3], p2, k7, p2, k1 [1, 2, 2, 2, 3, 3, 3], M1, k1, sm, k1, M1, k2 [2, 3, 3, 4, 4, 5, 5], p2, k5, p2, k7, p2, k5, p2, k2 [2, 3, 3, 4, 4, 5, 5], M1, k1, sm, k1, M1, k1 [1, 2, 2, 2, 3, 3, 3], p2, k7, p2, k1 [1, 2, 2, 2, 3, 3, 3], M1, k1, sm, k2, M1, k1, then turn—8 sts inc.

Note: Read through the next section carefully, as the front neck shaping is worked at the same time as the front/back and sleeve raglan increases are continued; the front/back raglan shaping is worked at a different rate than the sleeve raglan shaping.

Working inc sts into chart patt, cont working 1 more st at end of next 4 [4, 6, 6, 10, 10, 12, 12] rows, then 2 more sts at end of next 4 [4, 4, 4, 2, 2, 2, 2] rows. *At the same time*, cont inc at the front/back raglan every row 0 [0, 0, 3, 3, 7, 9, 13] more times, then every other row/rnd 18 [24, 26, 27, 29, 29, 30, 30] times, then every 4 rnds 2 [0, 0, 0, 0, 0, 0, 0] times. *And* cont inc at the sleeve raglan every RS row/every other rnd 16 [16, 16, 20, 20, 20, 24, 26] more times, then every 4 rnds 3 [4, 5, 4, 5, 6, 5, 5] times. *At the same time*, when 9 [9, 11, 11, 13, 13, 15, 15] rows have been worked, end with a WS row.

Join to Work in the Rnd

Next Short Row (inc): Sl 1, (work to 1 st before marker, M1R, k1, sm, k1, M1L) 4 times, work to 2 sts past last RS row turn—8 sts inc, and 13 [13, 13, 13, 15, 15, 15, 15] sts should rem unworked at center of front. Do not turn.

Cut yarn. Slip rem unworked front sts from LH needle to RH needle, then sl the left front sts from LH needle to RH needle. Rejoin yarn to beg rnds at left front raglan.

Cont raglan inc as established, work Chart A over front,

Key

- ☐ k on RS, p on WS
- ⊡ p on RS, k on WS
- ☐ MC
- ☒ CC1
- V CC2
- O CC3
- ☐ repeat

Chart A

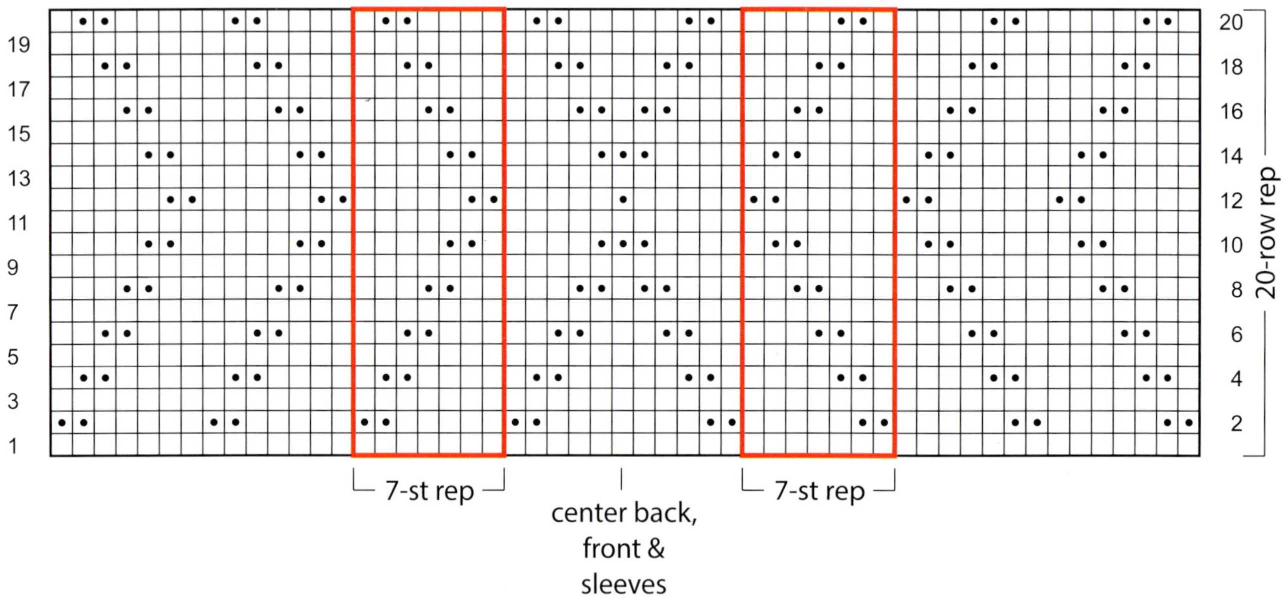

Notes: When working back and forth, read even-numbered (RS) rows from right to left and odd-numbered (WS) rows from left to right; when working in the round, read all chart rows from right to left.
Additional width has been added to the chart to help you work raglan increase stitches into the charted pattern.

Chart B

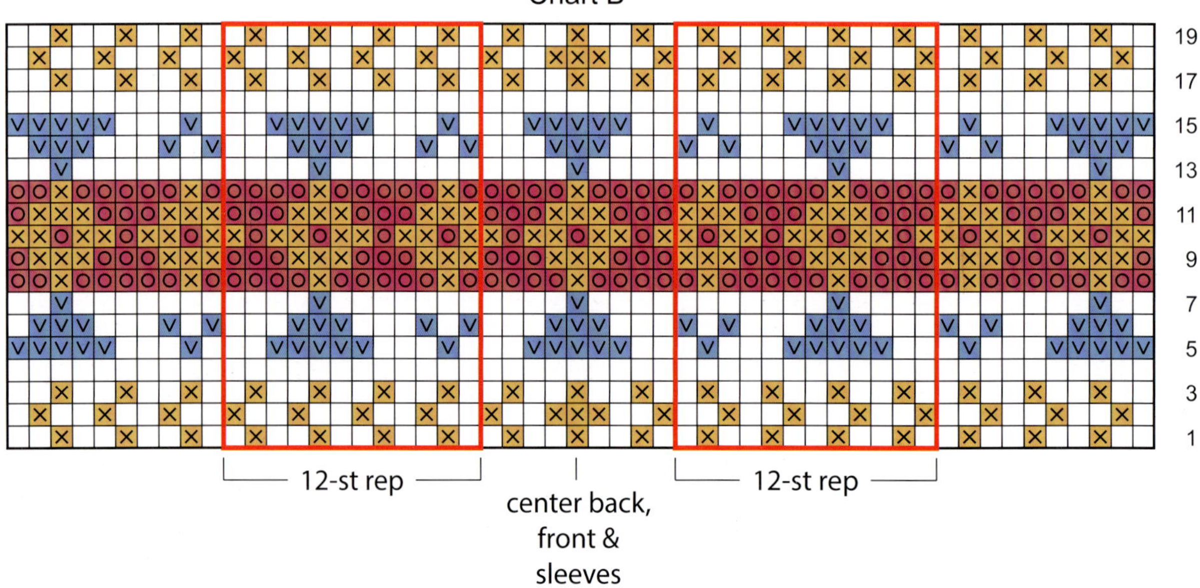

back, and sleeves for 13 [17, 17, 21, 21, 23, 25, 27] more rnds, work Rnds 1–19 of Chart B, making sure to center the chart patt on front, back, and sleeves, then cont in Chart A with MC only, making sure to center the chart patt on front, back, and sleeves again—256 [276, 296, 324, 340, 364, 392, 416] sts when all inc are complete, with 73 [81, 87, 95, 101, 109, 117, 125] sts each for front and back, and 55 [57, 61, 67, 69, 73, 79, 83] sts for each sleeve.

Work even until yoke measures 8 [8 ¾, 9 ½, 10, 10 ¾, 11 ½, 12, 12 ½]" (20.3 [22.2, 24.1, 25.4, 27.3, 29.2, 30.5, 31.8]cm) from CO edge at center of back.

Divide Body and Sleeves

Next Rnd: Remove marker, *place 55 [57, 61, 67, 69, 73, 79, 83] sleeve sts onto holder or scrap yarn, using Backward Loop method (see page 12), CO 6 [8, 10, 12, 16, 18, 20, 22] sts, work 73 [81, 87, 95, 101, 109, 117, 125] sts; rep from * once more, then k2 [3, 4, 5, 7, 8, 9, 10], pm for new beg of rnd—158 [178, 194, 214, 234, 254, 274, 294] sts rem.

■ BODY

Next Rnd: K2 (or p2 to beg garter st for faux side seam), pm, work next rnd of Chart A over next 77 [87, 95, 105, 115, 125, 135, 145] sts, pm, k2 (or p2 to beg garter st for faux side seam), pm, then work to end of rnd.

Keeping the 2 sts between both sets of marker in garter st, cont patt as established until body measures 14 ¼ [14 ¼, 14 ¼, 14 ½, 14 ½, 14 ½, 14 ¾, 15]" (36.2 [36.2, 36.2, 36.8, 36.8, 36.8, 37.5, 38.1]cm), or 2" (5.1cm) short of desired length from underarm CO, ending with an even-numbered rnd of patt and dec 3 [1, 1, 3, 1, 3, 1, 3] st(s) evenly spaced each over both front and back on the last rnd—152 [176, 192, 208, 232, 248, 272, 288] sts rem.

Next Rnd: *P2, k2; rep from * around.

Rep last rnd until ribbing measures 2" (5.1cm).

BO in ribbing.

■ SLEEVES

Return held sleeve sts to shorter circular needle. With RS facing and using MC, pick up and knit 6 [8, 10, 12, 16, 18, 20, 22] sts in underarm CO, 1 st in gap between underarm CO and sleeve sts, work sleeve sts, pick up and knit 1 in gap between underarm CO and sleeve sts, then work 2 [3, 4, 5, 7, 8, 9, 10] sts in patt—63 [67, 73, 81, 87, 93, 101, 107] sts. Pm and join to work in the rnd.

Set-Up Rnd: K2 (or p2 to beg garter st for faux underarm seam), pm, work 2 [3, 4, 5, 7, 8, 9, 10] sts, k2tog (or p2tog to maintain patt), work 53 [55, 59, 65, 67, 71, 77, 81] sts in established patt, ssk (or ssp to maintain patt), then work to end of rnd—61 [65, 71, 79, 85, 91, 99, 105] sts rem.

Man's Sleeves Only

Keeping the first 2 sts in garter st, cont Chart A over rem sts and work 13 [11, 11, 7, 7, 5, 5, 5] rnds even.

Dec Rnd: Work 2, sm, k2tog, work to last 2 sts, ssk—2 sts dec.

Change to double-pointed needles when there are too few sts to work on circular needle.

Rep Dec Rnd every 14 [14, 12, 10, 8, 8, 6, 6] rnds 7 [4, 4, 5, 12, 9, 20, 17] more times, then every 0 [12, 10, 8, 6, 6, 0, 4] rnds 0 [4, 6, 8, 3, 8, 0, 5] times—45 [47, 49, 51, 53, 55, 57, 59] sts rem.

Cont even until sleeve measures approx 17 ½ [17 ¾, 17 ¾, 18, 18 ¼, 18 ½, 18 ¾, 19 ¼]" (44.5 [45.1, 45.1, 45.7, 46.4, 47, 47.6, 48.9]cm), or 2 ½" (6.4cm) short of desired length from underarm CO, ending with an even-numbered rnd of patt and dec 5 [3, 5, 7, 5, 7, 9, 7] sts evenly spaced across last rnd, making sure not to dec over the faux underarm seam sts—40 [44, 44, 44, 48, 48, 48, 52] sts rem.

Next Rnd: *P2, k2; rep from * around.

Rep last rnd until ribbing measures 2 ½" (6.4cm).

BO in ribbing.

Woman's Sleeves Only

Keeping the first 2 sts in garter st, cont Chart A over rem sts and work 11 [11, 9, 7, 5, 5, 3, 3] rnds even.

Dec Rnd: Work 2, sm, k2tog, work to last 2 sts, ssk—2 sts dec.

Change to double-pointed needles when there are too few sts to work on circular needle.

Rep Dec Rnd every 10 [10, 8, 8, 6, 6, 6, 6] rnds 8 [5, 8, 2, 12, 10, 9, 3] more times, then every 0 [8, 6, 6, 4, 4, 4, 4] rnds 0 [4, 3, 12, 4, 8, 12, 20] times—43 [45, 47, 49, 51, 53, 55, 57] sts rem.

Cont even until sleeve measures approx 14 [14 ¼, 14 ¼, 14 ½, 14 ¾, 15, 15 ¾, 15 ¾]" (35.6 [36.2, 36.2, 36.8, 37.5, 38.1, 40, 40]cm), or 2" (5.1cm) short of desired length from underarm CO, ending with an even-numbered rnd of patt and dec 7 [5, 7, 9, 7, 9, 7, 9] sts evenly spaced across last rnd, making sure not to dec over the faux underarm seams sts—36 [40, 40, 40, 44, 44, 48, 48] sts rem.

Next Rnd: *P2, k2; rep from * around.

Rep last rnd until ribbing measures 2" (5.1cm).

BO in ribbing.

■ FINISHING

Weave in ends. Block to measurements *(Fig. 1)*.

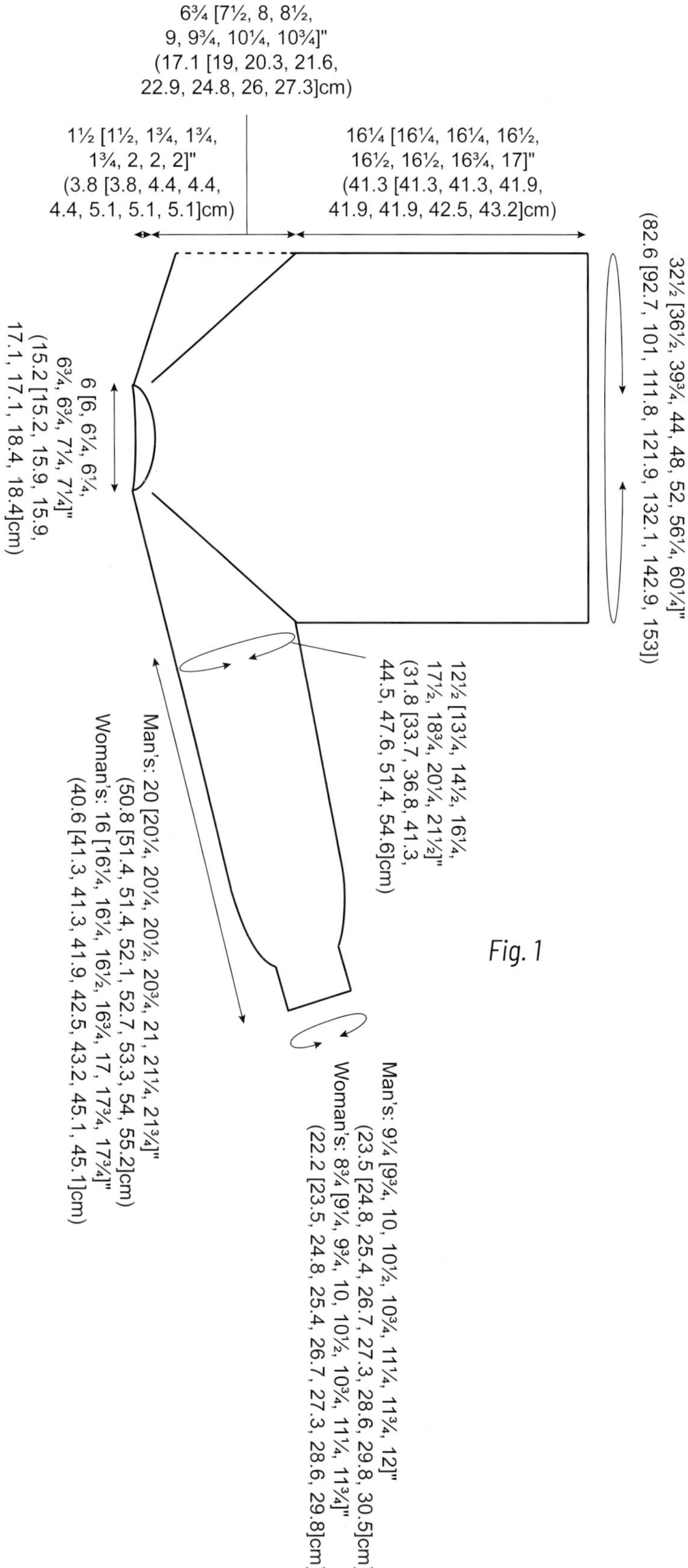

Fig. 1

INDEX